The Companion For The Orchard: An Historical And Botanical Account Of Fruits Known In Great Britain

Henry Phillips

AN

HISTORICAL AND BOTANICAL ACCOUNT

OF

FRUITS

KNOWN IN GREAT BRITAIN.

THE COMPANION FOR THE ORCHARD.

AN HISTORICAL AND BOTANICAL ACCOUNT OF FRUITS KNOWN IN GREAT BRITAIN:

BY

HENRY PHILLIPS, F.H.S.

AUTHOR OF

" THE COMPANION FOR THE KITCHEN GARDEN," &c. &c.

" I have often been astonished at our indifference respecting the applause of those who have introduced useful plants into their country, the fruits of which are to this day so delightful. The names of these public benefactors are chiefly unknown, whilst their benefits pass from generation to generation; whereas, those of the destroyers of the human race are handed down to us in every page, as if we took more account of our enemies than of our friends." ST. PIERRE.

NEW EDITION.

LONDON:

HENRY COLBURN AND RICHARD BENTLEY,

NEW BURLINGTON STREET.

1831.

TO THE RIGHT HONOURABLE

GEORGE O'BRYEN WYNDHAM,

EARL OF EGREMONT,

BARON COCKERMOUTH, LORD LIEUTENANT AND CUSTOS ROTULORUM OF THE COUNTY OF SUSSEX,

&c. &c. &c.

My Lord,

The being allowed the honour of dedicating this enlarged edition of my Work on Fruits to a Nobleman who has so greatly promoted the arts of Horticulture and Agriculture in my native country; is a gratification far beyond what can be derived by those who seek exalted rank for patronage only; and my ambition will be fully satisfied, should the labours I have bestowed on my orchard meet the approbation of one who possesses the discernment of your Lordship, whose favour, therefore, will be a strong recommendation to the dessert I have prepared.

I remain,

My Lord,

Your Lordship's most devoted,

And obedient Servant,

Henry Phillips.

Brighton,
Sept. 16, 1822.

INTRODUCTION.

———— "who studies Nature's laws,
Sincerest pleasures from the country draws;
And while the Arts his friendly aid receive,
For him, and him alone, does nature live."

Delille.

HISTORIANS generally seem to dwell with enthusiasm on the splendid achievements in which the cannon, the sword, and the bayonet, are chiefly instrumental; we, however, regard these implements of destruction with far less reverence than we bestow on the spade, the rake, and the pruning-knife, which enhance the beauties of the spring, and the luxuries of the summer, make our vats overflow in autumn, and secure us comforts for the winter. Not that we are insensible to the merits of the brave defenders of our country; but we wish to see those, whose talents and industry have so greatly enriched these kingdoms by their attention to horticulture, partaking of the admiration and gratitude of a people who are daily enjoying the fruits of their labours. Has the most splendid campaign which our history boasts secured the nation a treasure equal in value to the potatoe plant? or would we renounce the possession of ten of our best adopted fruits to double the acquisitions of the last ten wars? For it is not (says the elegant Bernardin St. Pierre) upon the face of vast dominions, but into the bosom of industry, that the Father of Mankind pours out the abundant fruits of the Earth.

The ingenuity of the horticulturist, and the industry of the cultivator may be said to have brought the south ten degrees nearer to our shores, within these last three centuries: a fact which, although imperceptible to us who have moved with the current, would be instantly acknowledged by our ancestors of the sixteenth century, could they be recalled to witness our gardens blushing with the fruits of Persia, our trees purpling with the drupes of Damascus, our hills ornamented with the cedars of Libanus, our valleys embellished by the spiral blossoms of the Asiatic chesnut, our cottages covered with the roses of China, and even some of our woods beautified by the violet blossoms of the American rhododendron, to say nothing of our numerous

"Ambrosial gardens, in which art supplies
The fervour and the force of Indian skies."

That the British nation has carried commercial enterprises to an unparalleled extent and success, all countries allow; that it excels in manufactures and arts, our works prove to all the admiring world: but that this northern island is beautified by plantations that surpass Italian scenery, and blessed with fruits that rival those of China, none will believe until they visit this land

——— "where mortals dare
To vanquish nature and correct the air."

Wars and dissensions are indigenous to barbarous soils; commerce and agriculture are natives of civilized lands; but horticulture is only to be found in countries where a high degree of refinement is cultivated. It was introduced to us by commerce, and flourished on the banks of the Thames when trade seated herself in our capital. They have journeyed together through every part of these realms, and where one has smiled, the other has prospered. Our intercourse with distant nations having enlightened the mind and refined the taste, men began to turn their attention to an employment, the most rational, because the most beneficial both to mind and body, as it is the most ancient and the most honourable. "The Lord took the man, and put him into the garden, to dress it, and to keep it,"—not to behold it only, and to revel in the enjoyment of the fruits, which unless earned by toil would cloy; but to rear the tender plant, and prop the beauteous blossom; to lend a staff to the gadding pea, or turn and fertilize the barren mould; these were the occupations that endeared man to earth, brought new relish to each fruit, and gave that humane delight which so greatly contributes to banish spleen and sullen sadness from the terrestrial globe.

Amongst civilized nations in ancient times, we find the greatest and wisest monarchs both studied and honoured this useful pursuit. Of Solomon it is written, that "he made cedars to be as sycamore trees that are in the vale for abundance;" and that he wrote a history of all the plants, from the cedar of Libanus to the moss growing on the wall.*

The Chinese have ever been celebrated for their attention to horticultural pursuits. Among the peasants in some parts of China, it is the custom to reward those whose gardens or fields are cultivated with the greatest care, by making them Mandarins of their class. It is related by the historians of China, that the Emperor Xi-Hoam-Ti, in the thirty-fourth year of his reign (213 years B. C.) ordered all the books in his dominions to be burnt, except those on Physic, Agriculture, and Astrology, which shews that despotism itself regarded this art as sacred.

* This is the literal meaning of the passage, and not *hyssop*.

Among the Persians, horticulture was most strictly attended to, according to Xenophon, who states that Cyrus the younger was accustomed to inform himself whether the private gardens of his subjects were well kept, and yielded plenty of fruit; that he rewarded the governors whose provinces were the best cultivated, and punished those who did not labour and improve their grounds. We must not omit the just compliment of Lysander to this monarch, who was telling him that many of the trees they were looking at had been planted by himself. The Lacedæmonian observed, "That the world had reason to extol the happiness of Cyrus, whose virtue was as eminent as his fortune, and who, in the midst of the greatest affluence, splendour, and magnificence, had yet preserved a taste so pure, and so conformable to right reason."

Socrates makes this noble encomium upon agriculture: —"It is," says he, "an employment the most worthy of the application of man, the most ancient and the most suitable to his nature; it is the common nurse of all persons in every age and condition of life; it is the source of health, strength, plenty, riches, and of a thousand sober delights and honest pleasures; it is the mistress and school of sobriety, temperance, justice, religion, and, in short, of all virtues, both civil and military."

To shew in what esteem those persons who encouraged or improved this art, were held by the ancients, Plutarch tells us that Ceres and Bacchus were mortals deified for having bestowed on mankind the knowledge of raising fruits. At Rome, especially during the Commonwealth, the greatest generals, consuls, and dictators, with the same victorious hands that overthrew the enemies of their state in war, turned up the earth in time of peace.

Pompey and Vespasian bore in their triumphs trees which they had procured from the conquered nations, as monuments more durable and useful than those of brass or marble; and long before their time, after the sacking of Carthage, the Senate reserved from the libraries of that great city only twenty-eight volumes, (the writings of Mago on Husbandry,) which they caused to be translated into the Latin language, notwithstanding Cato had so lately written on the same subject.

As soon as they had in some measure made themselves masters of Britain, the Romans began to clear the forests, and encourage agriculture, which in this country had previously been little attended to, except upon the coast; and at that period the island possessed but few fruits, which, for want of proper culture, must have been very inferior in quality.

The Romans were accustomed to convey to their native country the natural productions of the conquered nations, and by careful cultivation to make them flourish as well as those indigenous to the climate. It is probable that after the fall of their empire, the Crusaders, who often made that part of the world a rendezvous, observed and acquired a taste for many of those rarities; and brought back to their homes, not only new fruits, but those of their native soil in an improved state. Besides this, the intercourse of the Christian priests with Rome probably served to introduce other fruits, as the Catholic religion, enjoining frequent abstinence from animal food, must have increased the demand for fruits.

The monastic buildings appear to have been almost the only dwellings to which orchards and vineyards were attached, previously to the reign of Henry the Eighth.

But it was under that monarch and Elizabeth, that the most valuable fruits were introduced into this country; for at that time the desire of discovery pervading England, many fruits, plants, and vegetables, hitherto unknown, were brought hither from the New World. So little does horticulture seem to have advanced prior to that period, that Queen Catherine was obliged to procure her salads from Holland: and, according to Fuller, green peas were seldom seen except from that country. "These," says he, "were dainties for ladies, they came so far and cost so dear."

This politic Queen seems to have constantly patronized horticulture. Turner dedicated his Herbal to her in the first year of her reign, which is the earliest English work we possess on plants. She invited Tusser to her Court, who published the "*Five hundred Points of good Husbandry.*" But he, preferring his fields to a palace, remained in retirement at his farm in Essex. It was in this reign, also, that Leonard Mascall, or Maschal, printed his "New Art of Planting and Grafting." This author first introduced the pippin apple to our country.

In 1574, Thomas Hyll published "Art of Gardening." In 1597, John Gerrard, a surgeon in Holborn, sent out his History of Plants, a folio work of 1392 pages. The same year, William Lawson printed "A New Orchard and Garden."

In 1600, Sir Hugh Platt published "Paradise of Flora;" also, "Dyvers Snyles for manuring." In the following year Dr. Holland produced his Translation of the Works of C. Plinius Secundus.

Since this, there has been kept up a continued search for every kind of tree, shrub, and herb, that could either please the eye, gratify the taste, or contribute to the stores of medicine; the hottest and the coldest climates have been explored: and those plants that, for want of a warmer sun, would not flourish naturally in this country, have had an artificial clime and temperature furnished to them. The Agricultural Society has succeeded in improving our farms, the very meadows of which are clothed anew: this produces the grass of the Italian fields, and that the pasture of the Netherlands: the chalky hills wave with corn, our marshes are no longer stagnated, and famine, which formerly succeeded an unfavourable season, seems no longer to be dreaded.

The Horticultural Society was established in the year 1809, in order to give farther encouragement to this art, and to extend the best possible system to every part of the kingdom. By means of this company, what is discovered in one place, may be sent post as it were to others, through the remotest corners of the dominions, without travelling as before, by ages. Besides this advantage, individuals have sent out men of science to every quarter of the known world in search of plants, which have since been so diversified and multiplied, as to make it difficult to discover more varieties.

The author has ascertained, by the assistance of the Hortus Kewensis, that since the discovery of the New World, we have procured 2345 varieties of trees and plants from America, and upwards of 1700 from the Cape of Good Hope, in addition to many thousands which have been brought from China, the East Indies, New Holland, various parts of Africa, Asia, and Europe, until the list of plants now cultivated in this country exceeds 120,000 varieties.

But flowers have principally engaged the care and study of the lovers of horticulture and botany, while fruits have been, comparatively, rather too much neglected, though of the two the latter are intrinsically the most valuable; for since the more frequent use of fruits and vegetables in this country, many dreadful diseases, as the leprosy, &c. are no longer prevalent, or have lost their baneful effects.

With respect to the City of London, particularly, amongst the blessings which gardening has bestowed on it, one of the most important is the prevention of pestilence; cleanliness having become a matter of profit in this immense metropolis, whence the soil is carefully and expeditiously removed to fertilize the grounds occupied by gardeners in the environs, which are now calculated to exceed an extent of six thousand acres within twelve miles of London. These are constantly cultivated for the supply of the metropolitan markets with fruit and vegetables.

Stevenson informs us, that three thousand five hundred acres of ground in Surrey alone are employed as market gardens; and Middleton observes, that from Kensington to Twickenham, the land on both sides of the road for seven miles compose the great fruit-gardens north of the Thames, for the supply of the London markets. It is gratifying to see the number of hands this ground employs. Even during the six winter months, it is computed that each acre affords work to five persons, and at least double that number for the summer months; these are principally females; and if we add porters, hawkers, &c. the amount will be trebled, and the total number will be found to exceed ninety thousand persons, who are in the summer months daily employed by the gardeners within a circle of ten or twelve miles around London.

The author has been anxious to discover the names of the first introducers and cultivators of each particular fruit, but in this endeavour he met with considerable difficulty; for modern historians are silent on the subject, though they often dwell long on others not really so interesting; and the few works in our language on this head, are either too expensive, or too strictly botanical for general readers. Encouraged, however, by the observation of Sir Joseph Banks, that "every anecdote that tends to throw light on the introduction, or on the probable origin of plants now collected for use, is interesting, even though it is not quite perfect," he continued his researches till he was flattered by the suggestions of friends, that the work, originally intended only as a private instruction for his family, might, with care, become worthy the perusal of the public, and enable him to make farther inquiries and discoveries.

It has been the author's study to produce a History of Fruits, that may not only be read through, but referred to, with some amusement; to blend entertainment with useful information, as far as the subject would allow; to combine and compare the accounts of the ancients with those of the moderns which are more improved; and, in short, to treat on each species of fruit generally; for to have descended into varieties, would have filled volumes with names alone, since he finds one individual possessing four hundred kinds of strawberries, and others as great a variety of gooseberries; while the kinds of apples, pears, plums, &c. have been still more numerously multiplied—

And kinds are less material to *his* theme;
Which who would learn, as soon may tell the sands,
Driven by the western wind on Libyan lands,
Or number, when the blust'ring Eurus roars,
The billows beating on Ionian shores.

Dryden's Virgil.

HISTORY OF FRUITS.

ACORN—GLANS.

THE OAK TREE.—QUERCUS.

Natural Order, Amentaceæ. A genus of the Monœcia Polyandria Class.

Thresh the wood
For masts of Oaks, your fathers' homely food.

VIRGIL.

THE prince of the Latin poets having thus noticed the food of the early race of mankind, which Ovid tells us,

" Content with food, which nature freely bred
On wildings and on strawberries they fed;
Cornels and bramble-berries gave the rest,
And falling acorns furnished out a feast."

This, we trust, will justify our noticing a fruit, which the Horticulturists have banished from our board by the introduction of a more agreeable dessert. It is the fruit or nut of the oak-tree, and was called by the Greeks Βάλανος, while in Latin it is called *Glans*.

It appears to have been amongst the Grecian traditions that of all trees the oak was made first, and that among men the Arcadians were first created; who for this reason were compared to the oak. They were certainly celebrated for their partiality to that sort of diet, since they are distinguished in Lycophron by the name of βαλανηφαγοι, acorn-eaters. Hence it was customary in the marriage festivals of the Athenians, for a boy to bring in a bough full of acorns and a plate covered with bread, proclaiming 'Εφυγον κακον, ευρον άμεινον.'—I have escaped the worse and found the better — which was done in memory of their leaving the use of acorns for that of bread. Most other nations in Greece also made use of acorns. The inhabitants of Chios once held out a long siege, whilst they were destitute of all other food.

Strabo tells us that in the mountainous parts of Spain the inhabitants ground their acorns into meal. In a raw state they are eaten to this day by the Spaniards, who long retained them as a delicacy at the desserts. Cervantes mentions them in his Don Quixote. But the Spanish acorns are certainly of a sweeter nature than those of England. Mrs. Stothard says in her tour in Brittany, "I am informed that in the neighbourhood of Brest, the lower orders resort to acorns as well as chesnuts for food, which have some nutritious quality when boiled in milk." In times of scarcity and dearth of corn, they have been ground and baked into bread both in this country and in France; but the taste of this bread is rough and disagreeable; and indeed acorns are said to be hard of digestion and to cause head-aches and flatulence. Hence Turner, who is the earliest English author on this subject writes, "Oke whose fruite we call an Acorn or an Eykorn (that is ye corn or fruit of an Eike,) are harde of digestion and norishe very much, but they make raw humores. Wherefore we forbid the use of them for meates."

This species of mast was also eaten by the ancient Britons. The Druids taught that whatever grew on the oak was sent immediately from heaven; and nothing was held so sacred by them as the misletoe of an oak, which it was unlawful to cut except with a golden hook.

The Persians, and the Massagetæ, also thought the misletoe something divine.

The study of botany, and the encouragement given to agricultural and horticultural pursuits, have so wonderfully improved the state of this country, that what in early ages a king would have feasted on, the beggar now refuses; and the acorn is scarcely known as affording nourishment to the human species, even among the wandering vagrants who pitch their tattered tents, and cook their scanty fare beneath the branches of the trees that produce them.

Acorns continued to be of so much importance for many ages after they had been relinquished as the food of man, that a failure of them frequently caused a famine; as the swine which our woods and forests maintained, formed a principal part of the food of our ancestors. The author of the Saxon Chronicle, after describing the extraordinary famine and mortality of the year 1116, records particularly the failure of masts in that year.

We find that as early as the end of the seventh century our Saxon ancestors had a law and particular directions given them by King Ina, respecting the fattening of swine in woods, since his time called pawnage or pannage. In a succeeding century, Elfhelmus reserves the pannage of two hundred hogs for his lady, in part of her dowry: and acorns are particularly mentioned about the middle of the eleventh century in a donation of Edward the Confessor.

Before the conquest, the wealds of Sussex (which is the largest valley in Europe) were one continued forest from Hampshire to Kent, principally of oak-trees that were only valued for the number of swine which the acorns maintained. And so accurately was the survey taken in William the Conqueror's time, that woods are mentioned in the Domesday book, of one hog. The succeeding line of our Norman Kings, in their rage for extending forests for the chase, took away the right of pawnage from those on whose lands they had encroached: this was one of the grievances that King John was compelled to redress in the Charta de Forestâ.

Acorns are but little used at present, except to fatten hogs and deer; they are sometimes given to poultry, and would be found an advantageous food for them, were they dried, and ground into meal.

In the time of Strabo, Rome was principally supplied with hogs which were fattened on masts in the woods of Gaul; and we have observed that at the present time the swine fed in the woods of France, particularly those of Berry, afford a meat of a very superior firmness and flavour: and as many persons esteem it equal to that of Westphalia or Mentz, it brings a much higher price in the Parisian markets than the home fed bacon.

Tusser says,—

> "Some left among bushes shall pleasure thy swine;
> For fear of a mischief, keep acorns from kine."

They are considered injurious to cows because they swell in their stomachs, and will not come up to the cud again: which causes them to strain as it were, to remit, and draw their limbs together.

In medicine, a decoction of acorns is reputed good against dysenteries and colics. Pliny states, that acorns beaten to powder, and mixed with hog's-lard and salt, heal all hard swellings, and cancerous ulcers; and when reduced into a liniment, and applied, stay the hæmorrhage.

Every part of the oak is styptic, binding, and useful in all kinds of fluxes and bleedings, either inwardly or outwardly; the bark is frequently used in gargarisms, for the relaxation of the uvula, and for sore mouths and throats. An extract made from the bark is said by some to be equal to the Peruvian bark.

Dr. Cullen frequently employed the decoction with success in slight tumefactions of the mucous membrane of the fauces, in prolapsus uvulæ, and cynanche tonsillaris, to which some persons are liable upon the least exposure to cold: in many cases this decoction, applied early, has appeared useful in preventing these disorders, but in the improved state of medicine it is little employed although there is no doubt that oak bark will cure intermittents, both alone and joined with camomile flowers.

The gall nuts of the oak, are of many kinds, but they have all the same medicinal virtue. We learn from Pliny that they were used by the Romans to colour their hair black. Galls appear to be the most powerful of the vegetable astringents, striking a deep black when mixed with a solution of green vitriol, and are therefore preferred to every other substance for the purpose of making ink. As a medicine they possess a greater degree of astringent and styptic power than the bark, and have therefore an advantage over it, particularly for external use.

Two sorts of galls are distinguished in the shops, those brought from Aleppo, and therefore called *Aleppo* nuts;

or *Galla Spinosa*, are the most esteemed; the second sort is brought from the South of Europe.

All the varieties of galls are caused by insects, which prick the tender bud of the oak which begins to be turgid in June, and then deposit their eggs in the wound; these eggs swell with the excrescence, and first turn to worms, and then to flies, which, having perforated the galls make their escape. And as some eggs are unfruitful and remain in the gall, they are observed to yield a volatile salt. The gall insect is a species of the inchneumon fly, and so singularly differing from other insects that we refer the curious to Reaumer's Hist. Insects, vol. 4, p. 40. It is suspected that these insects eject some venomous ichor with their eggs, which effectually obstructs the regular vegetation of the bud, and causes those protuberances called galls, and oak apples, from their afterwards taking the shape and colour of that fruit.

At Rome the civic crown was composed of oak leaves. But the ancient veneration of this tree was not confined to the heathens, for it appears there were oak-trees in the temple of the true God; as the Bible informs us that Joshua "wrote the commandments and the precepts of the Lord, in the book of the law, and that he took a great stone, which he set up under an oak, which was in the sanctuary of the Lord."

In the valley of Mamre, which was in the beautiful country of the tribe of Judah, where Abraham was visited by the angels who announced to him the birth of Isaac, stood an oak, that became celebrated as the tree under which Abraham often went to repose and refresh himself. Bayle says, that this oak was said to have existed in the reign of the Emperor Constantius.

The biblical reader will recollect so many important notices of this tree as to induce us to think that the Israelites considered it almost as a sacred tree. As the oak in

Ophra, under which the angel of God appeared to Gideon, (*Judges* vi. 14.) The oak by Shechem, under which Jacob hid all the idols and ear-rings (*Genes.* xxxv. 4.) The oak near Bethel which marked the grave of Deborah, and was significantly called *Allor-bachuth*, (the oak of weeping. *Genes.* xxxv. 8.) The classical reader will scarcely want reminding that it was an oak-tree also which cost Milo of Crotona, the most celebrated wrestler of Greece, and who was always the conqueror in the games, his life. He possessed prodigious strength. It is related that he held a pomegranate in his hand so firmly, without smashing or hurting the fruit, that no person could open his fingers strait, so as to take it from him. He would put his naked foot on a quoit, greased with oil, and whatever effort was made, it was impossible to shake him. His confidence in his (almost supernatural) strength was fatal to him, for having once found in his way an old oak-tree, nearly opened by wedges, which had been forced by the hatchet and hammer, he undertook to finish the operation, by the power of his arms alone; but in the effort he displaced the wedges, and his hands were caught by the two parts of the oak, which joining together again, he was unable to liberate himself, and was devoured by the wolves.

The famous forest of Dodona, in Epirus, consisted of oaks that were consecrated to Jupiter: this was one of the most ancient oracles of which we have any particular account. Herodotus gives two accounts of the rise of this oracle, one of which clears up the mystery of the fable, *viz.* that some Phœnician merchants carried off a priestess of Thebes into Greece, where she took up her residence in the forest of Dodona, and there, at the foot of an old oak, erected a small chapel in honour of Jupiter, whose priestess she had been at Thebes; and this was the first temple that was ever seen in Greece. Suidas informs us that the answer was given by an oak. Homer has also delivered the same account; and as it was generally believed to proceed from the trunk, it is easy to conceive that the priestess had nothing more to do than to hide herself in the hollow of this oak, and from thence to give the pretended sense of the oracle; for the distance the supplicants were obliged to keep was an effectual means to prevent the cheat from being discovered. During the war between the Thracians and Bœotians, the latter sent deputies to consult this oracle of Dodona, when the priestess gave them this answer, of which she doubtless did not foresee the consequence, "If you would meet with success, you must be guilty of some impious action." The deputies suspecting that she prevaricated with them in order to serve their enemies, from whom she was descended, resolved to fulfil the decree of the oracle; and therefore seized the priestess and burnt her alive, alleging, that this act was justifiable in whatever light it was considered; that if she intended to deceive them, it was fit she should be punished for the deceit; or, if she was sincere, they had only literally fulfilled the sense of the oracle.

On Mount Lycæus, in Arcadia, was a temple of Jupiter with a fountain: when rain was wanted, it was thought that it would be obtained of the god by throwing into the fountain a branch of the oak-tree.

Socrates swore by the oak, perhaps because this tree was consecrated to Jupiter.

The veneration that the ancients had for the oak, gave rise to the Greek and Latin proverb, "Speak to the oak;" which signified, speak in good security. They had also another proverb on the oak: when they spoke of persons they did not know the birth of, it was said they were born of an oak, because the ancients often exposed children in the hollow of trees.

Lucan compares Pompey to an old oak, hung with superb trophies.

The oak is a tree of slow growth, requiring a century before it will arrive to its full perfection.

In Dodsley's Annual Register for 1758, p. 116, mention is made of an oak in Langley-wood, near Downton, Wilts, the property of the Bishop of Salisbury, supposed to be of near one thousand years growth. It was six feet two inches in diameter, contained about ten tons of timber, and was sold for forty pounds.

In the St. James's Chronicle, No. 5038, it is said that an oak was felled a few days before at Morley, in Cheshire, which produced upwards of a thousand measurable feet of timber. Its girth was fourteen yards, and one branch contained two hundred feet. Its existence could be traced back for eight hundred years, and it was supposed to be the largest tree in England; as a proof of it, the trunk had been used some years for housing cattle, and it is said Edward the Black Prince once dined under it.

Pliny, in his Natural History, states, that hard by the city of Ilium, there were oaks near the tomb of Ilius, which were planted from acorns when Troy was first called Ilium. He also says, "the great forest Hercynia is full of large oaks, that have never been topped or lopped. It is supposed," adds this naturalist, "that they have been there ever since the creation of the world, and (in regard to their immortality) surmounting all miracles whatever. The roots of these trees run and spread so far within the ground that they meet each other, in which encounter they make such resistance, that they swell and rise upwards to a great height, in the form of arches."

Linnæus mentions fourteen species of the oak-tree; Miller extended them to twenty-three; and Aiton describes twenty-eight species of this tree. The most common kind of the English oak produces the acorns close to the branches, without any stalk; but the species most esteemed for ship-building is found growing in the wealds of Sussex and Kent; and this tree often produces its acorns with foot stalks as long as the cherry stalk. Young says, "Oak is the staple commodity of Sussex, which, from the remotest antiquity, has been celebrated for the growth of oak: it is estimated that not less than from 170 to 180,000 acres are occupied by this timber, the quality of which is acknowledged by navy contractors preferring, and in all their agreements stipulating for, Sussex oak." This author adds, that the soil is so naturally adapted to the growth of oak, that if a field were sown with furze only, and the cattle kept out, the ground would, in a few years, be covered with young oaks, without trouble or expense of planting.

Sir William Ouseley observes, "However replete with interesting objects, the ample field of antiquarian research offers but few to our notice under a more attractive form than trees; whether we regard them as distinguishing remarkable spots, the scenes of memorable transactions; as dedicated to certain divinities; or as, in some cases, almost identified with those divinities themselves." This is peculiarly applicable to

—— the sturdy oak,
A prince's refuge once, th' eternal guard
Of England's throne, by sweating peasants fell'd,
Stems the vast main, and bears tremendous war
To distant nations, or with sov'reign sway
Awes the divided world to peace and love.

Phillips.

The scene of King William Rufus's death in the New Forest is still (or was within a few years) indicated by the remains of the tree, against which the arrow of Sir Walter Tyrrel glanced, and killed the King. Eighty years ago it became so decayed and mutilated, that the spot would probably have been forgotten, had not John Lord Delaware, who lived in one of the neighbouring lodges, erected a triangular stone, with an inscription on each face, before the stump was eradicated. On this subject Mr. Gilpin says, in his work on Forest Scenery, "They who think a tree insufficient to record a fact of so ancient a date, may be reminded that seven hundred years make no extraordinary period in the age of an oak." King William was killed in the year 1100.

The celebrated oak in Hainault Forest, Essex, known by the name of Fairlop, and under whose protecting shade so many city knights and dames have enjoyed their pic-nic meal, is no more. Whether it fell by a stroke of sound policy, the axe of avarice, or the shock of dice, it is not our intention to record, we have only in common with the lovers of ancient customs to regret its loss and record its wonders.

> "Nor could old age itself their pity reach,
> No reverence to hoary barks they knew."

It is thus mentioned by the late Rev. Mr. Gilpin: "The tradition of the country," says this ingenious writer, "traces it half way up the christian era. It is still a noble tree, though it has suffered greatly from the depredations of time. About a yard from the ground, where its rough fluted stem is sixty-six feet in circumference, it divides into eleven vast arms, which overspread an area of three hundred feet in circuit: beneath this shade an annual fair has long been held on the 2d of July; but no booth is suffered to be erected beyond the extent of its boughs."

This venerable oak was cut down previous to the fair in

1820. The founder of this fair was a Mr. Daniel Day, commonly called, the Good Day, who was born in the parish of St. Mary Overy, in 1682; his father was an opulent brewer, but Mr. Day followed the business of a block and pump-maker in Wapping, and possessing a small estate in Essex, at no great distance from this remarkable tree, he used, on the first Friday in July, annually, to repair thither, having given his accustomed invitation to a party of his neighbours to accompany him, for the purpose of dining under the shade of its branches and leaves, on beans and bacon. This benevolent as well as humorous man never failed to pay his annual visit to the public bean feast, and as regularly provided several sacks of beans, with a proportionate quantity of bacon, which he distributed from the trunk of the tree to the persons there assembled. For several years before his death, the pump and block-makers of Wapping, to the number of thirty or forty, went annually to the fair in a boat made of one entire piece of fir. This amphibious vehicle was covered with an awning, mounted on a coach carriage, and drawn by six horses; the whole adorned with ribbands, flags and streamers, and furnished with a band of musicians; it has thus been noticed in verse:

"O'er land our vessel bent its course,
Guarded by troops of foot and horse;
Our anchors they were all a-peak,
Our crew were baling from each leak,
On Stratford bridge it made me quiver,
Lest they should spill us in the river."

A few years before the decease of Mr. Day, (which happened on the 19th of October, 1767, being then eighty-four years of age) his favourite oak lost a large limb, out of which he procured a coffin to be made for his own interment.

We have been informed that the following circumstance

gave rise to the name of Fairlop, bestowed upon this celebrated oak. Some of Mr. Day's friends having promised that he should be buried in a coffin made from that tree, lopped off one of the branches, for which trespass an action was brought against the party, fortunately for whom some flaw was found in the pleadings, and the plaintiff was nonsuited. It was, however, proved that the fact committed was not injurious to the tree, but *a fair lop*. Mr. Day was buried in Barking Church-yard. As lately as 1794, this venerable oak, in the meridian of the day, shadowed an acre of ground, although then greatly decayed.

Fisher's oak, about seventeen miles from London, or half way to Tunbridge, is of a monstrous bulk; the trunk only remaining, of above four fathoms in compass. When King James the First made a progress that way, a schoolmaster of the neighbourhood, and all his scholars, dressed in oaken garlands, came out of this tree in great numbers, and entertained the King with an oration. They have a tradition at Tunbridge, that thirteen men on horseback were once sheltered in this oak.—*Martyn.*

Hern's oak, celebrated by Shakspeare, is still in existence in the Little Park at Windsor. The remains of an other oak stand at Heveningham, in Suffolk, called Queen Elizabeth's oak, which was hollow when that Princess was in her youth, and who, it is said, used to take her stand in this tree, and shoot the deer as they passed.

The large oak in Whinfield Forest, near Appleby, in Westmoreland, belonging to the Earl of Thanet, is also a great curiosity; a part of the trunk being broken away forms a portal, into which a person may ride on horseback and turn about at pleasure; it forms a convenient receptacle for deer in stormy weather. It is supposed to be upwards of 300 years old.

In Bloomfield wood, near Ludlow, in Shropshire, is an oak-tree belonging to Lord Powis, the trunk of which, in 1765, measured sixty-eight feet in girth, thirty-two in length, and which, reckoning ninety feet for the larger branches, contained in the whole 1455 feet of timber, round measure, or twenty-nine loads and five feet at fifty feet to a load.

In the vale of Gloucestershire, near the turnpike-road between Cheltenham and Tewksbury, stands the Baddington oak, the stem of whose trunk is fifty-four feet, and some of its branches extend to eight yards from the body of the tree.

The famous oak, Robur Britannicum, in Lord Norrey's Park, at Prescot, was computed to be able to shelter between three and four thousand men. Dr. Plot, in his Oxfordshire, tells us of an oak near Clifton, that spread eighty-one feet from bough-end to bough-end, and shaded 560 square yards.

In Worksop Park, the Duke of Norfolk had an oak which spread almost 3000 square yards, and near 1000 horse might stand under the shade.

We have been favoured with the particular dimensions of the large oak that was felled on the Gelin's estate, in the parish of Bassaly, and within four miles of the town of Newport, in the County of Monmouth, in 1810, as communicated by the Earl of Stamford to Sir Joseph Banks.

Body of the tree, ten feet long - -	450 ft.
Twelve limbs and collateral parts, contained	1850
Dead limbs - - - - - - -	126
	2426 ft. or

48 loads and 26 ft.—Quantity of bark, 65 cwt. and 16 stacks of wood.

Four men were three weeks and two days in felling and stripping the tree. There were 85 pieces of square or hewn timber: the squarers were three weeks and four days in squaring it. One pair of sawyers had been five months in sawing the tree, and had not finished when this account was sent. (Mar. 6th, 1811.) The tree was purchased by Mr. Thomas Harrison for one hundred guineas.

We could add the particulars of numerous other ancient oaks, had we not a fear of exceeding our bounds in describing the most picturesque kind of tree the world can boast. Its appearance has more of dignity than grace, yet it equally suits the Gothic tower or the modern villa, as it harmonises with the former, as beautifully as it contrasts with the latter; it is the grandest ornament of the embellished park, and the happiest protection to the woodman's hut, where

> "Hard by a cottage chimney smokes
> From between two aged oaks."

Part of an oak-tree, twenty feet in circumference, was drawn out of the Thames in September, 1815, near the Ferry at Twickenham, with great difficulty, by twenty-four horses: it is known to have lain in the river one hundred and fifty years.

The workmen, in cleaning the channel, at Brindisi, have drawn up many of the oak piles that were driven in by Cæsar. They are small oaks stripped of their bark, and still as fresh as if they had been cut only a month, though buried above eighteen centuries, seven feet under the sand. These piles were driven in by Julius Cæsar, to block up Pompey's fleet. *(Swinburn.)*

> *Thus* "oft conducted by historic truth,
> We tread the long extent of backward time."
>
> *Thomson.*

A great natural curiosity may be seen at the Imperial Museum at Vienna, at the entrance of the gallery of the portraits of the Emperors, in a block of oak about four feet high, and about nine feet in circumference, in which is the head of a Stag with the horns partly in the body of the tree and partly out. The hart was twenty-two years old when taken, as appears by the horns. This oak was cut in a forest in Hungary about three hundred years ago. We would wish the experiment to be made of binding a young oak with brass or iron hoops, to ascertain in what time the hoops would be surrounded by solid timber.

The timber of the oak-tree is so well known, and so justly esteemed, for a variety of purposes, that it would be superfluous to state the whole of them.

In building ships of war, one great advantage is, that it seldom splinters, which caused foreigners to attribute our naval victories to the excellence of our timber; but the late war has given so many proofs of our defeating our enemies with ships of their own building, that they must now acknowledge that the bravery of a British sailor is as firm as the heart of an English oak.

"The particular and most valuable qualities of the oak," says Mr. Gilpin, "are *hardness* and *toughness*. Box and ebony are harder, yew and ash are tougher than oak; but no timber is possessed of both these qualities together in so great a degree as British oak."

The beauty of oak timber was evidently known to the early Greeks, as Homer thus notices its use

> "Now gently winding up the fair ascent,
> By many an easy step the matron went:
> Then o'er the pavement glides with grace divine
> (With polish'd oak the level pavements shine)."
>
> *Odyssey.*

But it was not until we had manufactured into furniture all the curious woods of the New World, that the transcendent splendor of the English oak was brought to any degree of perfection, by the late Mr. Bullock, of Tenterdenstreet, and other eminent cabinet-makers. Mr. Penning, of Holles-street, Cavendish-square, has lately wrought up some old oak-trees of such matchless beauty, that one set of dining-tables brought him the unheard-of price of six hundred pounds. This far exceeds any thing of the kind we read of, even in the luxurious days of the Romans, although Pliny says, "Our wives at home twit us, their husbands, for our expensive tables, when we seem to find fault with their costly pearls."

"There is at this day to be seen," says this author, "a board of citron wood, belonging formerly to M. Tullius Cicero, which cost him ten thousand sesterces; a strange circumstance, as he was not rich." He also mentions a table that belonged to Gallus Asinius, which sold for eleven thousand sesterces, which is about equal to 70*l.* of our money; and he particularizes a table of citron wood that came from Ptolemæus, king of Mauritania, which was made in two demi-rounds, or half circles, joined together so cleverly, that the joints could not be discovered: the diameter of it was four feet and a half, and three inches in thickness. It is related that they set great store on woods of curious grains: some there are mentioned with curling veins, which were called *tigrinæ* (tiger tables); others, *pantherinæ* (panther); and some are described waved like the sea, and spotted like the peacock's tail. But those of the highest value were of the colour of honey wine, with shining and glittering veins, or lamprey veined, running across.

We venture to make this digression, having seen within these last few years oak of such various grains, that out of them the whole of the above-mentioned, and many other curious representations, might have been selected.

The bark of the oak-tree is a most valuable article for the purpose of tanning; it is also used to dye woollen of a purplish blue. The Highlanders of Scotland dye their yarn with it of a brown colour, and it is by the aid of this bark, that our English gardeners are able to supply us with pine-apples, and other fruits peculiar to the hottest climates; but as our stoves are now successfully heated by steam, we may expect that a less expensive article will be substituted, having witnessed that sea-sand will retain its heat so as to answer the same purpose.

Even the leaves of this valuable tree are used for the purpose of tanning, and many gardeners prefer them to dung for the purpose of making hot-beds for melons. See the History of Cultivated Vegetables, vol. ii. p. 96.

In medicine, oak-bark has long been esteemed as a powerful and useful astringent and tonic. It was at one time a celebrated remedy for intermittents, and considered as a good substitute for cinchona; but it certainly falls much short of that drug in these cases; for agues will often withstand the oak-bark, which readily yield upon administering a few doses of Peruvian bark. It is however an useful astringent in obstinate diarrhœa, and chronic forms of dysentery; also in leucorrhœa and other chronic serous discharges, depending on debility and relaxations of the secreting vessels.*

Oak sawdust is a principal ingredient in dyeing fustian; all the varieties of drabs and browns are made by the aid of oak sawdust. Oak apples are likewise used in dyeing: the black got from them is more beautiful than that obtained from galls, but not so durable.

For the sowing of acorns, we can take no better time than that which Nature directs, and the squirrels, who in all probability were the first planters of our forests, employ. When the fruit is perfectly matured, so that it may be easily taken from the cup, these little animals may be observed to descend from the oak each with an acorn

* Medical Botany.

in its mouth, and with the greatest rapidity they make a small hole in the earth and cover it over as a repository for their winter food: this they continue to repeat during the proper season. We may conclude that many of these hoards escape their subsequent search, and spring up to form Britannia's glorious bulwark. Can we see, and not estimate the admirable harmony of Nature?

John Ellis, Esq, discovered that acorns can be preserved in a state fit for vegetation for a whole year, by enveloping them in bees' wax: other seeds may be conveyed from distant countries by the same means.

In transplanting trees of any considerable size, more attention should be observed to the ancient practice of marking the bark so as to give them the same aspect they enjoyed in their original situation; an attentive observer will perceive that nature often clothes the northern bark with a coat of lichen, while the southern side is bare to the softer rains and warmer aspect; may not even the bark itself be formed for each particular aspect? Because we find some superstitious customs among the Romans, let us not condemn all their practices, but take a lesson from Virgil's unrivalled poem:—

Quinetiam Cœli regionem in cortice signant;
Ut quo quæque modo steterit, qua parte calores
Austrinos tulerit; quæ terga obverterit axi, restituant.

"Also Heaven's quarters on the bark they score,
That they may coast it as it was before,
Which Southern heat sustain'd, which view'd the Pole."

The oak principally used for wainscot, &c., is brought from Dantzic and Norway.

The evergreen oak *(ilex)* is a native of the south of Europe, and is planted merely to ornament our gardens and plantations: this variety was introduced into England in 1581, and is found to grow in great perfection on the banks of the Thames, west of London. There is an oak of this description in the grounds belonging to the Bishop of London's palace at Fulham, more than fifty feet high, and eight feet in circumference. We conclude it was planted by Bishop Compton, who introduced many new plants and forest trees from North America and other parts of the world.*

* The various species and varieties of the oak will be noticed in a future work on Plantations.

APRICOT.—ARMENIACA.

OR, PRÆCOCIA MALA.

Natural order, Pomaceæ. A genus of the Icosandria Monogynia class.

——And Apricots,
Seed of the sun, from Iran's Land.

THE name of the Apricot has been thought to be derived from *Apricus*, open and exposed to the sun; or from *præcox*, early ripe: but there can be no doubt that the word is a corruption of the Arabic name of the fruit, variously written in European characters, *barkuk*, *berkach*, or *berikach*.

M. L. Legnier has made some remarks on this subject, which appeared in the Revue Encyclopédique, for November 1815. Here he says, "I was struck with its mode of growth in Egypt, whither it was anciently brought from latitudes still more southern. In Egypt its leaves have scarcely fallen off before the blossoms appear again. The name of *berikokka*, first given to it even in Greece, approaches very near to its Arabian name of *berkach*, or *berikach*." M. L. Legnier adds, "that the inhabitants of the deserts called Oasis, gather and dry large quantities of apricots, which they bring down to Egypt for sale; and they are there called *michmich*." "The result of every inquiry I made," says this author, "was, that the apricot-tree grows there spontaneously, almost without cultivation: and as it is not known to grow in the natural state in any part of Armenia, we may very justly conclude that it is an Arabian fruit."

Dr. Turner, who wrote his Herbal soon after the introduction of this tree into the English garden, calls it *abrecok*. Gerarde, in 1597, writes it *abrecoke*, *aprecock*, and *aprecox*.

The apricot was, however, long considered, and in most botanical works stated, to be a native of Epirus; and the name of *pruneus Armeniaca* having been given to it in mistake, and which unquestionably belonged to another fruit, it has been transmitted down from one author to another, without particular enquiry. Theophrastus, one of the oldest authors, never mentions the apricot-tree as being cultivated in Greece, at the time when he lived: on the contrary, he alludes to it as an exotic, from an account transmitted to him. He also mentions the almond, as being the only tree in his country which produced the flowers before the leaves. (*Theoph. Hist. Plant. lib.* vii. c. 12.)

Columella is the oldest Roman author who has mentioned the tree that has been considered the apricot. He writes, that at the end of January we may graft the cherry-tree, the Armenian plum, the nectarine, the almond, the peach-tree, and others which blossom early.

Pliny also mentions the Armenian plum; and says there is a plum brought from a foreign nation, which is called *Armeniaca*, and is desirable for its smell. This great naturalist has particularly mentioned the apricot, as distinct from the Armenian plum: he states that it was not known above thirty years before he wrote the account; which would make its introduction into Italy about the sixtieth year of the Christian era. Pliny says, "at its first coming, each sold for a Roman denier:" he adds, "this fruit is harmless, and is in such request among invalids, that thirty sesterces are given for one of them, which is as great a price as is given for any fruit whatever. We have," continues he, "two sorts, *supernatia*, which we have from the Sabines; and *popularia*, which grow common everywhere." Thus Pliny has furnished us with an account of the apricot, and omitted to mention from whence it was first procured.

Sonnini, in his Travels in Egypt, observed that in some parts of that country near the plains of Siout, you find abundance of small apricots: they are called Mischmisch, and have an agreeable flavour. They dry them, and afterwards dress them as sauce to meats. These dishes, he observes, usually garnish the tables of the rich, and are of the best sort which come from Egyptian kitchens.

Thunberg describes the apricot-tree as growing to a large size in Japan. Grosier says it covers the barren mountains to the west of Pekin; and Pallas tells us that it is commonly wild on the whole tract of Caucasus.

The Chinese have a great variety of fruiting apricots, and they not only preserve the fruit both dry and in liquor, but make lozenges from the clarified juice, which dissolved in water yields a cool refreshing beverage. From the wild tree, the fruit of which has little pulp, but a large kernel, they extract a great quantity of oil.

The Persians have a delicious kind of apricot which they call *tokm ekshems*, signifying sun's seed.

The apricot-tree was first brought to England from Italy, in the year 1524, by Woolf, gardener of Henry the Eighth, who it appears introduced several valuable fruits about the same period. (*Gough's British Topography*, vol. i. page 133.)

Turner, whose work was written in 1564 and published in 1568, says, "I have sene many trees of thys kynde in Almany, and som in England." Gerarde in 1597 notices two varieties that he tells us "do grow in my garden, and now-adaies in many other gentlemen's gardens throughout all England." Parkinson notices but two varieties of this fruit, and Coles says also, in 1657, "I am not assured that there are more than two sorts of Apricot-trees."

We have now many varieties of this fruit, some of which, by their names, inform us whence they were procured, as the Algier, the Roman, the Turkey, the Breda, and the Brussels apricot, besides the Muscadine, the Orange, and several new varieties. It is one of our earliest wall-fruits, as well as one in the highest estimation.

The fruit, when gathered young to thin the crop, makes an excellent tart; and, when ripe, it is second to no fruit for preserves or jam: it gives an excellent flavour to ice, and makes a delicious *liqueur*. Of all the fruits used in pastry, none is more beautiful or agreeable than the ripe apricot: they should be placed in an open pastry, the stones taken out, and a kernel placed on each fruit, which adds as much to the flavour as to the appearance. To prolong the enjoyment of this fruit in its natural state, we should be careful to plant the earliest variety in the warmest situation, as the frost often injures the blossoms of the Muscadine apricot, unless it is protected by a glass shutter or some substitute. The Brussels apricot is the latest ripe, and it should be observed that this variety produces better fruit when not exposed to so full a sun. In this age which exerts so much ingenuity to accelerate the maturity of vegetation, we shall endeavour to point out the best means of retarding or prolonging the season of fruits. The apricot as well as the plum may be kept for our dessert two or three weeks later, by gathering it when half ripe and placing it in an ice-house, a dairy, or any cool place, where it slowly ripens.

Apricots, if not too ripe, agreeably astringe and strengthen the stomach, but like all other perfumed watery fruit, it loses its aromatic and tempting flavour, becomes clammy, and is less easy of digestion, when over-ripe: they should therefore be gathered at least twenty-four hours before they acquire the last degree of maturity.

The apricot-tree produces its blossom buds not only on the last year's wood, but also on the curzons, or spurs, from the two year old wood. Great care should be used, in pruning, not to injure them; and it is advisable to remove all foreright shoots in the growing time.

The Brussels and the Breda apricot are the best as standard trees: they are all propagated, by grafting them on plum stocks, excepting the Alberge, the seed of which will produce the same fruit, or with very little variation.

Madame de Genlis relates the following anecdote, which cannot be translated so as to retain the wit, which depends on the agreement of the French name for apricot-tree with the inscription alluded to.

Après la mort de Louis XI, au commencement de la régence de Madame de Beaujeu, plusieurs personnes furent disgraciées; entre autres, Cotier, premier médécin du feu roi, qui s'applaudissant d'être échappé de cette cour orageuse, fit sculpter sur la porte de sa maison un abricotier avec cette inscription, 'A l'abri Cotier.'

ALMOND.—AMYGDALUS.

Natural order, Pomaceæ. A genus of the Icosandria Monogynia class.

THAT the Almond-tree is a native of Syria and Arabia, we have the authority of the earliest writers.

Jacob mentions almonds among the best fruits of the land of Canaan, when he says to his sons, "Take of the best fruits in the land in your vessels, and carry down the man a present, a little balm, and a little honey, spices and myrrh, nuts and almonds." By the miracle of Aaron's rod we learn that this tree was growing in the wilderness—"the rod of Aaron for the house of Levi was budded, and brought forth buds, and blossomed blossoms, and yielded almonds." The Israelites did not use the same ornamental statuary that adorned the heathen temples, but copied the fruits and flowers of their country, where they admitted embellishment. The almond was selected to beautify the candlesticks for the tabernacle, which were made of pure gold, of beaten work: "Three bowls made after the fashion of almonds in one branch, a knop and a flower: and three bowls made like almonds in another branch, a knop and a flower; so throughout the six branches going out of the candlestick. And in the six candlesticks were four bowls made like almonds, his knops, and his flowers."

Theophrastus, who wrote about 300 years before Christ, mentions the almond as the only tree in Greece that produced the blossoms before the leaves. Servius relates the traditionary tale of Phyllis's being changed by the gods into an almond-tree, which was called *phylla* by the Greeks. Some days after this metamorphosis, Demophoon, her lover, revisited Thrace, of which Phyllis was queen: and when he heard of the fate of Phyllis, he ran and clasped the tree, which, though at that time stripped of its leaves, suddenly shot forth and blossomed, as if sensible of his tenderness and love.

The almond-tree was not cultivated in Italy in the time of Cato, who calls the fruit, *nuces Græcæ*, or Greek nuts. There are now orchards and whole fields of them in that country, as well as in the south of France.

The Jordan almond-tree was first planted in England in the reign of Henry the Eighth, 1548. *(Hortus Kewensis.)* Dr. Turner notices it in the year 1645, and says "almond-trees growe muche in hyghe Germany beside Sypre in a cytie called Newstat, and great plentye in Italye, and some growe in England, but I have hearde of no greate store of the fruyte of them that growe in England."

Lord Bacon, whose Natural History was written some years after this time, mentions it among the trees that blossom earliest, and whose fruit ripens latest: and which he accounts for as being a tree that hath much oily moisture. He recommends almond butter as an excellent nourisher to those that are weak; as also the oil of almonds, newly drawn, with sugar and a little spice, spread upon toasted bread, as a nourishing diet.

The Jordan almonds are the most esteemed for the table, and are named after the river Jordan, so celebrated in the Old Testament, and from whence they were first procured: these almonds, when taken in moderation, are wholesome, being cooling, healing, emollient, and nutritive: they are much prescribed in emulsions, and are found of good effect in all disorders arising from choleric and acrimonious humours. Dr. John Hill tells us that sweet almonds are good to be eaten in consumptive cases, if thoroughly chewed, as they supply many of the good offices of milk, when the stomach will not bear that fluid, and serve at once as a medicine and a food.

The oil of almonds is principally drawn from the Valentian and Barbary almonds, and is well known for its medicinal qualities. The bitter almond contains a great deal of oil; more salt than the sweet almond; and but little phlegm: it is for that reason, that the oil of the bitter almond will keep a longer time without growing musty, than the oil of sweet almonds.

Hoffman tells us that a family of ten persons, who had taken two ounces of arsenic by mistake in some water-gruel, were relieved and recovered from danger by the oil of almonds and milk which he administered. The same author says, " oil of sweet almonds taken to the quantity of some spoonfuls, in a little broth, is a most effectual medicine in all pains and spasms; even in such spasms as shake the most remote part of the body: for this reason, it is very properly prescribed in convulsive coughs, &c."

On triturating the almond with water, it unites with the fluid, into an emulsion or milky liquor. It is also useful for uniting substances with water, which of themselves are not miscible with it.

Bitter almonds were considered by the ancients as of use to prevent or relieve intoxication. Plutarch relates that Drusus's physician, who was a great drinker, took at every cup five bitter almonds, to allay the heat and fumes of the wine, and that though he became the greatest drinker of the age, he was never intoxicated. The bitter almonds are held aperient, detersive, and diuretic; they are therefore recommended in obstructions of the liver, spleen, &c. Pliny states, that a decoction of the roots of the bitter almond-tree supples the skin, prevents wrinkles, and gives a fresh, cheerful colour to the countenance; and that bitter almonds cause sleep, and create appetite. They were considered a cure for chilblains, as well as for the bite of a mad dog.

Neumann states, that these almonds are poisonous to birds, and all animals that come into the world blind. The Bohemians are said to bruise them, and to throw them where fowls frequent, which will stupify those that eat them, so that they are easily taken by the hand. The bitter almonds are more generally used for culinary purposes, and for flavouring cordials, &c. From the Jordan almond is produced one of the most exquisite and nourishing of all our soups.

As an ornamental tree, the almond deserves to be more generally cultivated in our shrubberies, and particularly as a foreground to clumps of evergreens in parks and plantations, which have a sombre appearance towards the spring, that would be much relieved by the blushing petals which grace the leafless branches of the almond-tree in the month of March, and give a gaiety to the plantations at a time when no other trees are in blossom. In favourable seasons, the fruit often comes to perfect maturity in this country; but these almonds will not keep so well as those produced in warmer climates; but when gathered young and preserved with their peachy pulp, they make an excellent sweetmeat, and we have no doubt but that they would be found an equally agreeable pickle.

It is observed that the handsomest almond-trees are those which have not been transplanted, but raised by planting well-ripened almonds in the month of October, or November; but they may be planted in February or March, if care be taken to preserve them in sand. Both the common and the dwarf almonds are, however, more generally propagated by inoculating a bud of either of these trees into a plum or peach stock, in the month of

July. For a wet or cold soil they should be budded on a plum stock; but where the soil is light and dry, the peach or almond stock is preferable. The nature of the soil, as well as the season, should be attended to in transplanting these trees. Where the ground is dry the month of October is a proper time; but in wet or cold lands the month of February is a better season. They should be trained with single stems; but when of a proper height they require no pruning, and are more graceful when allowed to branch out in their natural way.

Plate 1 THE APPLE BLOSSOM

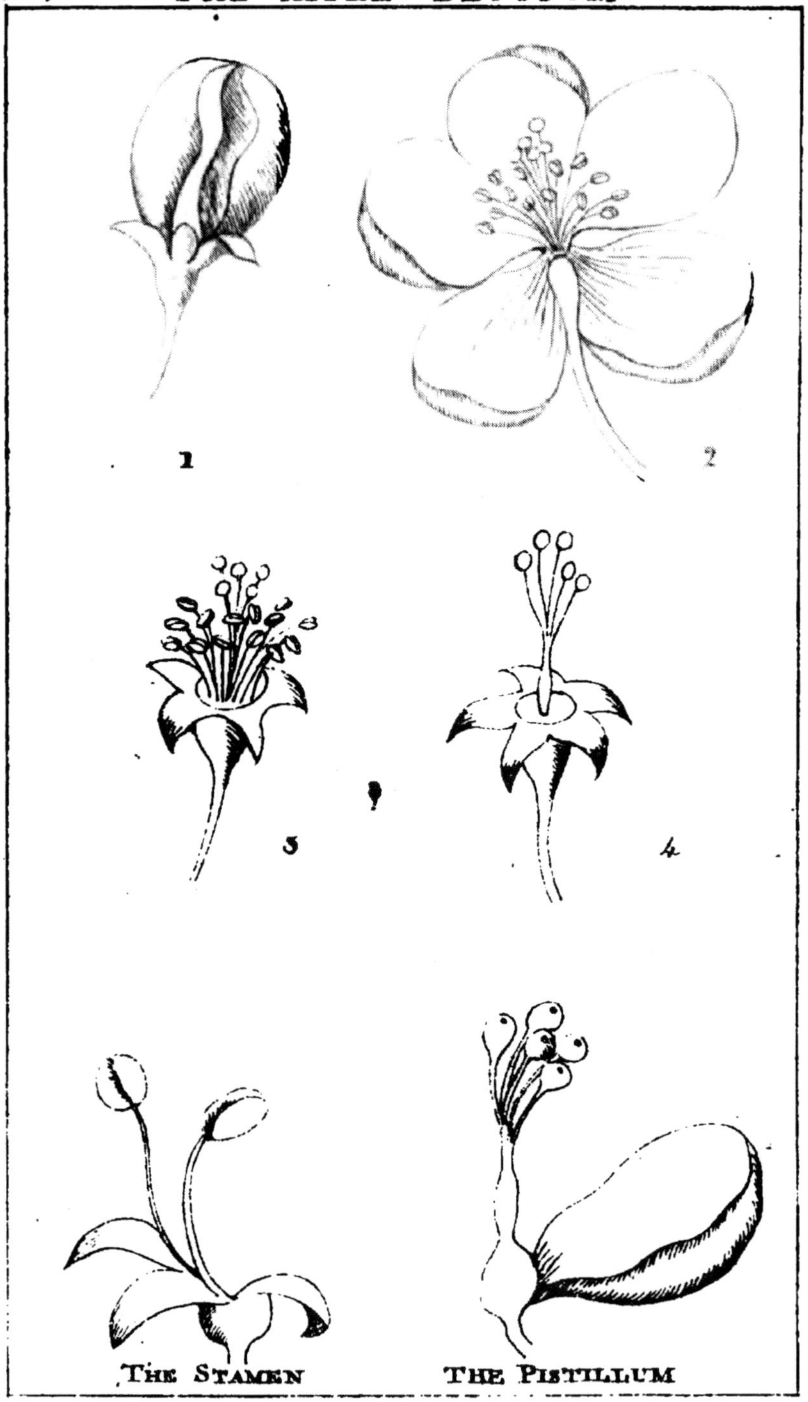

Magnified.

APPLE-TREE.—MALUS.

Natural order, Pomaceæ. A species of the Pyrus, belonging to the genus of Icosandria Pentagynia.

"Comfort me with Apples."
Song of Solomon.

The Apple-tree appears from the testimony of Sacred History, as well as that of the naturalists of ancient Greece and Rome, to be a native of the east. The prophet Joel, where he declares the destruction of the fruits of the earth by a long drought, mentions the fruits which were held in estimation, and among them names the apple-tree.

Solomon writes—"As the apple-tree among the trees of the wood, so is my beloved among the sons."

Apple-trees, from the earliest accounts, seem to have required the fostering care of man. Of all fruit-trees, Pliny says, the apple is the tenderest, and least able to bear heat or cold, particularly the early sweet apples. For a long time the apple-tree was of the highest value among fruit-trees with the Romans: "there are many apple-trees," says Pliny, "in the villages near Rome that let for the yearly sum of 2000 sesterces," which is equal to 12*l.* 10*s.* of our money; "and some of them," says this author, "yield more profit to the owner than a small farm, and which brought about the invention of grafting.

——— "Graft the tender shoot,
Thy children's children shall enjoy the fruit."
Virgil.

"There are apples," says Pliny, "that have ennobled the countries from whence they came; and many apples have immortalized their first founders and inventors. Our best apples," continues he, "will honour the first grafters for ever; such as took their names from Matius, Cestius, Manlius, and Claudius." This author particularizes the quince apples, that came from a quince grafted upon an apple stock, which, he says, smell like the quince, and were called Appiana, after Appius, who was of the Claudian house, and who was the first that practised this grafting. "Some apples," says he, "are so red that they resemble blood, which is caused by their being at first grafted upon a mulberry stock." But of all the apples he mentions, he says the one which took its name from Petisius, who reared it in his time, was the most excellent for eating, both on account of its sweetness and agreeable flavour. He mentions nine-and-twenty kinds of apples as being cultivated in Italy at about the commencement of the Christian era. The grafting of trees was carried to its greatest extent about this time. "I have seen," says Pliny, "near Thuliæ, in the country of the Tiburtines, a tree grafted and laden with all manner of fruits, one bough bearing nuts, another berries; here hung grapes, there figs; in one part you might see pears, in another pomegranates; and, to conclude, there is no kind of apple or other fruit but there it was to be found: but this tree did not live long." Modern grafters will condemn this account as fabulous or exaggerated; but what reason can we have to doubt the authority of a man, whose life was spent to the benefit of mankind, and whose death was caused by his perseverance in the research after truth in the wonderful works of nature? Let those who dispute this account be able to tell us why a graft, taking nourishment from a crab-stock, shall have a fruit more noble than its nurse and parent.

Lord Bacon mentions apple scions that were grafted upon the stock of a colewort, which produced great flaggy apples. This great man observes, "that grafting should be done on a drier stock, as the apple upon the crab, the pear upon the thorn," &c.

Thornton says, in his History of Turkey, that "apples are among the most common fruits of Wallachia, and that one variety appears natural to the climate, as it bears without culture a fruit called *domniasca*, which is perhaps the finest in Europe, both for size, odour, and flavour."

Sir William Ouseley tells us, in his account of the Eastern Nations, that "in the territory of *Istakhr*, a kind of apple grows, the half of which is sweet and the other half sour."

The wild crab is the only apple indigenous to this country; and it is on this stock that most of our valuable apples have been grafted and raised by the ingenuity of the gardeners, who have, by sowing the seeds and studying the soil, so improved and multiplied the varieties of this most excellent fruit, that it has now become of great national importance, affording an agreeable and wholesome diet, in a thousand shapes, to all classes of society.

The English name of this valuable fruit is evidently derived from the Saxon word æppel; and from which circumstance we may safely conclude that the fruit was cultivated in this country under the Saxon government, if not previously by the Romans.

Maliciously barking of apple-trees, or other fruit-trees, is made felony by 37th Henry VIII. c. 6.

But it was not until the 16th year of the reign of that monarch, that pippins were first introduced into England, by Leonard Maschal, who, in Fuller's words, "brought them from over sea," and planted them at Plumstead, in Sussex, a small village on the north side of the South Downs, near the Devil's Dyke. Maschal brought the first carp to England, and thus, at one time, furnished our orchards and our ponds with the rarest variety of each kind.

Pippins take their name from the small spots or pips, that usually appear on the sides of these apples. The golden pippin is a native of Sussex, and is said to have been first reared at Parham Park, which is also situated on the north side of the South Downs. The Dutch acknowledge it to be an English apple in their catalogue of fruits, where it is called the "Engelsche goud Pepping." The French call it "Pippin d'Or," which is a translation of the English name. Worlidge notices the golden pippin, and says, "it is smaller than the orange-apple, else much like it in colour, taste, and long keeping." Evelyn observes in his Diary, 22d October, 1685, that "at Lord Clarendon's seat at Swallowfield, Berks, there is an orchard of 1000 golden and other cider pippins."

Catherine, Empress of Russia, was so fond of this apple, that she was regularly supplied with it from England; and in order that she might have it in the greatest perfection, each apple was separately enveloped in silver paper before it was packed.

Our earliest apple is ripe at the end of June, hence called June eating, and now corrupted into Juniting and Jenniting.

The Ribston pippin is a native of Ribston Park, Yorkshire. Hargrave, in his History of Knaresborough, (p. 216,) says, "This place is remarkable for the produce of a delicious apple, called the Ribston Park pippin. The original tree was raised from a pippin brought from France, from which tree such numbers have been propagated, that they are now to be met with in almost every orchard in this and many other counties." The old tree is yet standing: and in the year 1787 produced six bushels of fruit. Mr. Speechly says, "he has seen the tree within these last few years, and that it was without decay, or any indication of dissolution."

Hargrave adds, "This fruit still retains its value, being preferred before every other apple this country produces." While Philips says in his Poem on Cider :—

"Let every tree in every garden own
The Redstreak as supreme ; whose pulpous fruit
With gold irradiate, and vermilion, shines
Tempting, not fatal, as the birth of that
Primeval interdicted plant, that won
Fond Eve in hapless hour to taste, and die.
This, of more bounteous influence, inspires
Poetic raptures, and the lowly Muse
Kindles to loftier strains ; even I perceive
Her sacred virtue. See ! the numbers flow
Easy, whilst, cheer'd with her nectareous juice,
Her's and my country's praises I exalt.
Hail, Herefordian plant, that dost disdain
All other fields ! Heaven's sweetest blessing, hail!
Be thou the copious matter of my song,
And thy choice nectar ! on which always waits
Laughter, and Sport, and care-beguiling Wit,
And Friendship, chief delight of human life.
What should we wish for more ? Or why, in quest
Of foreign vintage, insincere, and mix'd,
Traverse th' extremest world ? Why tempt the rage
Of the rough ocean, when our native glebe
Imparts from bounteous womb annual recruits
Of wine delectable, that far surmounts
Gallic or Latin grapes, or those that see
The setting sun near Calpe's tow'ring height.
Nor let the Rhodian nor the Lesbian vines
Vaunt their rich must, nor let Tokay contend
For sov'reignty ; Phanæus' self must bow
To th' Ariconian vales."

Gerard, who wrote his History of Plants about seventy years after the introduction of pippins, has given no account of this variety of the apple. He describes but seven kinds: the pome water, the baker-ditch apple, the king of apples, the quining, or queen of apples, the summer pearmain, the winter pearmain, and the Paradise apple. In his description of apples, he says, "The fruit of apples do differ in greatness, forme, colour and taste; some covered with a red skin, others yellow or greene, varying infinitely according to the soyle and climate; some very great, some little, and many of a middle sort; some are sweet of taste, or something sour; most be of a middle taste, betweene sweet and sour; the which to distinguish I think it impossible, notwithstanding I heare of one that intendeth to write a peculiar volume of apples, and the use of them." This author continues, "The tame and grafted apple-trees are planted and set in gardens and orchards made for that purpose: they delight to grow in good and fertile grounds. Kent doth abound with apples of most sorts; but I have seen in the pastures and hedge-rows, about the grounds of a worshipful gentleman dwelling two miles from Hereford, called M. Roger Bodnome, so many trees of all sortes, that the seruants drink for the most part no other drinke but that which is made of apples. The quantitie is such, that by the report of the gentleman himselfe, the parson hath for tithe many hogsheads of cyder." "Like as there be divers manured apples, so is there sundry wilde apples, or crabs, not husbanded, that is, not grafted. We have in our London gardens, (Gerard's garden was in Holborn) a dwarfe kind of sweet apple called the Paradise apple, which beareth apples very timely without grafting."

From this account we may conclude, that the pippin apples were still rare, or that they had not been cultivated out of Sussex, although I find Gerard must have seen the fruit of the pippin kind, for, in his account of the pomum amoris, or love-apple, he says it is the bigness of a goose egg or a large pippin. The pippin appears to have been scarce even in the time of Charles the First; for in the valuation of the fruit-trees at the royal gardens of his queen at Wimbledon, there is only one pippin-tree mentioned.

For some years past, it has been stated by several ingenious writers, that many of our best varieties of apples could no longer be cultivated with success; that by length of time they have become degenerated and worn out. Mr. Knight, the president of the Horticultural Society, seems to have been the first that gave birth to this idea. He says, in his Pomona Herefordiensis, that those apples which have been long cultivated are on the decay. The Redstreak and the Golden Pippin can no longer be propagated with advantage. The fruit, like the parent-tree, is affected by the debilitated old age of the variety. Again, he says, in his Treatise on the Culture of the apple and pear, page 6, " the Moil, and its successful rival the Redstreak, with the Must and Golden Pippin, are in the last stage of decay, and the Stire and Foxwhelp are hastening rapidly after them." " It is much to be regretted," says Speechly, " that this apparently visionary notion of the extinction of certain kinds of apples should have been promulgated by authors of respectability, since the mistake will, for a time at least, be productive of several ill consequences." Pliny notices the decay of apple-trees in his time, and observes that the apple-trees become old sooner than any other tree, and that the fruit becomes less, and is subject to be cankered and worm-eaten, even while on the trees. *Book* 16. *c.* 27.

Columella seems to make the same allusion in his 10th book :—

"And Autumn, glutted with all sorts of fruit,
Shaking his hoary head, with apples deck'd."

Having observed among the apples in Covent-garden market, in 1819, a great quantity of the real Golden Pippin in a perfect state, the author was induced to make particular inquiries respecting this fruit; and has received satisfactory accounts from all quarters that these trees are fast recovering from a disease, or canker, which appears to have been brought on by a succession of unpropitious seasons; but that the summer of 1818, and the following year, have greatly improved them.

When the author had decided to publish this History of Fruits, he waited on some gentlemen who are well known in all parts of the world for their practical knowledge in the cultivation of apples. Mr. Hugh Ronalds, jun. of Brentford, informed him that he had lately seen a tree of the Golden Pippin kind, which had been planted against a wall in a south aspect, which was in a thriving condition, and the fruit in a perfect state. Mr. Ronalds, sen. assured him it was the true Golden Pippin, and that there is no fear of losing this variety.

Mr. Lee, of Hammersmith, who politely shewed me 500 various kinds of apple-trees, was decidedly of opinion that the apparent decay of some trees was owing to the unfavourable springs we have had for several years.

Mr. Knight, of the King's Road, Chelsea, has also favoured us with his opinion, which perfectly agrees with that of Mr. Ronalds and Mr. Lee. Mr. Knight added, that if this spring and summer should be as favourable as the two last seasons, he should be able to shew this and other old varieties of the apple-tree in as perfect a state as they have ever been known. Since the first edition of this work was printed, we have had opportunities of making observations and farther inquiries as to the state of these trees both in this and other countries, the result of which has been that of confirming the opinions of the gentlemen before named. We are informed by Thomas Harrison, Esq. who resided several years in the Island of Madeira, that there are at this time a considerable number of the true Golden Pippin-trees growing on the mountains in Madeira, about fourteen miles from the capital of that island, and at an elevation of about 3000 feet above the sea, which regularly produce abundance of fruit, notwithstanding the trunk and branches are covered with a white lichen or moss. Grafts which were sent from these trees about three years ago, produced fruit at Cheshunt in Hertfordshire the second year, and proved to be the original Golden Pippin. These trees are also in a thriving state in several parts of America, as has been shewn by the excellent quality of the fruit lately sent to this country. We observed them also in several parts of England during the summer of 1821 in as healthy a state as most other apple-trees, particularly in the gardens of Mr. Kirk of Old Brompton, and Messrs. Humphreys at Chichester, where the fruit was of a size and perfection which has been rarely surpassed: thus it appears that the Golden Pippin only requires the most genial situation of the orchard, to render it as prolific as formerly.

Mr. Knight, the ingenious president of the Horticultural Society, we conclude, had watched these trees during the unfavourable wet seasons we have had from the commencement of the present century, and finding the disease increase, he attributed it to the old age of the varieties; for, as the great friend of Pomona, his object evidently was to encourage the obtaining and cultivation of new kinds, to replace those which he apprehended would be lost to the country. We have made this digression, to prevent if possible our best apples from being stigmatized as a decaying fruit, and unprofitable to the grafter, which would be the cause of their becoming scarce, and, in time, totally lost. We have not presumed to set our judgment in opposition to that of Mr. Knight, who is so justly celebrated for his attention to horticultural pursuits; but it behoves all who may write of this most valuable fruit, to recommend the graftings to be of the best kinds, and to throw out no hint that may cause our nurserymen to neglect its propagation. Gerard, when he published his Account of the Apple in 1597, was a warm advocate for the cultivation of apples. "Gentlemen that have land and living," says he, "put forward, in the name of God; graffe, set, plant, and nourish up trees in euery corner of your grounds; the labour is small, the cost is nothing, the commoditie is great, your selues shall have plentie, the poor shall have somewhat in time of want to relieve their necessitie, and God shall reward your good mindes and diligence."

Thomas Andrew Knight, Esq. has, for some years past, been benefiting his country, by creating, if I may be allowed the expression, a new variety of fruits; but before we disclose the ingenious method he has adopted to procure new varieties, it is but justice to departed merit to notice by whom the invention was first deemed possible: and we have great pride and satisfaction in stating, that, after an unprejudiced research, we find this wonderful discovery has been left for the perseverance of the English, who, although late in taking up botanical studies, have now surpassed whatever was done by the ancient world in this science.

Lord Bacon, who has been called the Prophet of Arts, and who looked into nature with a most curious eye of inquiry, evidently suspected that it was possible to cross the breed of plants, and so procure kinds, by art, as novel as those which Nature has sometimes produced by accident.

"We see," says the great Verulam, "that in living creatures that have male and female, there is copulation of several kinds, and so compounded creatures; as the mule that is generated betwixt the horse and the ass; and some other compounds which we call monsters.

"The compounding or mixture of kinds in plants is not found out; which nevertheless, if it be possible, is more at command than that of living creatures; wherefore it were one of the most notable experiments touching plants to find it out, for so you may have great variety of new fruits, and flowers yet unknown. Grafting does it not:" adds this great man: "*that* mendeth the fruit, or doubleth the flowers, &c.; but it hath not the power to make a new kind, for the scion ever overruleth the stock."

Bradley, whose works were published in 1718, about a century after those of Lord Bacon, is the first author who wrote on this subject as being accomplished; but the exact method was not then clearly understood, as he only describes it by bringing the branches of different trees together when in blossom. But, on this hint, the gardeners in Holland and the Netherlands practised before it was much attended to in this country, where the discovery was made and published; and, to do them justice, they have the honour to acknowledge they owe the art to the English.

In the Monthly Review for November 1750, (vol. I. p. 55,) an account of the mixed breed of apples is noticed by Mr. Benjamin Cooke of the Isle of Wight, and is clearly explained by the editor's observation.

It now appears to have reached its highest perfection; and we shall proceed to relate the manner in which Mr. Knight has so successfully produced new varieties of apples and other fruits. Although he has most clearly explained himself, yet we have thought it advisable to elucidate it more plainly by plates from drawings which we have made from the blossoms for the express purpose, knowing how little even the botanical terms are understood by the farmers, and many gardeners in the country.

Mr. Knight, in his *Pomona Herefordiensis*, says, "It is necessary to contrive that the two trees from which you intend to raise the new kind, should blossom at the same time; therefore if one is an earlier sort than the other, it must be retarded by shading, or brought into a cooler situation, and the latest forwarded by a warm wall or a sunny situation, so as to procure the blossoms at the same period."

The apple-blossom contains about twenty stamina or males, which are represented in Plate I. No. 3. and generally five pointals or females, which form the centre of the cup or cavity of the blossom, as in Figure No. 4. The males stand in a circle, just within the bases of the petals, or flower leaves, and are formed of slender threads, each of which terminates in a small yellow ball or anther, as in Fig. 5. As soon as the blossoms are nearly full grown, as in Fig. 1, they must be carefully opened, and all the male stamina cut or extracted, so as not to injure the pointals or females, which will then appear as in Fig. 4. The blossoms are then closed again, as in Fig. 1, and suffered to remain till they open spontaneously. From the blossoms of the tree, which it is proposed to make the male parent of the future variety, must be taken a portion of their pollen or farina, when ready to fall from the mature anthers; and this pollen must be deposited upon the pointals of the blossoms of the tree which is intended to bear the variety, which consequently will afford seed. By shaking the blossoms over a sheet of white paper, you will ascertain when the pollen is ready. It is necessary in this experiment, to cover the branches on which the prepared blossoms are, with a thin muslin or gauze, so as not to touch the flowers, or keep off the sun or air, but to prevent the bees or other insects from inoculating them with the pollen of other blossoms, which would make the experiment uncertain; and in order to obtain the fruit and the seeds of a large size, it is best to leave but few blossoms on the tree, and, at all events, to clear the branches on which the prepared flowers are, from all other blossoms. When the fruit is quite ripe, the pips or seeds should be sown at a proper season, and in suitable soil, and in about four or six years fruit may be expected. Mr. Knight has also made some curious experiments between the peach and the almond, which will be found in the account of the former fruit. Among the new apples which the world have to thank Mr. Knight for, is the Grange apple, which fruited first in 1802, and obtained the prize of the Herefordshire Agricultural Society: it is the offspring of the Orange Pippin and the Golden Pippin. He also obtained the annual premium of the same society, in 1807, for the Siberian Harvey, an apple which fruited for the first time in that year. This tree was raised from the seed of the Yellow Siberian Crab and the pollen of the Golden Harvey. Mr. Knight also raised the Foxley apple, from the seed of the yellow Siberian crab and the pollen of the orange pippin: this fruit also received the premium in 1808, and it is said to rival the golden pippin in sweetness.

Apples and pears may be raised from seed in the short space of four years, by the following mode: Sow the kernels in separate pots in November, and place them in a green-house during winter. They will vegetate in February; at Midsummer remove the plants into a seed-bed in rows, about fourteen inches apart. In the autumn of the following year transplant them into a nursery at a distance of six feet. Every succeeding winter prune away all small lateral shoots, leaving the stronger laterals to the bottom, and so disposing the branches, that the leaves of the upper shoots may not shade those underneath.

The Chinese method of raising fruit trees has of late years been practised with success, and with the great advantages of keeping the varieties perfect and an early production of fruit. They strip a ring of bark, of about an inch in width, from a bearing branch, surround the place with a ball of fat earth or loam, with a mixture of cow dung, bound fast to the branch with a piece of sacking or mat: over this they suspend a pot or horn, with water, having a small hole in the bottom just sufficient to let the water drop, in order to keep the compost constantly moist. The branch throws roots into the earth just above where the bark has been stripped off. The operation is performed in the spring, and the branch is sawn off and put into the ground at the fall of the leaf. The following year it will bear fruit.

The cultivation of this our most valuable fruit, has been attended to with so much care of late years, that one of our principal nurserymen (Mr. Hugh Ronalds, of Brentford,) exhibited at the Horticultural Society, in August 1818, sixteen varieties of apples, and in September he exhibited fifty-eight other sorts, all grown in his own garden, and considered the finest collection ever exhibited. In the month of October of the same year, he exhibited fifty-three sorts, making in the whole a variety of 127 kinds of this our staple fruit, which, in point of real value, takes place of all others, and affords a variety for all seasons of the year, both for the dessert and for culinary purposes, as well as the drink, of which Philips in Miltonian verse has sung,—

> Some ciders have, by art or age, unlearn'd
> Their genuine relish, and of sundry vines

Assumed the flavour: one sort counterfeits
The sparkling nectar of Champagne; with that,
A German oft has swill'd his throat, and sworn,
Deluded, that imperial Rhine bestow'd
The gen'rous rummer, whilst the owner, pleased,
Laughs inly at his guest, thus entertain'd
With foreign vintage from his cider cask.

Thomson has thus beautifully described the cider season:—

The fragrant stores, the wide projected heaps
Of apples, which the lusty-handed year,
Innumerous, o'er the blushing orchard shakes;
A various spirit, fresh, delicious, keen,
Dwells in their gelid pores; and, active, points
The piercing cider for the thirsty tongue.

The word *Cider* is a slight abbreviation from the *Seider* of the ancient Britons, and which having some analogy with the Greek word Sikera, induces us to believe that it is a beverage of great antiquity in this country. Huet is of opinion that the use of cider was first introduced into Neustria by the Normans, who had learned it of the Biscayans, as these latter had done from the inhabitants of the northern coast of Africa.

Dr. Short informs us, that cider was first invented by a Norman, who much admired the delicate flavour of apples; and "long observation," says he, "assures us, that such as chiefly drink cider, are more healthy and strong, and have better complexions, than those that are accustomed to wine or ale." Both Lord Bacon and Dr. Baynard tell us of several persons near a hundred, and some above, who, having seldom used any other liquor, were very active and vigorous at that age. It is certainly more nourishing than wine, for, not being so thoroughly fermented, its spirits are less subtile and impetuous.

It has been also remarked that those who drink cider are free from apoplexy, which often overthrows the strongest ale tippler. But we are decidedly of opinion, that our beverage, like our diet, ought not to be too uniform. The constant use of any one particular kind of drink, as of food, might have some bad effects. Nature seems to give us this opinion by the aliments which she has provided for man, and likewise by giving him an appetite for different kinds of food.

Many estates might be improved, the country enriched, and the people benefited, were the planting of cider fruit more attended to, particularly on those grounds not fit for corn. Cider is always a marketable commodity, it costs no fuel to make it, and when well made it brings as high a price from the press as the Frenchman obtains for his boasted wines from the vat: lét us then imitate the Parsis, who hold few good works in more estimation than the planting of trees. They have also a great unwillingness to cut down any fruit-tree.

Apple-wine is admired as a summer beverage, but it is by no means equal to the cider made from Golden Pippins, which, when given in good condition, and well timed, surpasses every other refreshing drink. The spirit extracted from cider is equal to brandy for preserving fruit, or mixing in made wines or liquors.

A solution of iron in the juice of the golden rennet, evaporated to a thick consistency, proves an elegant chalybeate.

Apples were formerly used as a cosmetic to soften the skin and take away freckles.

"There is made an ointment," says Gerard, "with the pulp of apples and swine's grease and rose-water, which is used to beautify the face, and to take away the roughness of the skin, which is called in shops pomatum, of the apples whereof it is made."

As the Horticultural Society of this country has been established for the purpose of benefiting the world by its attention to the improvement of our various fruits, and as it is the study of the members to induce the planters of orchards to cultivate and propagate the best kinds of apples only, we may expect that by their attention we shall soon have our markets supplied with a superior kind of apples to what is now generally offered for sale, as the same land that will produce an ill-flavoured apple will afford a good one; and it is as easy to raise the best kinds of apple-trees as those of inferior value.

Virgil says in his Pastorals:—

> ——"New cheese and chesnuts are our country fare,
> With mellow apples for your welcome cheer."

Coles tells us in his "Paradise of Plants," that "Apples in moderation expel heaviness, and procure mirth." Dr. Veitch, when before the Committee of the Commons on the treatment of insane persons, particularly recommended that their proportion of animal food should be lessened, and that puddings should be substituted: he also says, "The occasional use of cooling fruits, particularly at the warm season of the year, would be attended with advantage."

M. Duduit de Maizieres, a French officer of the king's household, has invented, and practised with great success, a method of making bread with common apples very far superior to potatoe bread. After having boiled one-third of peeled apples, he bruised them while quite warm into two-thirds of flour, including the proper quantity of yeast, and kneaded the whole without water, the juice of the fruit being quite sufficient; when this mixture had acquired the consistency of paste, he put it into a vessel, in which he allowed it to rise for about twelve hours. By this process he obtained a very excellent bread, full of eyes and extremely palatable and light.

The Siberian crab apple was not cultivated in this country until 1758, and the small fruited variety was first introduced in 1784. The flavour of this latter kind is highly esteemed in tarts and puddings, and the tree is often planted to beautify our shrubberies. The dwarf apple-tree, when allowed to spread naturally, is the greatest ornament that can be planted on our lawns, both when in blossom and in fruit, particularly the red varieties.

In pruning apple-trees, nothing more should be done than to cut out all those branches which cross each other, to prevent the rubbing of the bark; but never to shorten any of their shoots, except those shoots or suckers which proceed from the stem, which should be entirely taken off, as also all branches broken by the wind or accident, which should be cut off close to the division of the branch. November is the best time to prune apple-trees, as it injures them to prune in frosty weather, or when the sap begins to rise. Pruning is to be avoided as much as possible, as it creates useless shoots, and prevents the fruiting; but if trees are becoming too full of branches, which will be the case in espaliers, the better way is to rub off the buds and shoots which are irregularly produced in the growing season. All sorts of apples produce their fruit upon curzons, or spurs, therefore it is necessary to be careful not to cut off or destroy them, as they continue to be fruitful for several seasons.

The apples intended to be preserved for the winter should remain on the trees until quite ripe, when they should be gathered in dry weather, and placed in a heap for five or six weeks, in order to sweat: they should then be carefully wiped dry, and those that are perfectly sound, packed in large jars or boxes so as to be excluded from the air, which will keep them sound and plump, and retain their flavour. Tusser tells us in his "Points of Good Husbandry."

> "Fruit gathered too timelie, will taste of the wood,
> Will shrink and be bitter, and seldome proue good:
> So fruit that is shaken, or beat off a tree,
> With brusing in falling, soon faultie will be."

He adds,

> "The moon in the wane, gather fruit for to last,
> But winter fruit gather when Michel is past."

We have found the wood of old apple-trees, when used as a fuel, produce a most agreeable perfume.

The various diseases to which the apple-tree is subject, have occupied the attention and the pen of some of our greatest naturalists, as well as many of our eminent practical gardeners. Dr. John Hill considered the blight on trees to be occasioned by debility or ill-health. Animals of different species are found to engender different kinds of insects, particularly where cleanliness is not attended to. Trees, according to their kinds, attract different blights: our endeavours, therefore, would be in vain to avoid the blight affecting the leaves and blossoms of large trees; but as the trunk and branches of the apple-tree are often injured, and sometimes destroyed, by animalculæ, an attention to the cleanliness of these trees cannot fail of being beneficial to their growth. It has therefore occurred to us, from observations and experiments made since compiling this work, that if the trunks of the apple-trees were rubbed with the leaves and young shoots of the elder, to which every kind of blight has an antipathy, those injurious, although minute insects, would not only be destroyed, but it would prevent their fixing themselves on these trees. As this is a matter of importance to the public, we shall feel obliged by the remarks of any gentlemen who may be disposed to try the experiment. Brimstone pounded and put on lighted charcoal, has been found a successful fumigation for destroying the blight on apple-trees. The canker of apple-trees, we apprehend, is principally occasioned by the uncongenial quality of the soil. We lately travelled with a gentleman, who informed us, that having observed all his apple-trees become cankered at a certain state of growth, he was induced to examine the nature of the soil at the greatest depth the roots had penetrated, and which he found consisted of gravel. Not being willing to give over the propagation of apple-trees, he caused a pavement of bricks to be made on the bed of gravel, which obliged the roots to take a horizontal direction, and thereby prevented their reaching the gravel, since which they have been free from canker. This seems to have been an ancient practice, as many of the gardens which were formerly attached to the monasteries in this country have been found paved with tiles a few feet beneath the earth.

There is an apple-tree now growing on the leads of Romsey Church in Hampshire, which regularly produces two sorts of apples; and we have gathered nuts from a hazel which grows on the top of the Church steeple at Henfield in Sussex.

In planting of orchards we attend more to the fruits that please our fancy, than to kinds that are most congenial to our soil and situation; thus we often see pear-trees unfruitful where apples might be produced, and *vice versa.* Columella notices " Apple-bearing Tibur," and Virgil, " Those whom the walls of Apple-bearing Abella look down upon." Indeed throughout the writings of these authors we are reminded that particular spots were set apart for particular plants.

BARBERRY.—BERBERIS;

OR, THE PIPPERIDGE-BUSH.

A genus of the Hexandria Monogynia class.

The Greeks called this bush ὀξυάκανθα, from the sharpened points of its thorns; which name was adopted in Latin; but the barberry is distinguished as *Oxyacantha Galeni,* there being some difference between Dioscorides and Galen concerning this plant: the latter is the name still used in the shops. *Berberis* is an Arabic name, used by Averroes and the officinal writers; and from which the English name is derived.

The common barberry-bush is a native of this country; and notwithstanding the high state of cultivation this kingdom is now arrived at, it is still to be found growing wild in many parts of the northern counties. Gerard says, in his time (1597) most of the hedges near Colnbrook were nothing else but barberry-bushes.

It is now very properly introduced into our gardens and shrubberies, being both ornamental and useful; but it should not be planted near the house or principal walks, on account of its offensive smell when in blossom. The flowers are small, but beautiful; and on their first appearance have a perfume similar to that of the cowslip, which changes to a putrid and most disagreeable scent, particularly towards the evening and at the decay of the flowers. The author had a barberry-tree in his garden near twenty feet in height, the branches of which extended over a circumference of sixty feet. When covered with blossom in the spring, it had a pleasing effect in the shrubbery; but was so offensive for about a fortnight, that no one could walk near it during that time. It seems particularly attractive to singing-birds, especially the bullfinch and the goldfinch, both of which often build in these bushes.

A very singular circumstance has been stated respecting the barberry-shrub;—that corn sown near it, proves abortive, the ears being in general destitute of grain; and that this influence is sometimes extended to a distance of three or four hundred yards across a field. This, if correct, is a just cause for banishing it from the hedgerows of our arable fields, for which, otherwise, its thorny branches would have made a desirable fence.

Mr. Macro, a very respectable farmer at Barrow, in Suffolk, planted a barberry-bush in his garden, on purpose to ascertain the fact. He set wheat round it three succeeding years, and it was all so completely mildewed, that the best of the little grain it produced, was only about the size of thin rice, and that without any flour. He adds, that some, which he set on the opposite side of his garden one of the years before mentioned, produced very good grain, although the straw was a little mildewed. From this observation the author was induced to try the experiment by sowing clumps of canary seed in his shrubbery. Those which were planted immediately under the barberry-bush certainly produced no seed; but other plants of this grass yielded seed, although not at many yards distance. The celebrated Duhamel, and Mons. Broussonet, who have paid such particular attention to agriculture, assure us that there is no just reason for ascribing this baneful effect to the barberry-bush.

The flowers of the barberry have this singular property, that if you touch the chives which support the stamen with a pin or a straw, &c. they incline towards the pistillum, and they often draw with them the petals, and the flower closes when its sensitive organs are pressed.

On close inspection it appears to us that the parts of fructification could not perform their office without being slightly touched, and that to remedy this apparent inconvenience, the blossoms contain particles that seem particularly attractive to various kinds of insects, who, while seeking their food, press on the chives, and thus assist nature in the procreation of the seed. May not this in some degree account for the blighting effects of this shrub, that by its May-flowers allures insects which breed on the branches, and then feed their progeny on the nutritious juices of the surrounding blades of young corn? Probably these very insects are the cause that the barberry-bush is so much frequented by small birds.

Linnæus observed, "that when bees in search of honey touch the filaments, the anthers approximate to the stigma, and explode the pollen."

Dr. Smith thus notices this curious phenomenon. "The stamens of such flowers as are open, bend back to each petal, and shelter themselves under their concave tips. No shaking of the branch has any effect upon them; but if the inside of the filaments be touched with a small bit of stick, they instantly spring from the petal and strike the anther against the stigma. The outside of the filament has no irritability, nor has the anther itself any; as may easily be proved by touching either of them with a blunt needle, a fine bristle, a feather, or any thing which cannot injure the structure of the part. If a stamen be bent to the stigma, by means of a pair of scissors applied to the anther, no contraction in the filament is produced. From all this it is evident, that the spring of the stamens is owing to a high degree of irritability in the side of the filament next the germ, by which, when touched, it contracts, that side becomes shorter than the other, and, consequently, the filament is bent towards the germ.

"This irritability is perceptible in stamens of all ages; in flowers only so far expanded as to admit a bristle; and in old flowers ready to fall off. If the germ be cut off, the filaments will still contract, and nothing being in their way, will bend over quite to the opposite side of the flower. After irritation, the stamens will return to their original place. On being touched, they will contract with the same facility as before: and this may be repeated three or four times.

"The purpose which this curious contrivance of nature answers, is evident. In the original position of the stamens, the anthers are sheltered from rain by the concavity of the petals. Thus probably they remain, till some insect, coming to extract honey from the base of the flower, thrusts itself between the filaments, and almost unavoidably touches them in the most irritable part: and as it is chiefly in the fine sunny weather that insects are on the wing, the pollen is also in such weather most fit for the purpose of impregnation."

When this coral-like fruit is ripe, it adds much to the beauty of the garden; but its acidity is so great, that even the birds refuse to eat it.

It is concluded that this is the fruit called *appendices* by the ancients. Pliny says, "There is a kind of thorny bush called *appendix*, having red berries hanging from the branches which are called *appendices*:" he adds, "these berries, either raw by themselves, or dried, and boiled in wine, are good to stay the flux of the body." We find, by Gerard's account, that the leaves were formerly used in salad, and to season meat with: he also says, "The green leaves of the barberry-bush stamped and made into sauce, as that made of sorrel called green sauce, doth cool hot stomachs, and those that are vexed with hot burning agues, and procureth appetite."

Barberries are of an agreeable, cooling, astringent

taste, which creates appetite. A conserve is made from this fruit that is refreshing, and strengthens the stomach, and is good against diarrhœas and dysenteries. The juice, or decoction, abates the inflammation of the fauces and tonsils, and heals scorbutic gums.—*Brookes.*

This fruit gives an agreeable acid to soup, and the young leaves may also be used for the same purpose. According to Prosper Alpinus, the Egyptians employ a diluted juice of the berries in ardent and pestilential fevers. Their manner is to macerate them in about twelve times their quantity of water, afterwards to let them stand for about twenty-four hours, and then to add a little fennel seed.

Pickled barberries make a handsome garnish for all white dishes, where acids can be introduced: this fruit is also used for making syrup, lozenges, &c.

The bark of the tree is a good medicine against the jaundice, and all obstructions and foulness of the viscera. The inner bark of this tree, with the assistance of alum, dyes a bright yellow: in Poland it is used for colouring leather.

The French use it for dyeing both silk and cotton, and also for staining wood for cabinet and other purposes.

Valmont Beomare says, that the scratches of these thorns are difficult to cure; therefore hedges made of these bushes are to be avoided. Cows, sheep, and goats are said to feed on the barberry; but horses and swine refuse it.

We have now several varieties of the barberry-shrub cultivated in England, one of which was brought from Candia in 1759, and another from Siberia in 1790; but they possess no advantage over our native kind of this fruit. The variety with a white berry seldom produces much fruit, but they are considerably larger, and of a more agreeable acid.

BEECH.—FAGUS.

Natural order, Amentaceæ. A genus of the Castanea, or Chesnut Tree, and of the Monœcia Polyandria class.

——" And the beech
Of oily nuts prolific."——

The fruit of this tree having been the food of mankind before the use of corn, claims our attention. The Greeks called the beech $\varphi\eta\gamma o\varsigma$, from the old verb $\varphi\eta\gamma\omega$, I eat: hence the Latin name of *Fagus*. It is, however, maintained that our beech is the $o\xi\upsilon\alpha$ of the Greeks. The fruit is often called buck-mast, in England, from the eagerness with which deer feed upon it.

The beech is one of the handsomest of our native forest-trees, and, in stateliness and grandeur of outline, vies even with the oak. Its silvery bark, contrasting with the sombre trunks of other trees, renders its beauties conspicuous in our woods; while the gracefully spreading pendulous boughs, with their glossy foliage, mark its elegance in the park or paddock. If none but painters were planters, we should oftener see this tree cultivated for the sake of its autumnal tint, which harmonizes so happily with the oak, the elm, and the ash, and relieves so cheerfully the gloom of the cedar, the fir, and the cypress. The German or purple beech is particularly ornamental to the plantation. Cæsar remarks in his Commentaries, that during his stay in Britain he had never seen either the beech-tree or the fir; but from our reading we have never discovered that he penetrated into Sussex or Hampshire, where the beech most abounds, or that he visited Scotland, from whence we have transplanted the fir. The beech seems to have been greatly admired by the ancients. Pliny says, "There was a little hill called Carne, in the territory of Tusculum, not far from the city of Rome, that was clad and beautified with a grove and tufts of beech-trees, which were as even and round in the head as if they had been curiously trimmed with garden shears." He adds, "this grove was, in old times, consecrated to Diana, by the common consent of all the inhabitants of Latium, who paid their devotions there." To one of these beech-trees, he says, "Passienus Crispus, an excellent orator, who was twice consul, and afterwards married the Empress Agrippina, was so much attached, that he not only reposed under it, but sprinkled it plentifully with wine, and would even embrace it."

Manlius Curius protested with an oath, that of all the booty and pillage taken from the enemy, he had reserved nothing for himself but a cruet, or little ewer, made of beech-wood, wherein he intended to sacrifice to the gods.

The beech, it will be observed, from the class in which it is ranged, produces both male and female flowers on the same tree. The fruit succeeds the latter blossoms, which have a one-leafed empalement, cut into four parts, but have no petals: the germen is fixed to the empalement, which afterwards becomes a roundish capsule, armed with soft pines opening in three cells, each containing a triangular nut, called the beech mast. This nut is palatable to the taste, but when eaten in great quantities occasions head-aches and giddiness; nevertheless, when dried and ground into meal, it makes a wholesome bread.

An oil, equal in flavour to the best olive oil, with the advantage of keeping longer without becoming rancid, may be obtained from the nuts by pressure. It is very common in Picardy and other parts of France, where the masts abound; in Silesia, it is used by the country people instead of butter. The cakes which remain from the pressure are given to fatten swine, oxen, or poultry. A bushel of masts is said to produce a gallon of clean oil; but the beech-tree seldom produces a full crop of masts oftener than once in three years.

A few years ago an attempt was made to introduce the making of beech-oil in this country, and a patent was granted to the projector; but the difficulty of bringing the country-people into any new measure, however beneficial to them, is so great, that it often destroys the best-concerted projects. In this instance it was found, that they would rather let the swine consume the masts, than suffer their children to collect them for sale to the patentee; and thus failed the making of salad oil in England.

In the reign of George the First, we find a petition was made for letters patent for making butter from beech-nuts. At the beginning of the last century Aaron Hill had a project for paying off the national debt with the oil of beech nuts! We conclude that he intended to have used it with a spunge!

The finest beech-trees in England are said to grow in Hampshire. The forest of St. Leonard, near Horsham, in Sussex, abounds with noble beech-trees. The cottagers of this forest inform you, that when St. Leonard wished to rest beneath these trees, he was disturbed during the day by the biting of vipers, and that his repose was broken in the night by the warbling of nightingales, and on that account they were removed by his prayers, since which time tradition says of this forest,—

The viper has ne'er been known to sting,
Or the nightingale e'er heard to sing.

The shade of the beech-tree is very injurious to most sorts of plants that grow near it, but is generally believed to be very salubrious to human bodies. The leaves of the beech are collected in the autumn, to fill mattresses, instead of flock or straw, as they remain sweet, and continue soft, for many years. Thus Juvenal observes,

——*Silva domus, cubilia frondes.*
The wood 's a house, the leaves a bed.

To chew beech-leaves is accounted good for the gums and teeth. The Romans used beech-leaves and honey to restore the growth of hair, which had fallen off in sickness.

Mr. Arthur Young, in his "Travels in France, speaks of a Beech at Chantilly about seventeen miles from Paris, which he says "is straight as an arrow, and not less than eighty or ninety feet high ; forty feet to the first branch, and four yards in diameter at five feet from the ground."

In the "*Extraits et Notices des MSS., &c.*" *Tome* 3. *p.* 300, it is stated that on Ascension Eve, the curate of Douremy, on the borders of Lorraine, usually performed a religious ceremony under a beech called the Tree of the Fairies, for the express purpose of keeping the fairies at a distance. It was under this tree that the unfortunate heroine Joan of Arc paid homage to those imaginary creatures, according to her absurd accusers.

One charge against the Maid of Orleans (when tried in 1431 for witchcraft and heresy) was her declaration, that Saint Margaret and Saint Catharine had revealed themselves and spoken to her near the great tree, which, as was commonly reported, the fairies frequented. Joan acknowledged that she had gone with other girls, who amused themselves innocently singing and dancing near the beech called "Handsome May," or "Fairy-tree," formerly haunted, as old people said, by the fairies; but she employed herself there in making nosegays for the holy Virgin of Douremy: she had seen angels and the two saints above-mentioned, not exactly at the Fairy-tree, but at the fountain near it. (See her Trial in the "*Extraits et Notices des MSS.*" *Tome* 3. *p.* 58.)

The timber of these trees, in point of actual utility, follows next to the oak and the ash, and is little inferior to the elm for water-pipes. Between the years 1790 and 1800, when John Aldredge, Esq. of New Lodge, St. Leonard's Forest, was causing fish-ponds to be dug in that neighbourhood, the workmen found scantlings of beech timber, and trunks of these trees, squared out, which were supposed to have been buried in the earth since the time of the Romans, as there is no record mentioning that part of the forest having been cleared, or of ponds made there since. Beech-timber is subject to worms when exposed to the air without paint. It is used by wheelwrights and chairmakers, and also by turners for making domestic wooden ware, such as bowls, shovels, &c. Bedsteads and other furniture are often made with this timber; and no wood splits so fine, or holds so well together, as beech, so that boxes, sword-sheaths, and a variety of other things, are made from it. When the art of splitting this wood was first known in England, the parties who used it kept the method a profound secret for many years.

The inhabitants of London are indebted to this tree for the baskets called pottles, in which they are so well supplied with strawberries.

> "———No wars did men molest,
> When only beechen bowls were in request."
>
> *Tibullus.*

Of the ancient use of beech-timber the poet tells us:—

> " ——In the world's best years, the humble shed
> Was happily and well furnished:
> Beech made their chests, their beds, and the join'd-stools,
> Beech made the board, the platters, and the bowls."

Virgil notices its use in husbandry:—

> " Of beech the plough-tail, and the bending yoke."

In the pastorals of the same author we learn how highly the rustics of his country esteemed their beechen bowls, and to what perfection carving was carried even in common furniture:—

> " The pawn I proffer shall be full as good:
> Two bowls I have, well turn'd, of beechen wood;
> Both by divine Alcimedon were made;
> To neither of them yet the lip is laid;
> The lids are ivy, grapes in clusters lurk
> Beneath the carving of the curious work;
> Two figures on the sides emboss'd appear;
> Conon, and—what's his name,—who made the sphere,
> And shew'd the seasons of the sliding year."

Damœtas replies to Menalcas:—

> " And I have two, to match your pair, at home;
> The wood the same, from the same hand they came:
> The kimbo handles seem with bear's-foot carved;
> And never yet to table have been served."
>
> *Dryden.*

The beech-tree thrives in a chalky or stony ground, where most other timber-trees will not prosper, and it is found to resist winds on the declivities of hills better than most other trees; where the soil is tolerably good, beech will become fit to be felled in about twenty-five years. There is no tree better calculated to train as espaliers for the purpose of screening the garden or orchard from winds than the beech, which when so grown is often found to retain its brown leaves all the winter.

This tree is propagated by sowing the mast, which should be gathered about the middle of September, when they begin to fall, and spread them out on a mat in an airy place for a week to dry, when you may either sow them immediately, or put them into bags to be sown in the spring, when there is less danger of their being destroyed by vermin. These nuts do not require to be covered more than one inch deep in mould, and it will be observed that only a part of them germinates the first year.

BLACKBERRY.—RUBUS;

OR, BRAMBLE BERRY.

Natural order, Senticosæ. A species of Raspberry.—A genus of the Icosandria Polygynia class.

"But check the progress of thy vasty toil:
First choose thy objects from thy native soil;
Where, daily seen, they own thee for their lord,
And, born with thee, shall greater joy afford."

Delille.

"—————— Berries, that emboss
The bramble, black as jet,————
Hard fare! but such as boyish appetite
Disdains not.

Cowper.

The bramble which creeps along the hedge of every soil, derives its Latin name, *rubus*, from the redness of its twigs and the juice of its fruit. Pliny informs us, "that the propagation of trees by layers was taught the ancients by the bramble-bush."

Some bow their vines, which buried in the plain,
Their tops, in distant arches, rise again.

Dryden's Virgil.

"The berries," says Pliny, "have a desiccative and astringent virtue, and are a most appropriate remedy for the gums and inflammation of the tonsils." The flowers also, as well as the berries of the bramble, were considered by the ancients as remedies against the most dangerous serpents. They are diuretic; and the juice pressed out of the tendrils, or young shoots, of brambles stamped, and afterwards reduced into the consistency of honey by standing in the sun, is, says the above author, "a singularly efficacious medicine taken inwardly, or applied outwardly, for all the diseases of the mouth and eyes, as well as for the quinsy," &c. The young shoots, eaten as a salad, will fasten teeth that are loose. The roots of the bramble, boiled in wine, were esteemed one of the best astringents by the Roman physicians, who preferred the juice of blackberries to that of mulberries for the infirmities of the mouth. Brookes says, "the fruit, when ripe, is cooling, and quenches thirst; and the leaves pounded, and applied to ringworms, and ulcers of the legs, was thought to heal them in a short time." Boerhaave affirms, that the roots taken out of the earth in February or March, and boiled with honey, are an excellent remedy against the dropsy.

Turner, one of the earliest English writers on Plants, says, "The bramble bindeth, drieth, and dieth heyre."

The jam made from blackberries is now much used in sore throats caused by colds, and is given in slight fevers.

The juice of blackberry mixed with raisin wine, before it has fermented, will give it both the colour and flavour of claret.

The green twigs are still found of great use in dyeing woollen, silk, and mohair, black. Silk-worms will feed upon the leaves of the bramble; but the silk they produce is not so good as when they are fed on mulberry-leaves.

However generally the bramble is reprobated as a troublesome weed, we must acknowledge that when either in fruit or flower, it forms a principal among the numberless hedge-row beauties; and its utility in particular soils is equally valuable, especially in poor sandy lands where the growth of other hedges is slow. When planted in such situations, it will by its quick growth soon entwine its thorny branches in the dead hedge, which it binds fast from the pilfering vagrant, and proves equally hostile to the legs of idle boys, thus forming a fence

> "Not pervious to the cattle, or the thief."

Of the *Rubus fruticosus*, or common bramble, we have five varieties; and as one has been discovered in a hedge near Oxford by Bobart, which produces a white fruit, it will be necessary to adopt the proper name of bramble-berry for this fruit, to avoid the contradictory appellation of *white blackberry*. The variety with a double flower is now one of the ornaments of the shrubbery: the other varieties are, one with variegated leaves, one with cut leaves, and the bramble without thorns.

Of the species of bramble named *Rubus cæsius*, or dew-berry, but which Gerard calls *Rubus saxatilis*, or stone-berry, the protuberances are much larger, and fewer in number, than those of the common blackberry. It is generally found trailing on the banks of hedge-rows, or in hazel copses, seldom growing above a foot high, with leaflets considerably larger than those of the common bramble. This is a berry of excellent flavour, and quite free from the faint taste of the common bramble-berry. It is therefore well deserving a place in cultivated grounds, as it must be equally beneficial to society that our native fruits should be improved, as that new varieties should be imported from climates that afford but little hope of their thriving here without the aid of artificial heat.

CACAO.—THEOBROMA ;

OR, CHOCOLATE TREE.

Natural order, Columniferæ. Agenus of the Polyadelphia Decandria class.

THE generic name is derived from Θεων Βρῶμα, signifying the food of the gods.

Coles, who wrote in 1657, and is one of the best etymological herbalists that we have been able to consult, says "It is called by the West Indians, amongst whom it was first knowne, and not in any part of the christian world till after the discovery of America, *Cacao* or *Cacavate*, besides which name it hath received none, either Greek or Latin; in English it is called, the pear-bearing wholesome almond-tree: the confection wherein the *Cacao* is the maine ingredient, is in the Indian language called *Chocolate*, being compounded of *Ate* as some say, or as others, *Atle*, which in the Mexican language signifieth water, and *Choco* the noise that the water (wherein the chocolate is put) maketh when it is stirred in a cup, until it bubbles and rises into a froth. It may be called, in English, a compounded or confectioned drink, yet it is better known by the names of Chocolate and Chocoletto." The native Mexicans call this tree *Cucuhua guahuitl*, and the Spaniards *Cacastal*.

The cacao, or chocolate-tree, is a native of South America, and is said to have been originally conveyed to

Hispaniola from some of the provinces of New Spain, where, besides affording the natives a principal part of their nourishment, it also serves the purpose of money, 150 of the nuts (which are about the size of Windsor beans) being considered of the same value as a rial by the Spaniards.

Dampier says that the cacao tree grows nowhere in the north seas but in the bay of Campeachy, on Costa Rica, between Portabel and Nicaragua, chiefly up Carpenter's river, and on this coast as high as the Island of Trinidada. In the South Seas it grows by the river of Guiaquil, and in the valley of Collima, on the south of Mexico. The nuts of the coast of Caraccas, though less than those of Costa Rica, which are large and flat, are better and fatter.

It is not only an article of great internal consumption, but for exportation it is one of the most valuable fruits. Guthrie considers the cacao, from which chocolate is made, as the next considerable article, in the natural history and commerce of Mexico, to gold and silver. A garden of cacao is said to produce the owner twenty thousand crowns a-year.

Chocolate was not known in England until the eleventh year of the reign of Heury the Eighth, although twenty-three years had elapsed since Columbus had discovered the country of which it is a native. It is esteemed the most restorative of all aliments, insomuch that one ounce of it is said to nourish as much as a pound of beef.

An acquaintance, on whose veracity we can rely, informed us, that during the retreat of Napoleon's army from the North, he fortunately had a small quantity of little chcoolate cakes in his pocket, which preserved the life of himself and a friend for several days, when they could procure no other food whatever, and many of their brother officers perished for want.

In all countries where chocolate is known, it is esteemed, and found to be a suitable diet for all ages; more particularly for infants, old persons, those of consumptive habits, and such as are recovering from sickness: but with all these advantages the author does not know of one chocolate-house now remaining in the vast metropolis of the British Empire. White's chocolate-house near the Palace in St. James's Street, kept by Mr. Arthur, was burnt down on Saturday, 28th April, 1733.

It is related in Hawkesworth's Voyages, that Commodore Byron, in his passage through the South Seas, found plenty of cacao in the island called King George's Island; and that many of his men, who were so afflicted with scorbutic disorders that their limbs were become black as ink, and who could not move without assistance, and suffering excruciating pain, were in a few days completely cured by eating these nuts, and able to resume their accustomed duties.

The sons of Æsculapius who wrote on the properties of the chocolate-nut when first known in Europe, recommend it strongly to Venus and all her disciples.

We have often been surprised that the making of the small chocolate cakes for eating should not have been attempted by some persons in London, when they are in such demand at Paris, where a celebrated manufacturer of these chocolate trifles assured us that he had then, in 1816, received an order from a late high personage in England that would exceed 500*l*.

The oil of the cacao-nut is the hottest of any known, and is used to recover cold, weak, and paralytic limbs. The Mexicans are said to eat the nuts raw, to assuage pains in the bowels. The Spanish ladies make use of the oil drawn from the cacao-nut, as a good cosmetic to soften and smooth the skin, as it does not render it greasy or shining, being a quick drier and without smell.

Should we ever revive the ancient custom which formerly existed amongst persons of all ages, of rubbing themselves with oil to give pliability to the muscles, and to preserve them from rheumatism, this oil would obtain the preference, as we conclude the practice was discontinued from the greasy and rancid smell which common oil must naturally leave on the body.

We cannot but regret that the cultivation of this valuable plant should have been discontinued in our West-India islands; nor can we be surprised, when we find that the duty, including the customs and excise, amounted to upwards of four hundred and eighty per cent. on its marketable value when manufactured.

It is carefully cultivated in all the French and Spanish settlements in the warmer parts of America. For what reason our ministerial policy should have so widely differed from that of the neighbouring courts, we are unable to guess; but we trust that the alteration which has lately taken place in the duty on chocolate, will prove a benefit to our revenue, an advantage to our colonies, and a credit to the ministers who adopted this measure.

It is certain that the cultivation of the cacao plantations was both extensive and successful in the British sugar islands, for many years after they had become subject to our government. Blome, who published a short account of Jamaica in 1672, speaks of cacao as being at that time one of the chief articles of export: "There are," says he, "in this island, at this time, about sixty cacao walks, and many more now planting." At present, we believe, there is not a single cacao plantation from one end of Jamaica to the other. A few scattered trees, here and there, are all that remain of those flourishing and beautiful groves which were once the pride and boast of the country. "They have withered with the indigo manufacture," says Edwards, "under the heavy hand of ministerial exaction."

The produce of one tree in Jamaica was generally estimated at about twenty pounds of nuts. The produce per acre was rated at one thousand pounds per annum, allowing for bad years.

The chocolate-tree grows to about six feet high before the head spreads out, and it seldom exceeds from sixteen to twenty feet in the whole height, the boughs and branches beautifully extending themselves on every side, resembling the heart cherry-tree, the leaves being much of the same shape. The tree bears leaves, flowers, and fruit, all the year through; but the usual seasons for gathering the fruit are June and December. The flowers spring from the trunk and large branches; they are small, but beautiful, and sometimes pale red, but most commonly of a saffron colour: the pods are oval and pointed, and contain from ten to thirty nuts each, almost like almonds, adhering to one another by soft filaments, and enclosed in a white pulpy substance, soft and sweet, which some persons suck when they take them out of the shells. The pods change from green to a yellowish colour when they reach their maturity, which is known by the rattling of the nuts, when the pods are shaken. When gathered, it is usual to lay the pods in heaps to sweat for three or four days before they are opened; they are then exposed upon mats or skins, to the sun, every day for about a month.

The cacao-tree is permitted to bear a moderate crop of fruit the fourth year after the seed has been sown: but if the plant is weak, a greater quantity of the blossoms are gathered, in order that it may recover strength. The tree attains its full perfection in eight years: after that it will continue to produce fruit for thirty years or more, if planted in a good soil; but it is obnoxious to blights, and shrinks from the first appearance of drought. In early times the planters had many superstitious notions concerning this tree; and among others, the appearance of a comet was always considered as fatal to the cacao plantation.—*Lunan.*

It is from the wood of this tree that our most esteemed German flutes have for some years past been made, as they are not so subject to swell by using as those made from Box-wood; which swelling often causes a variation of half a note, as after being played on for a short time the tone becomes sharper. The cacao flutes have also an objectionable quality, viz. as they are subject to crack by use, and will not stand the breath of different persons. A respectable professor of this instrument, among other instances, informed us of a gentleman who after having played on a cacao flute for seven years without accident, sold it to a friend, by whose breath alone three joints were split, in the course of a few months practice.

The chocolate-tree was grown in our stoves as early as the year 1739.

Chocolate-nuts will not retain their growing faculty long after they are taken from the trees, so that there is no possibility of transporting them to any great distance for planting: they are, therefore, generally planted in boxes of earth when transported to Europe. They may also be encreased by cuttings. Naturalists observe that the germ of these nuts or almonds is placed in the large end, whereas the common almond is placed in the small end.

Although it is thought that grafting would improve this fruit, we believe it has never been attempted.

CASHEW-NUT.—ANACARDIUM.

Natural order, Holoraceæ. A genus of the Polygamia Monœcia class.

The generic name is derived from two Greek words, signifying, without a heart; because the fruit, instead of having the seed enclosed, has the nut growing at the end.

The cashew-tree is a native of the East Indies, and of the Brazils, and other parts of America, where it grows to the height of twenty feet or more, in favourable situations. Lunan gives the following account of it in his *Hortus Jamaicensis*. The fruit is full of an acrid juice, which is frequently used in the making of punch. To the apex of the fruit, grows a nut of the size and shape of a hare's kidney, but much larger at the end which is next the fruit than at the other end. The shell is very hard, and the kernel, which is esteemed the finest nut in the world, is covered with a thin film. Between this and the shell is lodged a thick, blackish, inflammable liquor, of such a caustic nature in the fresh nut, that, if the lips chance to touch it, blisters will immediately follow. The fruit is said to be good in disorders of the stomach; for the juice of it cuts the thick tough humours, which obstruct the free circulation of the blood, and thus removes the complaint. This juice, expressed and fermented, makes a fine rough wine, useful where the viscera or solid system has been relaxed. Barham, who has written on this fruit, says, "the stone of this apple appears before the fruit itself, growing at the end in the shape of a kidney, as big as a walnut. Some of the fruit are all red, some entirely yellow, and some mixed with both red and yellow, and others perfectly white, of a very pleasant taste in general; but there is a great variety, some being more sharp, some in taste resembling cherries, others very rough like unripe apples. The taste of most of them is sweet and pleasant, but generally goes off with an astringency or stipticity upon the tongue, which proceeds from its tough fibres, that run longwise through the fruit. When cut with a knife, it turns as black as ink. The generality of the fruit are as big and much of the shape of the French Pippins, and make an excellent cider or wine." Barham adds, that he has distilled a spirit from the nut far exceeding arrack, rum, or brandy, of which an admirable punch is made.

The flowers are very small, grow in tufts of a carnation colour, and are very odoriferous. The leaves much resemble those of the common walnut-tree in shape and smell, and a decoction of them is equally effectual in cleansing and healing old wounds.

The oil cures the herpes, takes away freckles and liver spots, but draws blisters, and therefore must be cautiously used; it also takes away corns, but it is necessary to have a very good defensive round the corn to prevent inflaming the part. The inside kernel is very pleasant to eat when young, and, before the fruit is too ripe, exceeding any walnut; and when older and drier, roasted, is very agreeable, excelling pistachio nuts or almonds; and ground up with cocoa, makes an excellent chocolate.

It has been observed, that poor dropsical slaves, who have had the liberty to go into a cashew-walk, and eat what cashews they pleased, as well as to eat the roasted nuts, have been recovered. These trees are of quick growth: Barham says he has planted the nuts, and the young trees have produced fruit in two years after. They will continue bearing fruit for more than a hundred years. Many are now flourishing in Jamaica that were planted when the Spaniards had it in their possession.

The author of this work lately received from Jamaica a cashew apple, bearing two distinct nuts, which was considered so rare a circumstance that it was preserved in spirits. Its appearance is unnatural, resembling a lemon pippin apple, with two lambs' kidneys stuck on the end.

The wood of the cashew is excellent, strong, and lasting timber.

These trees annually transude in large quantities, *viz*. often to ten or twelve pounds' weight, a fine, semi-transparent gum, similar to gum-arabic, and not at all inferior to it in virtue and quality, except that it contains a light astringency, which perhaps renders it the more valuable in many respects: for this reason it is often used as a succedaneum in the Jamaica shops.

The thick oil of the nut or shell tinges linen of a rusty iron colour, which can be hardly got out; and if any wood be smeared with it, it preserves it from decay. From the body of this tree is procured, by tapping, or incision, a milky juice, which stains linen of a deep black, and cannot be discharged. Dr. Grew mentions the juice being used for staining of cottons; but it is doubtful which of the species he means, though Sir Hans Sloane supposes it to be of the acajou or cashew, here mentioned.

Long seems of opinion that this juice has the same property as the Japan lac.

The oil between the rinds of the nut, if held to the candle, emits bright salient particles. This oil is used as a cosmetic to remove freckles and sun-burning, but the pain suffered makes its use not very frequent. *Grainger*.

The pith, or medullary part of the anacardium, is extremely pungent and acrimonious; whence the ancients made great use of it in cold diseases of the head, particularly to strengthen the memory; but the abuse of it sometimes made them stupid, delirious, or even mad; the moderns rarely venture on its use, at least not without great correctives. *Chambers.*

The cashew-nut tree was cultivated in this country as early as 1699, by the Duchess of Beaufort; but, as it requires the stove even in the summer months, it has not become common in Europe.

CHERRY.—CERASUS.

Natural order, Pomaceæ.. A genus of the Icosandria Monogynia class.—It was formerly considered by Botanists as a distinct genus; but Linnæus pronounces it of the Prunus species.

Χεράσια, the Greek name for the Cherry, was derived from the Latin; of most other plants and fruits the Latin names are derived from the Greek: but this beautiful fruit was procured and brought into Europe on occasion of the overthrow of Mithridates, king of Pontus, when he was driven from his dominions by Lucullus, the Roman general, who found the cherry-tree growing in Cerasus, a city of Pontus, (now called Keresoun, a maritime town belonging to the Turks in Asia,) which his army destroyed, and whence this fruit derived the present name of Cherry. Lucullus, who was as great an admirer of nature as he was of the arts, thought this tree of so much importance, that when he was granted a triumph, it was placed in the most conspicuous situation among the royal treasures which he obtained from the sacking of the capital of Armenia; and we doubt much if there was a more valuable acquisition made to Rome by that war, which is stated by Plutarch to have cost the Armenians 155,000 men. We may very justly style it the fruit of the Mithridatic war.

Botany seems to have been more studied in early times by distinguished persons than at present. In this instance we find the conquered and the conqueror both botanists.

Mithridates, whom Cicero considered the greatest monarch that ever sat on a throne, and who had vanquished twenty-four nations, whose different languages he had learnt, and spoke with the same ease and fluency as his own, found time to write a treatise on botany in the Greek language. His skill in physic is well known: there is, even at this day, a celebrated antidote, called Mithridate, a particular translation of the account of which will be found in the history of the walnut.

It was in the 68th year before the birth of Christ, that Lucullus planted the cherry-tree in Italy, which "was so well stocked," says Pliny, "that in less than twenty-six years after, other lands had cherries, even as far as Britain beyond the Ocean." This would make their introduction to England as early as the forty-second year before Christ, although they are generally stated not to have been brought to this country until the early part of the reign of Nero, A.D. 55.

Some idea may be formed of the Roman gardens, by the luxurious manner in which Lucullus lived in his retirement from Rome and the public affairs. He had passages dug under the hills, on the coast of Campania, to convey the sea-water to his house and pleasure grounds, where the fishes flocked in such abundance, that what were found at his death sold for more than twenty-five thousand pounds. Pliny mentions eight kinds of cherries as being cultivated in Italy when he wrote his Natural History, which was about the seventieth year A.D. "The reddest cherries," continues he, "are called *apronia;* the blackest, *actia;* the Cæcilian are round. The Julian cherries have a pleasant taste, but are so tender that they must be eaten when gathered, as they will not endure carriage." The Duracine cherries were esteemed the best; but in Picardy the Portugal cherries were most admired. The Macedonian cherries grew on dwarf trees; and one kind is mentioned by the above author, which never appeared ripe, having a hue between green, red, and black. He mentions a cherry that was grafted in his time on a bay-tree stock, which circumstance gave it the name of *laurea*: this cherry is described as having an agreeable bitterness. "The cherry-tree could never be made to grow in Egypt," continues Pliny, "with all the care and attention of man."

The county of Kent has long been celebrated for the quantity of cherries which it produces, and, in all probability, they were first planted in this part of England, of which Cæsar speaks more favourably than of any other part which he visited. Some authors assure us, that the whole race of cherries that had been brought to this country by the Romans, were lost in the Saxon period, and were only restored by Richard Harris, fruiterer to Henry the VIIIth, who brought them from Flanders, and planted them at Sittingbourn in Kent. This appears to be an error, as Gerard says, "the Flanders' cherrie-tree differeth not from our English cherrie-tree in stature or in forme," &c.

The Kentish-cherry is considered to be the original kind, and it is also thought to be the most wholesome; great quantities of this variety of the cherry are cultivated in the neighbourhood of Paris, where they are generally preferred, particularly the variety with a short stalk, called *Montmorency*, from the fertile and delightful valley of that name, in the northern vicinity of Paris, where they are cultivated for the well-supplied markets of that city.

De Heem seldom painted any other than the Kentish cherry in his admirable fruit-pieces, from which we should judge that it was the favourite cherry in Flanders two hundred years ago.

Mr. T. A. Knight has raised a new variety of this fruit,

called after him *Knight's early Black cherry*, and which seems to possess a very desirable property, that of ripening its fruit considerably earlier than the May-duke; it is of a fine dark hue, and its flesh is firm and juicy. It blossoms much earlier than any other sort.

There is an account of a cherry-orchard of thirty-two acres in Kent, which, in the year 1540, produced fruit that sold in those early days for 1000*l*., which seems an enormous sum, as at that period good land is stated to have let at one shilling per acre. We can only reconcile our minds to this great price, from the deficiency of other fruits in this country, and the splendour in which Henry the VIIIth and his ministers lived. Evelyn tells us, that in his time, an acre planted with cherries 100 miles from London, had been let at 10*l*.

Fruit orchards are still considered the most valuable estates in Kent; and we learn from Boys's Kent, that cherry-gardens, while in full bearing, pay better than orchards; but the cherry-tree does not generally continue more than thirty years in perfection. Mr. Randall says, he has known a single cherry-tree produce fruit that he has sold for above five pounds per annum, for seven years in succession.

Gerard says, "the Luke Warde's cherrie is so called, because he was the first that brought the same out of Italy. Another we have called the Naples' cherrie, because it was first brought into these parts from Naples: the fruit is verie great, sharpe pointed, somewhat like a man's heart in shape, of a pleasant taste, and of a deepe blackish colour when it is ripe." This author mentions the Spanish and the Gascoigne cherry, &c. and says, "there are many other sorts in our London gardens."

The cherry seems to have been a fruit highly esteemed by the court in the time of Charles the First, as we find, by the survey and valuation of the manor and mansion belonging to his queen, Henrietta Maria, at Wimbledon in Surrey, which was made in 1649, there were upwards of two hundred cherry-trees in those gardens. (*Archæologia*, vol. x. p. 399.)

We have observed, that the cherry-gardens in the vicinity of London have what is termed an upper and an under crop, which is produced by planting strawberries or currants, &c. between the trees; and the latter fruit, we have noticed, has been as fine, and as productive, as when planted by itself, and engrossing the whole garden. Philips says, the apple-tree is

> " Uneasy, seated by funereal yew,
> Or walnut, (whose malignant touch impairs
> All generous fruits,) or near the bitter dews
> Of cherries; therefore weigh the habits well
> Of plants, how they associate best, nor let
> Ill neighbourhood corrupt their hopeful grafts."

Lord Bacon has clearly elucidated what the ancients considered the sympathy or antipathy of plants. " For it is thus," says this great man: " wheresoever one plant draweth such a particular juice out of the earth as it qualifieth the earth, so that the juice which remaineth is fit for the other plant: there the neighbourhood doeth good, because the nourishments are contrary, or several;—but where two plants draw much the same juice, there the neighbourhood hurteth; for the one deceiveth the other."

The cherry, like many other kinds of fruit, has had its sorts so multiplied by various graftings and sowing the seeds, that we now enjoy a great variety of this agreeable fruit, and for a considerable portion of the summer, as it is one of the first trees that yields its fruit in return for the care of the gardener. From the ripening of the Kentish and the May-duke, to that of the Yellow Spanish and the Morello, we may reckon full one third of the year that our desserts are furnished with this ornamental fruit; and to those who have the advantage of housed trees, the cherry makes a much earlier appearance, as it is a fruit that bears forcing exceedingly well.

Cherries have ever been found more tempting than wholesome. Pliny says, "this fruit will loosen and hurt the stomach; but, when hung up and dried, has a contrary effect." He relates, that some authors have affirmed that cherries, eaten fresh from the tree when the morning dew is on them, and the stones being also swallowed, will purge so effectually, as to cure those who have the gout in their feet. Dr. John Quincey says in his English Dispensatory, "Many of the sorts, and particularly the Kentish red cherries, are a very wholesome fruit and grateful to the stomach, but the black only are used in medicine: they are prescribed in all diseases of the head and nerves; and by some are accounted diuretic, especially the water distilled from them."

Dried cherries are much esteemed for winter puddings; and the wine made from this fruit much resembles the red Constantia, both in colour and flavour. The small black cherries, with good brandy, produce one of the most wholesome as well as agreeable liqueurs. *Eau de Cérises* is an admired liqueur of France.

The wood of the cherry-tree, which is hard and tough, is next to oak for strength, and comes the nearest to mahogany in appearance: it is in much request with the turners for making chairs, &c. and is esteemed by musical instrument makers, who pretend that it is sonorous.

The common black cherry-tree prospers in a cold soil. Evelyn observes that they afford considerable timber; and he mentions some that were eighty feet in length. In all probability these trees originally sprang from the seed of the cultivated cherry that had been introduced by the Romans, as they do not partake of the character of any of our native trees.

It is observed of stone-fruit in general, that, if sown immediately after they are excarnated, they will appear the following spring, but, being kept too long, they will not germinate under two years.

The timber of the wild cherry-tree comes to perfection in about forty years.

The cherry-tree produces its fruit generally at the extremity of the branches; therefore, in pruning, they should never be shortened. In trees that are trained to a wall, displace all foreright shoots by the hand, in the summer; for if they are suffered to grow till winter, they will not only deprive the bearing branches of their supply of nourishment, but, when they are cut out, will occasion the tree to gum in that part. Cherries bear the knife worse than any other sort of fruit-trees: we would therefore impress upon the mind of the pruner, that although this fruit was gained by the sword, it may be lost by the knife. He must be also careful not to rub off the sides or spurs which are produced upon the two or three year old wood; for it is upon these that the greatest part of the fruit is produced; and it will continue fruitful for several years. "It is," says Miller, "for want of duly observing this caution that cherry-trees are often so unfruitful, especially the Morello, which shoots the weaker the more it is cut.

Judiciously planted, the cherry-tree is very ornamental in a shrubbery, its early white blossoms contrasting with the sombre shades of evergreens in the spring, and its graceful ruby balls giving a pleasing variety in the summer; particularly the Morello, which, when planted as a standard, decorates the pleasure-grounds by its gracefully pendent boughs, whose snowy blossoms opening early to receive the sedulous bee, gives a pleasure that is scarcely surpassed by its autumnal transparent fruit.

There is a feast celebrated at Hamburgh, called the "Feast of Cherries;" in which troops of children parade the streets with green boughs ornamented with cherries, to commemorate a triumph obtained in the following manner: In 1432 the Hussites threatened the city of Hamburgh with immediate destruction, when one of the citizens, named Wolf, proposed that all the children in the city, from seven to fourteen years of age, should be clad in mourning, and sent as supplicants to the enemy. Procopius Nasus, chief of the Hussites, was so touched with this spectacle, that he received the young supplicants, regaled them with cherries and other fruits, and promised them to spare the city. The children returned crowned with leaves, holding cherries, and crying "*Victory.*"

CHESNUT.—CASTANEA.

Natural order, Contortæ. In Botany, it is ranged in the class of Monœcia Polyandria, and is of the genus of Fagus, or Beech. The Fruit is more properly a Mast than a Nut.

Or whose discourse with innocent delight
Shall fill me now, and cheat the wint'ry night?
While hisses on my hearth the pulpy pear,
And black'ning chesnuts start and crackle there.

The chesnut-tree was first brought to Europe from Sardis (now Sart), a town of Asia Minor, by the Greeks, who called the fruit the Sardinian nut, until it was honoured by the appellation of Διὸς Βάλανος, or Jupiter's nut. Sardis was burnt by the Athenians 504 years before Christ, which caused the invasion of Attica by Darius. We may therefore venture to conclude that the chesnut was thus early known to the Greeks. Pliny mentions eight kinds of chesnuts as being known to the Romans in his time, and says they were ground into meal, and made into bread, by the poor; "but when roasted," he adds, "they are pleasanter and better food." He also mentions one kind, *coctivæ* (chesnuts to be boiled). Chesnuts were considered nutritive by the ancients, and good for those who vomited blood.

"Chesnuts," continues Pliny, "were much improved when men began to graft them."

The Romans called them *Castanea*, after a city of that name in Thessalia, from whence they first procured them, and where they were grown in great abundance by the Grecians; they still retain the same appellation in all the European languages. In German *Castanienbaum;* in Swedish and Danish *Castanietræe;* in French *Châtaignier;* in Italian *Castagno;* in Spanish *Castano;* in Portuguese *Castanheire*. In Russian *Keschtan*.

Some authors affirm that the chesnut-tree is a native of this country. Dr. Ducarel maintains, in his Anglo-Norman Antiquities, that it is an indigenous, or native tree of this island; in proof of this he alleges, that many of our old buildings in London, and other places, contain a great quantity of this timber; and among the ancient records to which he appeals, produces a deed of gift from Henry the Second to Flexley abbey, of the tithe of all his chesnuts in the forest of Dean.

The remains of very old decayed chesnut-trees may be seen in the Forest of Dean, Enfield Chase, and in many parts of Kent. At Fortworth, in Gloucestershire, is a chesnut-tree fifty-two feet round: it is proved to have stood there since the year 1150, and was then so remarkable, that it was called "*The great chesnut of Fortworth*." It fixes the boundary of a manor. Mr. Marsham states that this tree is 1100 years old. It is mentioned by Sir Robert Atkyns in his history of that county, as a famous tree in King John's time;—and by Evelyn in his Sylva, to have been so remarkable for its magnitude, in the reign of King Stephen, as then to be called the great chesnut, as already noticed; from which it is presumed to have been standing before the Conquest.

Cheshunt, or Chestrehunt, in Hertfordshire, is supposed to have been so called from the chesnut-trees with which it formerly abounded. Camden remarks, that Cowdery Park, near Midhurst in Sussex, abounded in fine chesnut-trees. It is therefore evident that chesnut timber has been long known in this country; but we are induced to believe that it was one of the fruits which was introduced by the Romans to this island, who, having been masters of the country for nearly four hundred years, and being much attached to horticultural pursuits, we may naturally conclude, would not fail to transport hither their hardier kinds of fruits, and particularly those which were used as a substitute for bread.

Chesnuts were certainly considered as a proper food for man by Lord Bacon, who, in his " Essay on Plantations," says, " In a country of plantation, first look about what kind of victual the country yields of itself to hand; as chesnuts, walnuts, pine-apples, olives, dates, &c. &c." Chesnuts are the usual, and in some places almost the only food of the common people, in the Apennine mountains of Italy, in Savoy, and some parts of the south of France; not only boiled and roasted, but also in puddings, cakes, and bread. They afford great part of the food of the peasants in the mountains of Madeira. M. Valmont Bomare says, the inhabitants of Perigord and Limousin and the mountains of Cévennes make great use of these nuts for bread, which is thought to give them a swarthy complexion: they are also said to be flatulent and hard of digestion; yet there are instances, in Italy, of men's living to ninety or one hundred years of age, who have fed wholly on chesnuts. Roasted chesnuts make a good substitute for malt in making beer.

Chesnuts stewed with cream make a much-admired dish, and many families prefer them to all other stuffings for turkeys: they make an excellent soup; and we have no doubt that chesnuts might be advantageously used in cooking, so as to make many agreeable and wholesome dishes. The author has had them stewed and brought to table with salt fish, when they have been much admired;

but it is exceedingly difficult to introduce any article as food that has not been established by long custom; and it is not more strange than true, that the difficulty increases, if the object be economy. Nievhoff tells us that the Chinese grow chesnuts in the province of Suchuen that will melt in the mouth like sugar. We hope to hear that this tree will be inquired for and brought to England.

The importation of chesnuts is very considerable both from Spain and Portugal, yet we believe it is rarely if ever there is a single meal made from them in this country. The Catalonians have this strange religious practice: on the first of November, the eve of All Souls, they run about from house to house to eat chesnuts, believing that for every chesnut they swallow, with proper faith and unction, they shall deliver a soul out of purgatory.

As ornamental and profitable for parks, chesnut-trees are exceeded by no others, which all must acknowledge who have seen the picturesque and stately trees in the domains of the Earl of Egremont at Petworth, or the fine avenues in Greenwich Park. It is this tree which graces the landscapes of Salvator Rosa, who painted in the mountains of Calabria, where it flourishes. Its ramifications are more straggling than even those of the oak, while its foliage, which is more loose and brilliant in colour, is less subject to the attacks of insects, and its yellow and umber tints greatly relieve the sable hue of the fir and the pine, and act like a blossom to enliven the month of November. The male flowers, which appear in May, have for a short time a strong spermatic and disagreeable odour; the female blossom attracts our attention by the curious manner in which nature has provided for the impregnation of this seed. There are generally four chesnuts in each of their thorny habitations, that have a small hole at the point, out of which each nut thrusts its stigma, which opens into five claws, however crowded they may be, to receive the farina and conduct it to the proper channel. When the fruit is matured and becomes of that reddish brown colour, which gives a name to horses, its prickly dwelling opens into four quarters, and the sap having discontinued to supply the ripened fruit, it drops from its plush-lined dwelling to form future trees, and to feed the various animals that await its fall, as is noticed by the author of the Farmer's Boy, who says of the swine:—

> " From oak to oak they run with eager haste,
> And wrangling share the first delicious taste
> Of fallen acorns; yet but thinly found,
> Till the strong gale has shook them to the ground."

There is no better food for deer than chesnuts, and they fall from the trees when other sustenance is often scarce from the dryness of the season.

The timber is of equal value with the best oak, and, for many purposes, far exceeds it; to which we may add that it grows twice as fast. No wood is preferable to this for making casks to hold wine and other liquors, as it imparts no taste to the contents, and has the property of maintaining its bulk constantly, without shrinking or swelling, which most other timber is apt to do, and which often causes casks to burst.

M. Bourgeois says, " that casks made of the chesnut-wood contribute much to the quality of the wine, as well as to the preservation of it; the fermentation," he adds, " is very slow, and the wine made in those vessels is sweeter. This wood being less porous than the oak must certainly prevent the evaporation of the spirituous parts.

It has also the quality of lasting longer than elm, or any other timber, when used for water-pipes, or other purposes, under ground.

Its durability when exposed to the weather is sufficiently ascertained from its use for gate-posts at Wellington in Somersetshire, of which the following account is extracted from the Transactions of the Society of Arts for 1789.—" In or about the year 1763, some gate-posts of oak, and others of chesnut, were to be repaired: they had the appearance of being put in at the same time, but the latter were much more sound, insomuch that some of them were adjudged good enough to remain as gate-posts, and are now to be seen there (1788) Such as were too small were taken up, and set as posts to fix rails to. At the same time some new posts of oak were put in, there not being enough of the old chesnut posts. Though these were old when put in, twenty-five years ago, they are now (1788) more sound than the oak posts which were then new. One side of the chesnut posts was the outside of the tree, but the timber is as sound there as in any other part, which would not have been the case with oak, the sap of which, next the bark, soon decays. The chesnut gate-posts had been put down many years before 1745; they have therefore probably stood the weather above half a century."

Another account says, that the branch of a chesnut about thirteen inches square, which in the year 1726 was put down as a hanging post for a gate, and carried the gate fifty-two years, when taken up appeared perfectly sound, and was put down for a clapping post in another place.

Its durability when employed in buildings has been shewn in the most ancient houses of our metropolis, while its beauty has been displayed in the doors and balustrades of our modern dwellings. It appears to be noxious to spiders and other insects, which must rather increase than diminish its value in buildings.

These and similar recommendations have induced the

Earl of Fife and other land-proprietors to enrich their northern estates, by the planting of chesnut-trees: while in the more congenial southern counties the tree is scarcely known, and seldom seen without the boundaries of the park fence.

M. Valmont Bomare makes the same observation on the neglect of his countrymen that without offence we would make to our own, on the unaccountable neglect of the cultivation of this tree, when it is the general opinion that, the oak excepted, it should be attended to before any other forest-tree.

"It is to be regretted," says this able French writer, "that there are not to be found so many chesnut-trees in our provinces where this timber used to abound." Yet we find that they have many large forests composed entirely of those trees in Britanny; where you see the fruit piled up within their cabins as a winter food for the poor, who seldom taste the luxury of wheaten bread.

The chesnut-wood has recently been successfully applied to the purposes of dyeing and tanning, thus forming a substitute for log-wood and oak-bark. Leather tanned by it, is declared, by the gentleman who made the experiment, to be superior to that tanned with oak-bark; and in dyeing, its affinity for wool is said, on the same authority, to be greater than that of either galls or sumach, and consequently the colour given is more permanent: it also makes admirable ink.

The great chesnut-tree near Mount Etna is perhaps one of the most extraordinary trees in the Old World. It is called "The chesnut-tree of a Hundred Horses," from a traditionary tale that Joan of Arragon, when she visited Mount Etna, being attended by her principal nobility, a heavy shower obliged them to take refuge under this tree, the immense branches of which sheltered the whole party. According to the account given of it by Mr. Howel, this chesnut-tree is 160 feet in circumference. Mr. Brydone, who measured it in 1770, says, "it was then 204 feet round;" and, although quite hollow within, the verdure of the branches is not affected; for this species of tree, like the willow and some others, depends upon its bark for subsistence. The cavity of this enormous tree is so extensive, that a house has been built in it, and the inhabitants have an oven therein, where they dry nuts, chesnuts, almonds, &c. of which they make conserves: but, as these thoughtless people often get fuel from the tree that shelters them, it is feared that this natural curiosity will be destroyed by those whom it protects.

These trees seem to delight in the cinerated substances thrown out of volcanos, as is shewn by the thick woods of chesnut-trees, which cover the surface in the neighbourhood of Vesuvius. They grow luxuriantly on Mount Somma, on the heights of the Camaldoli near Naples, on the Pyrenees near medicinal springs, and in general, in the neighbourhood of subterraneous fires, not to mention the numerous and gigantic trees that have for ages darkened the sides of Etna.

We strongly recommend the grafting of chesnut-trees where planted for the sake of the fruit, and to those who plant for timber it may be only necessary to notice that the months of November and February are the best seasons for sowing the nuts, which should be done on fresh undunged earth: and the fruit of English trees answers equally well for the latter purpose, provided care is taken to reject all the nuts that swim upon the surface of the water. Evelyn says, "they need only to be put into holes with the point upmost as you plant tulips. October is the season recommended for transplanting the young trees; and the younger they are planted, the better they succeed.

This fruit should be gathered on a sunny day, and then exposed for a week to the influence of the sun on wicker mats, which should be removed to the hottest part of the house in the evening. By this treatment chesnuts will retain their native relish and their reproductive energy, though conveyed to a great distance and even across the seas.

HORSE-CHESNUT.—ÆSCULUS.

Natural order, Trihilatæ. A genus of the Heptandria Monogynia class.

The generic name of this tree is derived from *esca*, food. It had the old names *Hippocastanum* and *Castanea equina*, from the similitude of the fruit to that of the chesnut, and from its being given to horses. The class and order of the tree being as widely different from the *Castanea* chesnut, Linnæus altered the old title to that of *Esculus*.

The Horse-chesnut was first brought from the northern parts of Asia into Europe about the year 1550, according to Martin's edition of Miller, and was sent to Vienna about the year 1558; but of this statement we are doubtful, as it was certainly not introduced into French Flanders before the year 1576, when C. Clusius, a celebrated botanist of Arras, received it from the Imperial Ambassador at the Porte, together with a considerable variety of trees new to Europe; but the horse-chesnut and the cherry-laurel were the only two he succeeded in rearing.

When planted in well-chosen situations, this tree is one of the greatest ornaments to our parks or extensive grounds, particularly during the month of May, when its bold and elegant spiral blossoms are conspicuous at a distance and pleasing on approach: but the large digitated leaves form a heavy foliage, that requires to be relieved by the birch, the ash, the elm, or the poplar. It tells well as a fore-ground to clumps of firs, whose dark tapering points are relieved by the early and soft green of the Esculus, and their naked limbs are obscured by its branches, which in return show their flowery spikes to greater advantage by the contrast.

Where unsightly buildings are to be hidden, or where grounds are too much overlooked by public roads, this tree by its rapid growth and ample foliage is preferable to most others. Even when raised from the nut it has frequently attained so considerable a height in twelve or fourteen years as to form a complete screen, or to shade by its branches a space sufficient for several chairs. The horse-chesnut is only objectionable when planted too near our dwellings or the walks of the shrubbery, as its leaves fall early and are unsightly in the path.

This tree does not appear to have been planted in England in the time of Gerard, who, in 1597, says, "the Horse-chesnut groweth in Italie and in sundry places of the East countries." But in Johnson's edition of that author, printed in 1633, we are told, "it is now growing with Mr. Tradescant at South-Lambeth."

Parkinson, in 1629, seems to have been unacquainted with the tree: he says, "our Christian world had first the knowledge of it from Constantinople." He places it as a fruit-tree between the walnut and the mulberry, and adds, "it is of a greater and more pleasant aspect, for the fair leaves, but also of as good a use for the fruit, which is of a sweet taste, roasted and eaten as the ordinary sort." He also, like Gerard, describes and figures the corolla with four petals.

It appears to have been rare even as late as the year 1700, as Mr. Houghton notices some at Sir William Ashhurst's, at Highgate, and at the Bishop of London's, at Fulham.

Those which now afford shade to the pensioners of

Chelsea college were then very young; but we are told that there was a very fine one then growing in the post-house garden near Old-street, and another not far from the ice-house under the shadow of the Observatory in Greenwich Park.

The grand avenue of horse-chesnut-trees in Bushey Park, near Hampton-Court Palace, is the finest in England, and attracts many parties from London to see it when in full blossom.

The fruit of the horse-chesnut-tree is ground, and given to the horses in Turkey, particularly to such as have coughs, or are broken-winded. The Turks also give it to milch-cows, it being found to increase the quantity of milk, without injuring the quality.

The author, when in Paris, found the milk which he obtained from the porter of the hotel so superior in flavour to what he had ever met with in the country, that he was induced to investigate the cause, and found that the goats which supplied the hotel with milk, were then kept entirely on the leaves of the horse-chesnut-tree, which were brought to Paris as a covering to the numberless baskets of fruit that then furnished the markets of that city.

In France and Switzerland horse-chesnuts are used for the purpose of bleaching yarn, and are recommended as capable of extensive use in whitening, not only flax and hemp, but also silk and wool. These nuts contain a great deal of farinaceous and nutritive matter, and when deprived of their astringent principle, constitute a very good article of food for cattle.

A patent was granted, in the year 1796, to Lord William Murray, for his discovery of a method of extracting starch from horse-chesnuts; and a paste or size has been made from them, which is preferred by bookbinders, shoemakers, and paper-hangers, to that made from wheaten flour. It is thought that the meal of this fruit can be converted into many useful articles, such as soap, &c.; and as it loses its bitter astringent taste after it has been rasped into water, it is concluded that it would be a wholesome food mixed with flour or potatoes. The prickly husks are valuable for tanning leather.

Zannichelli affirms, that he has made a great many trials, and has found the bark of the horse-chesnut-tree to have the same effect as the Peruvian bark; but the generality of practitioners tell us it is much inferior to that article.

The bark of horse-chesnut is inodorous, but has an astringent and agreeable bitter taste; it should be taken from those branches which are neither old nor young: it may be preserved for several years without having its virtues impaired, for they do not reside in any volatile matter, but in a substance called tannin, which may be extracted from the bark by spirit or water. Its medical properties are astringent and tonic.—*Medical Botany*.

The common horse-chesnut is propagated by sowing the nuts in the same manner as the eatable chesnut. This tree will grow luxuriant and healthy even in very cold, barren, and hungry earth, being, as Dr. Hunter observes, "not very nice in its diet;" but in a sandy loam it makes the greatest progress, and retains its verdure longest in a moist soil. After horse-chesnuts have been transplanted, neither knife nor hatchet should come near them, but they should be left to Nature to form their fine parabolic heads, and assume their utmost beauty; for the fine spikes of flowers come out at the extremity of each branch, therefore when pruned or crowded by other trees they lose half their splendour.

The timber is not considered valuable; but as Mr. Hanbury justly observes, "It grows rapidly to a considerable magnitude, and is therefore well worth the planting for the sake of the timber." It is used by the turner, and often by the cabinet-maker as a substitute for wainscot-oak, to which in appearance it approaches so nearly that none but those who are accustomed to work on these woods can discern the difference. It is also said to be more durable than many harder kinds of timber when used for under-ground pipes, &c.

The most common observer of Nature must have admired with what wonderful security the buds of these trees are guarded against the inclemency of the winter, and the rapacity of insects. No sooner are the flowers fallen, than the buds for the succeeding year are formed, which continue swelling till autumn, at which time the folding covers are spread over with a thick tenacious juice, which, like pitch, hardens with the cold, and thus defends its tender buds from the frost and rain in winter, but which is never so far hardened but it melts and runs off upon the first return of warmth in the spring: the young bud then escapes and grows with such rapidity that in less than three weeks it is often found to have made a shoot of eighteen inches in length, and to have fully expanded its fine leaf.

On opening the fruit we find a vacuum so perfectly formed for the shape of the leaf, that even the impression for the veins is distinctly to be seen. That part of the germ which forms the root escapes without opening the nut, and as it extends in the earth it sends up moisture, which swells the germ until the vacuum is filled and the first leaves are perfectly formed by the impression, when the fruit opens and the bud escapes.

COCOA-NUT.—COCOS.

Natural order, Palmæ; a genus of the Monœcia Hexandria class.

"Give me to drain the Cocoa's milky bowl,
And from the palm to draw its freshening wine!"

THE Cocoa-nut appears to have been known to the ancient Greeks, as we find the Macedonian soldiers, who accompanied Alexander the Great in his expedition into India, met with various Indian fruits, amongst which, although they were not able to give the names of them, this nut was evidently one; and their account of it has been faithfully transmitted to us in the twelfth book of Pliny's Natural History, chap. 6. "The fruit," he says, "is put forth at the bark, having within it an admirably sweet juice, and in such abundance, that one of them is sufficient to regale four men." The Macedonians described the leaves as being of great size, resembling birds' wings.

From this period, which was about 325 years before Christ, little or nothing more was known of the cocoa-nut by the Europeans, for more than 1800 years, when the discoveries of Columbus opening a wide field of speculation for the naturalist as well as the trader, this fruit became once more known to the Old World; but it is only of late years that the cocoa-nut has been brought to

England as an article of commerce. It is now used by the West-India captains instead of wedges of timber, to fill up the vacua between the casks and other packages in their ships. The freightage of these large nuts is consequently considered as of no charge: they are therefore now become as common in the shops and streets of London, as the orange.

We learn from the Travels of two Mahomedans who visited India in the years of the Hegira 831 and 851, and which have been translated from the Arabic by Eusebius Renaudot, a learned member of the French Academy, that there were then some Indians, who, making profession of piety, went in search of unknown islands, or those newly discovered, on purpose to plant cocoa-nut trees and to sink wells for the use of ships. These travellers farther tell us, " there are people at Oman who cross to these islands that produce the cocoa-nut trees, from the planks of which they build ships, sewing them together with the yarn made from the bark of the tree. The mast is made of the same wood, the sails are formed from the leaves, and the bark is worked up into cordage: and having thus completed their vessel, they load her with cocoa-nuts, which they bring to Oman for sale."

The tree which produces this fruit is, indeed, of the first importance to the Indians, as it furnishes them with meat, drink, physic, clothing, lodging, furniture, and fuel. Chambers states, that many travellers aver, that from a single cocoa-nut tree and its fruit, a ship might be built, equipped, and laden with merchandize and provision.

It is supposed to be a native of the Maldive, and some desert islands in the East Indies, and from thence to have been transported to all the warmer parts of America. The largest cocoa-nut trees grow on the river Oroonoko, which reach to the height of sixty feet, and, bearing all their foliage at the top, produce a beautiful, waving, feather-like appearance.

The leaves have a strong mid-rib from twelve to fourteen feet long, on which the leaflets are placed alternately; these are from six to nine inches long, and are nearly triangular, having very sharp points. The flowers come out round the top of the trunk of the tree in large clusters: they are inclosed in a large spathe or sheath, and the nuts afterwards are formed in large clusters, ten or twelve together. When all the parts of the flowers have gained a due degree of perfection, the spathe splits on the under side, from the bottom upwards, and exposes the common bunch, with all its flowers, to the open air. Most of these are males, and fall off gradually as the spathe withers, leaving the embryo fruit, which is generally fixed to the lower and stronger part of the stalk, to increase and ripen gradually.

This fruit is properly a berried Drupe, superior, very large, ovate, rounded-three-cornered, umbilicate both ways, tawny or reddish, becoming finally of a very pale red or brownish colour: the skin is thin and very tough; the substance under this, investing the shell, is extremely fibrous. The shell itself is of a bony substance, ovate, three-sided, and acuminate, marked with three raised spurious sutures, and having three holes at the base closed with a black membrane. The kernel adheres all round the inner wall of the shell, and the cavity is filled with a milky liquor.—*Browne, Gærtner, Lunan.*

The Spaniards call it *Palma de las Indias;* and the Portuguese *Coco,* from the three holes in the shell, which give it the appearance of a monkey's head.

The kernel, or substance which adheres to the interior of the shell of the cocoa-nut, is very nourishing, and is used instead of almonds in milks, emulsions, &c. These emulsions, when added to coffee instead of cream, give it an exquisite taste; excellent cakes and fritters are also made from the kernel, when rasped. The tender shoots of this tree, when boiled, afford an excellent substitute for cabbage.

A large cocoa-nut will produce upwards of a pint of milk; and when young, it is esteemed one of the greatest dainties of America. As the fruit gets older, the milk becomes more sharp and cooling, consequently more agreeable to those of feverish habits. It is also esteemed highly antiscorbutic. Custards, blanc-mange, rice puddings, &c. are made with this milk.

An agreeable sweet oil, fit for the table, is procured by concentrating the milk of the cocoa-nut over a moderate fire, by ebullition. The oil obtained from this nut by pressure is an excellent lamp oil, burning with a clear bright flame, without exhaling any odour or smoke. The cocoa-nut oil, composed with the emulsion, is a gentle purgative, without being nauseous or producing colic: it is also recommended in coughs, and complaints of the lungs. The substance from which this oil has been squeezed, is given to cattle, mixed with their forage, and greatly promotes the quantity of milk when given to cows.

A juice is obtained by tapping the trunk of this tree, or by cutting off the shoots which produce the nuts, and which is caught in jars attached to the trees. This liquor, after it has fermented, is distilled into a spirit called Arrack, which is very superior to that drawn from rice: it also improves the flavour of rum when used in the distillation of that spirit. This juice, when exposed to the sun, produces vinegar.

The filings of the hard shell, applied to old wounds, will cleanse and heal them rapidly. In Maldivia, this nut is thought a powerful antidote against the venom of serpents and other poisons.

The milk is of the greatest importance in dyeing silks, cotton, or woollen stuffs, as it prevents black and other caustic colours from burning them, and gives a brilliancy to the colour. The emulsion of the kernel is used in painting chintzes, and in scouring the cloth after the colours have been applied. The Hindoos procure their fine violet and rose colours by the assistance of this fruit.

The tough fibres, or substance which encloses the shell, being steeped in water and beaten like flax, are then manufactured into linen. The palms of this tree are made into mats for sleeping on; the leaves, which are of great length, are made into baskets, hammocks, mats, brooms, racks, &c. and are used for the thatching of houses: the trunk of the tree is employed for gutters, and split into laths for covering buildings, &c. The shell of the fruit, when polished, is formed into basins, drinking-cups, and a variety of useful articles. The Emperors of Mogul highly esteemed the cocoa-nut for making goblets, which they had set with precious stones and edged with gold, believing that poison would lose its baneful qualities in these vases.

The cocoa-nuts have three holes closely stopped; one of these being both wider, and more easily penetrated than the rest: from this, when the nut is planted, rises the germen, or young tree, first having ramified and filled the whole cavity of the nut; it then shoots out at the before-mentioned hole in the top, and soon appears above ground in two narrow leaves: through these holes likewise is the water copiously distilled into the nut from the roots: thus wonderfully has nature made an egress for the future tree.

M. Le Goux de Flaix, an officer of engineers, and a member of the Asiatic Society of Calcutta, in his account of the cocoa-nut tree, says it is a well-known fact, that the fibrous covering of the cocoa-nut is converted into good ropes, which are useful in navigation and for various purposes on shore. Cables for anchors made of this substance are much better than those made of hemp. They are exceedingly elastic, stretch without straining the vessel, and scarcely ever break—advantages which are not possessed by those of hemp. They are also lighter, and never rot in consequence of their being soaked with sea-water; nor do they exhale damp or miasmata, which are exceedingly hurtful to the crews of ships who sleep on the same deck where ropes are kept when ships are under sail. These ropes are also more easily managed, and run better in the pulleys during nautical manœuvres.

Some time since a cocoa-tree was cut down on Mr. Hanson's land, in Jamaica, which had been planted about a century, when, in grubbing up the root, the shell from which the tree had been raised was found quite sound and perfect.

The Chili cocoa produces a fruit not larger than a walnut, but this is more esteemed than the large kind which is brought to England.

The cocoa-nut-tree was cultivated in Chelsea garden as long back as the year 1739.

COFFEE.—COFFEA.

Natural order, Stellatæ. A genus of the Pentandria Monogynia class.

Coffee is named after Caffa, in Africa, where it grows abundantly. This berry, which affords such a wholesome and agreeable beverage, is said to have been drunk from time immemorial in Ethiopia, but for this we have no satisfactory authority; and as the use of most plants has been accidentally discovered, it is probable that the properties of coffee might have been first found out in the manner related by Chambers, who says that a goatherd having observed that his cattle, after browsing on this tree, would wake and caper all night; this fact the prior of a certain monastery, being informed of it, first tried it on his monks, to prevent their sleeping at matins.

About the fifteenth century the use of coffee appears to have been introduced from Persia by Gemaleddin, Mufti of Aden, a city near the mouth of the Red Sea. He, finding it dissipate the fumes which oppress the head, give cheerfulness, and prevent sleep, without injury, recommended it to his dervises, with whom he used to spend the night in prayer. It was soon after this drunk at Aden by all studious persons and those who travelled by night. It was progressively used at Mecca, Medina, &c. and Grand Cairo: hence it continued its progress to Damascus and Aleppo. From the two latter places, it was introduced into Constantinople by persons of the name of

Shems and Hekin, in the year 1554, each of whom opened a public coffee-house in that city. These coffee-houses becoming a rendezvous for newsmongers, who made too free with state-affairs, were suppressed by Cuproli, the Grand Vizier.

Rauwolfus, who was in the Levant in 1573, was the first European author who made any mention of coffee; but the first who has particularly described it is Prosper Alpinus, in his *Medicina Ægyptiorum*, 1591, and in his History of Egyptian Plants, published at Venice in 1592.

The Venetians seem to be the next who used coffee. Pietro della Valle, a Venetian, writes from Constantinople in 1615, informing his friend, that upon his return he should bring him some coffee, which he believed was a thing unknown in his country. This beverage was noticed by two English travellers at the beginning of the seventeenth century: Biddulph about 1603, and William Finch in 1607. The former says, "the Turks have for their most common drink *Coffa*, which is a black kind of drink, made of a kind of pulse like peas, called *Coava*." The latter observes, "that the people in the island of Socotora have, for their best entertainment, a China dish *Coho*, a black bitterish drink, made of a berry like a bayberry, brought from Mecca, supped off hot."

Lord Chancellor Bacon mentions it in 1624: he says, "the Turks have a drink they call coffee, made with boiling water from a berry reduced into powder, which makes the water black as soot, and is of a pungent and aromatic smell, and is drunk warm."

M. La Roque, who published his journey into Arabia Felix in 1715, contends that his father having been with M. de la Haye, the French ambassador at Constantinople, did, when he returned to Marseilles, in 1644, drink coffee every day; but the same author acknowledges that it was M. Thevenot who taught the French to drink coffee, on his return from the East, in 1657. It was made fashionable and more known in Paris, in 1669, by Soliman Aga, ambassador from Sultan Mahomet the Fourth, who gave coffee at all his parties with great magnificence; and it could not fail to be pronounced an agreeable beverage by the Parisian ladies, after they had received it from his slaves on bended knee. If it were a matter of policy with the Turks to get coffee introduced into France, the ambassador's splendid porcelain, equipage, and gold-fringed napkins, were the best recommendation that could have been given to a people who are so naturally fond of show.

Two years after, it was sold in public at the Foire St. Germain, by Pascal, an Armenian, who afterwards set up a coffee-house on the Quai de l'Ecole; but, not being encouraged in Paris, he left that city, and came to London. However, soon after this, some spacious rooms were opened in Paris for the sale of coffee, and they soon increased to upwards of three hundred.

It is said to have been first brought to England by Mr. Nathaniel Conopius, a Cretan, who made it his common beverage, at Baliol College, at Oxford, in the year 1641; but it must evidently have been a few years prior to this date, as Evelyn says in his Diary, 1637, "There came in my tyme to the Coll: one Nathaniel Conopios out of Greece, from Cyrill the Patriarch of Constantinople, who, returning many years after, was made (as I understand) Bishop of Smyrna: he was the first I ever saw drink coffee, wch custom came not into England till 30 years after."

The first coffee-house in England was kept by one Jacob, a Jew, at the sign of the Angel in Oxford, in 1650. Coffee was first publicly known in London in

1652, when Mr. Daniel Edwards, a Turkey merchant, brought home with him a Ragusan Greek servant, whose name was Pasqua Rossée, who understood the roasting and making of coffee, and kept a house for that purpose, in George Yard, Lombard Street, or rather, according to Mr. Houghton, in a shed in the Churchyard of St. Michael's, Cornhill. This seemed to give alarm to the ale-sellers, who, taking advantage of Rossée's not being free of the City, petitioned the Lord Mayor against him; but Mr. Edwards having married a daughter of Alderman Hodges, the Alderman joined Bowman his coachman, who was a freeman, as a partner with Pasqua Rossée. The Greek was afterwards obliged to leave the country for some misdemeanor; and Bowman, by his business and the aid of a subscription of one thousand sixpences, was enabled to convert his shed into a coffee-house. The famous Dr. Harvey used it frequently. Mr. Ray affirms that, in 1688, London might rival Grand Cairo in the number of its coffee-houses, so rapidly had it come into use; and it is thought that they were augmented and established more firmly by the ill-judged proclamation of Charles the Second, in 1675, to shut up coffee-houses as seminaries of sedition: this act was suspended in a few days.

The first mention of coffee in our statute books is in 1660, (12 Char. II. cap. 24.) by which a duty of fourpence was laid upon every gallon of coffee bought or sold. Kæmpfer says, "that Mocha is the peculiar region of coffee:"—"Kahwah; quæ nullibi terrarum quàm circa Mocham Arabiæ felicis colitur."—(*Amœn. Exot. p.* 123.)

Bruce, however, would trace it to Caffa, "the South province of Narea, whence it is first said to have come." (*Travels, &c.* vol. ii. p. 411.)

The Arabs seem to have been very jealous of letting this tree be known; and in order to confine the commodity to themselves, they destroyed the vegetable quality of the seeds; but Nicholas Witsen, burgomaster of Amsterdam and governor of the East-India Company, desired Van Hoorn, governor of Batavia, to procure from Mocha, in Arabia Felix, some berries of the coffee-tree, which were obtained and sown at Batavia; and about the year 1690, several plants having been raised from seeds, Van Hoorn sent one over to Governor Witsen, who presented it to the garden at Amsterdam. It there bore fruit, which in a short time produced many young plants: from these the East Indies and most of the gardens in Europe have been furnished. In 1696, it was cultivated at Fulham, by Bishop Compton; and in 1714, the magistrates of Amsterdam presented Louis the Fourteenth with a coffee-tree, which was sent to the royal garden at Marli. In 1718, the Dutch colony, at Surinam, began first to plant coffee; and in 1722, M. de la Motte Aigron, governor of Cayenne, contrived by an artifice to bring away a plant from Surinam, which, by the year 1725, had produced many thousands. The French authors affirm that it was planted in the Isle of Bourbon, in the year 1718, having been obtained from Mocha. This seems doubtful; but it is ascertained that M. Declieux carried the first coffee-plant to Martinico in 1720.

This passage was long and dreary, and fresh water being scarce in the vessel, made it necessary to limit every one to a small portion daily, to make it last out the voyage, when this gentleman deprived himself of a great part of his allowance in order to keep these valuable trees alive. M. Fusée Aublet states that one tree only survived in the Isle of Bourbon, which bore fruit in 1720. From Martinico it spread to the neighbouring islands. Sir Nicholas Laws first introduced it into Jamaica, in the year 1728, and planted it at Townwell Estate, now called Temple Hall, in Liguanea: the first berries produced from this tree sold at a *bit* each, which is equal to 6*d*. In the year 1752 the export of coffee from Jamaica was rated at 60,000lbs.; and it has continued regularly to increase since that time, except when additional duties have been laid on, which have as regularly lessened the exports and the revenue also; an important proof, among others, how frequently heavy taxation defeats its own purpose. In 1791 there were 607 coffee-plantations in Jamaica, employing 21,000 negroes. In 1808, the exports from Jamaica were 29,528,273lbs.; the next year they were lessened about four millions of pounds; in 1812, the export was 18,481,986lbs. The Abbé Raynal says, that 12,550,000 pounds of coffee are annually exported from Arabia Felix.

Almost every species of the vegetable creation has an apparent enemy peculiar to itself in the animal tribe, but which is undoubtedly intended for some wise purpose, although often beyond our investigation. The finest coffee-tree in our colonies, and sometimes a whole plantation, is seen to perish in a short time. This is often occasioned by an insect called the coffee fly: this fly is very long, and has attached to its head two saws with which it sometimes cuts these trees to the very heart. The white vine-fretters also attack the coffee-tree, to prevent which, pine-apples are planted between the trees, because these insects, preferring the juice of this fruit, eat of it, which causes their death.

Every gentleman who has stoves should raise this tree for the beauty of its appearance. It is an evergreen, whose leaves continue three years; and being of a fine dark green, make a beautiful contrast with the clusters of pure white blossoms, which perfume the air with an odour like jasmine. Nothing can be conceived more delightful and grateful than the appearance and perfume of a field of coffee-trees when in full bloom: it resembles a shower of snow, which nearly obscures the dark green branches. The tree, like the walnut, produces smaller fruit, and better-flavoured, as it becomes older.

Sonnini, in his Travels in Egypt, says, "If you wish to be supplied with excellent coffee, you must go to Kous, Kenné, or Bonoub; for when one had arrived at Cairo, or had crossed the Nile, it was no longer pure. Merchants were waiting there to mix it with the common coffee of America. At Alexandria it underwent a second mixture by the factors who forwarded it to Marseilles, where they did not fail again to adulterate it; so that the pretended Mocha coffee, which is used in France, is often the growth of the American colonies, with about one-third, and seldom with half of the genuine coffee of Yemen. When I was at Kous, the unadulterated coffee of the first quality sold for about ten-pence halfpenny the pound. If to prime cost is added the expense of conveying it to Cairo, the duties which are paid there, the charges for loading and unloading, those for transporting it to Alexandria, freight to Marseilles, the exorbitant and arbitrary duties with which that commodity is there loaded, and if to these are added commission and the expense of grinding, &c. how is it possible to believe that they should have real Mocha coffee at Paris, at the rate of five shillings per pound?

The Turkey coffee is a small berry, and is more esteemed for its flavour than that which grows in the West Indies. We conclude that one great cause of the American coffee being inferior in point of flavour, is owing to the practice, in that part of the world, of gathering the berries before they are quite ripe, whereas the Arabians shake their trees, and by this means obtain the berries in full perfection. Mr. Lunan observes, that the West-Indian berries being considerably larger than those of the Turkey coffee, require much longer keeping; but Mr. Miller, the celebrated gardener, is of opinion, that coffee does not require long keeping, and that it loses a part of its flavour. He states that two gentlemen, who resided some years in Arabia, assured him that the berries, when first ripe, were very superior to those which had been kept. He also states, that from plants brought from the West Indies, and raised in English hot-houses, coffee-berries have been produced, which, at a proper age, were found to surpass the very best Mocha that could be produced in Great Britain. Jamaica coffee is often sold as Turkey coffee in London, and there have been many samples sent from Jamaica, that have proved quite equal to any Arabian berries. As coffee readily imbibes the smell or flavour of any article it comes in contact with, it is often injured in the voyage home, by being stowed near sugar, rum, pimento, &c. &c.; and the flavour which it thus contracts, cannot be separated again, even by roasting.

The most eminent physicians of every country have recommended the use of coffee for various complaints. It greatly relieves the head-ache, and is recommended to those of constitutionally weak stomachs, as it accelerates the process of digestion, removes languor and listlessness, and affords a pleasing sensation. Coffee is often found useful in quieting the tickling vexatious cough. Sir John Floyer, who had been afflicted with the asthma for sixty years, was relieved by strong coffee. The great use of coffee in France is supposed to have abated the prevalency of the gravel; for where coffee is used as a constant beverage, the gravel and the gout are scarcely known. Voltaire lived almost wholly on coffee, and said nothing exhilarated his spirits so much as the smell of it; for which reason he had what he was about to use in the day roasted in his chamber every morning, when he lived at Ferney.

A friend writes me from Constantinople, that many of

the Turks will subsist almost entirely on coffee, except during the rigid fast of the Ramadan, or Turkish Lent, which lasts forty days; during which time they neither eat, drink, nor smoke, while the sun is over the horizon; and the use of coffee is then so strictly forbidden, that those who have even the smell of coffee on them, are deemed to have violated the injunctions of their prophet: yet it is estimated that as much money is spent in coffee at Constantinople as in wine at Paris. Among the legal causes of divorce with the Turks, the refusal to supply a wife with coffee is one. Notwithstanding the immense consumption of coffee in the Turkish capital, they have but one building where it is allowed to be roasted; a great number of persons are employed in pounding it in mortars; this is performed as soon as the coffee is taken from the oven, which causes the surrounding neighbourhood to smell strongly of this aromatic drug.

Among the various qualities of coffee, that of its being an antidote to the abuse of opium must make it an invaluable article with the Turks, who drink it without either sugar or milk. The Persians, who sip their coffee extremely hot, take it also without either of these additions; but they have an accompaniment that would not be quite so agreeable to our fair countrywomen. The Persians have a saying, that "coffee without tobacco is like meat without salt." How greatly must the habits of the Mahomedans have been changed by the introduction of these two vegetable luxuries, which now contribute to solace even the poorest inhabitants of Turkey and Persia, as much as the Chinese leaf does the English.

An interesting analysis of coffee was made by M. Cadet, apothecary in ordinary to the household of Napoleon, when emperor; from which it appears, that the berries contain mucilage in abundance, much gallic acid, a resin, a concrete essential oil, some albumen, and a volatile aromatic principle, with a portion of lime, potash, charcoal, iron, &c. Roasting developes the soluble principles. Mocha coffee is, of all kinds, the most aromatic and resinous. M. Cadet advises that coffee be neither roasted nor infused till the day it be drunk, and that the roasting be moderate.

M. Bigio, of Venice, has succeeded in extracting from coffee a green gum lac, said to be useful and beautiful in painting.

Dr. Moseley, in his learned and ingenious Treatise, states, that "the chemical analysis of coffee evinces that it possesses a great portion of mildly bitter, and lightly astringent gummous and resinous extract, a considerable quantity of oil, a fixed salt, and a volatile salt. These are its medicinal constituent principles. The intention of torrefaction is not only to make it deliver those principles, and make them soluble in water, but to give it a property it does not possess in the natural state of the berry. By the action of fire, its leguminous taste and the aqueous part of its mucilage are destroyed; its saline properties are created and disengaged, and its oil is rendered empyreumatical. From thence arise the pungent smell, and exhilarating flavour, not found in its natural state.

"The roasting of the berry to a proper degree, requires great nicety. If it be underdone, its virtues will not be imparted, and in use it will load and oppress the stomach: if it be overdone, it will yield a flat, burnt, and bitter taste; its virtues will be destroyed, and in use it will heat the body, and act as an astringent. The closer it is confined, at the time of the roasting, and till used, the better will its volatile pungency, flavour, and virtues, be preserved.

"The influence which coffee, judiciously prepared, imparts to the stomach, from its invigorating qualities, is strongly exemplified by the immediate effect produced on taking it when the stomach is overloaded with food, or nauseated with surfeit, or debilitated by intemperance, or languid from inanition. In vertigo, lethargy, catarrh, and all disorders of the head, from obstructions in the capillaries, long experience has proved it to be a powerful medicine: and in certain cases of apoplexy, it has been found serviceable even when given in clysters, where it has not been convenient to convey its effects to the stomach. Mons. Malebranche restored a person from apoplexy by repeated clysters of coffee.

"Du Four relates an extraordinary instance of the effect of coffee in the gout: he says, Mons. Deverau was attacked with the gout at twenty-five years of age, and had it severely until he was upwards of fifty, with chalk stones in the joints of his hands and feet: he was recommended the use of coffee, which he adopted, and had no return of the gout.

"A small cup or two of coffee, immediately after dinner, promotes digestion. With a draught of water previously drunk, according to the eastern custom, coffee is serviceable to those who are of a costive habit."

The generality of English families make their coffee too weak, and use too much sugar, which often causes it to turn acid on the stomach. Almost every housekeeper has a peculiar method of making coffee; but it never can be excellent, unless it be made strong of the berry, any more than our English wines can be good, so long as we continue to form the principal of them on sugar and water. When coffee is used as a breakfast beverage, we would strongly recommend it to be served in the manner of the French *Café au Lait*:—with a small pot of very strong coffee, they send a large jug of boiling milk, and it is generally used from about one-fourth of coffee, to three-fourths of milk; thus you get nourishment from the milk and sugar, and more refreshment from a small quantity of strong coffee, than a larger portion of weak.

After dinner we would recommend it strong and hot, but without sugar or cream.

Count Rumford says, " Coffee may be too bitter; but it is impossible that it should ever be too fragrant. The very smell of it is reviving, and has often been found to be useful to sick persons, and to those who are afflicted with the head-ache. In short, every thing proves that the volatile, aromatic matter, whatever it may be, that gives flavour to coffee, is what is most valuable in it, and should be preserved with the greatest care, and that, in estimating the strength or richness of that beverage, its fragrance should be much more attended to, than either its bitterness or its astringency. This aromatic substance, which is supposed to be an oil, is extremely volatile, and escapes into the air with great facility, as is observed by its filling a room with its fragrance, if suffered to remain uncovered, and at the same time losing much of its flavour.

We would recommend those who give coffee to evening parties, to let their attendants hand empty cups, with a coffee-pot on the tray, which would ensure its being warm and with flavour.

CRANBERRY.—VACCINIUM.

Natural order, Bicornes. A genus of the Octandria Monogynia class.

THIS fruit, which is so much esteemed in tarts, or with cream, is a native of England, and is found growing in the peaty bogs of Sussex, Cumberland, Norfolk, Lancashire, and in other marshy lands. Gerard calls the fruit *fen-berries:* " they grow, "says he, " in fennie places, in Cheshire and Staffordshire, where I have found them in great plentie." Valerius Cordus called them *oxycoccon;* the Dutch term them *fen grapes.*

They are thought to have derived the name of cranberry from the peduncles being crooked at the top, and, before the expansion of the flower, resembling the head and neck of a crane.

Dr. Withering states, that at Longton, in Cumberland, there is a considerable traffic carried on in cranberries; that on the market-days, during the gathering season, the sale of these berries amounts to from twenty to thirty pounds sterling per day. Many people in that neighbourhood make wine from cranberries; but never having tasted this liquor, we can give no account of its quality. The English cranberries, which are preserved in bottles with no other care than keeping them dry, are very superior to those large cranberries imported from the northern parts of America, which are now so common in the shops of London. These berries, being packed in large casks, must undergo a fermentation during the voyage, which consequently deprives them of a part of their natural flavour. Cranberries are also imported from Russia and Germany; and during this last year great quantities have been brought from New Holland, which are smaller, and darker coloured, than those brought from America, and very superior in flavour. Cranberries are found growing in many parts of Spain and Hungary. They are the produce of damp swampy lands only; but the idea that they will not bear transplanting is erroneous, the late Sir Joseph Banks having planted some near a pond in his grounds at Spring Grove, which have produced fruit beyond calculation. This information may be worth the attention of those who have marshy or brook land, as a matter of profit; and to those who have ornamental water in their gardens or parks, it would be found an embellishment to the banks; it being an elegant little fruit on the ground, where it trails, and spangles the grass with its red and variegated berries. When transplanted into the garden, they require a moorish or boggy soil, and the bed should be kept about six inches lower than the general surface of the ground, by which means they may be kept in a swamp by a small channel, or temporary shoot from a pump; they will soon cover the surface, and produce fruit abundantly.

This fruit is now also grown in dry beds:—the experiment was first made by Robert Hallett, Esq. of Axminster, Devonshire, who in a letter to the Horticultural Society (read 5th June, 1821,) says, "Having cultivated the American cranberry with great success in Devonshire, I beg to submit to the Horticultural Society a detail of the practice by which I have satisfactorily ascertained that the fruit of this plant may be obtained in *dry*, as well as in *moist situations*, to any extent that may be desired; and since it makes such excellent tarts, and as no other trouble is required than putting them into dry bottles, and corking them up close, I trust this communication will be acceptable.

"In April 1814, I procured four plants of the American cranberry (*Vaccinium macrocarpon*), the kind cultivated by the late Sir Joseph Banks at Spring Grove, whose method I followed, placing them in a small bed over part of a pond which was fenced off. These plants flourished, and produced me some very fine fruit, which I found so useful that I was induced to attempt to obtain, if possible, a larger supply; but not having another piece of water, which I could conveniently devote to this purpose, I resolved to try to grow them in a dry bed.

"In April 1818, I filled half-a-dozen shallow boxes, each about eighteen inches square and four inches deep, with peat earth, and planted in them, at one inch apart, cuttings of the cranberry, about an inch and a-half in length, placing them in my melon bed, where they were frequently watered: the cuttings rooted freely and threw out strong shoots, and in the June following they were fit to plant out. Having collected from a dry hill, where wild heath flourished in abundance, a sufficient quantity of peat earth, such as Cushing in his *Exotic Gardener* (second edition, page 156,) describes under that name, I formed a bed one hundred and fifty feet long by four feet wide. In order to give the plants room to extend their roots freely, I caused eighteen inches in width of the centre part of this bed to be excavated throughout its whole length to the depth of two feet; and having first covered about two inches of the bottom of the trench with small wood, I filled it up with the peat earth, well trod in; on the sides of the bed, to the extent of its width, I put only six inches depth of this mould. About the end of June 1818, I placed one row of plants in the centre of this bed, about two feet apart from each other in the row: these soon put forth luxuriant runners, extending before the winter to the edges of the bed.

"At the close of the year 1819, the bed was covered with the plants, and the runners of the former year had thrown out a number of upright bearing shoots, from which, last year, I gathered several bottles of excellent fruit, much superior in flavour to any imported berries I have ever tasted. In the autumn of 1820 I had the satisfaction to see the entire bed filled so completely by the plants, as to form a mass through which scarcely a weed could penetrate, the whole exhibiting a profusion of bearing branches, which are now (May 1821) putting forth such an abundance of blossoms as not only to make a very handsome appearance, but to promise a supply of berries far exceeding my expectations.

"The plants, after the first supply, may be easily propagated to any extent that may be required; for though they root more freely under glass, yet a hot-bed is not absolutely necessary to raise them.

"I have known the cuttings strike well, and make good plants in pots in the open air, and after being rooted they require no trouble to preserve them. One of the boxes of those raised in 1818, has been left exposed to the open air throughout three summers and as many winters, and though no care was bestowed on the plants, and the depth of earth did not exceed four inches, yet neither the summer's heat nor winter's cold affected them, and last year they produced some very fine berries. This proves their hardy nature, and that an exposed situation will not be inimical to the health of the plants. The berries I have likewise found to be as little susceptible of injury from being allowed to remain out late in the season; for on examining my bed in April last, I discovered that out of a considerable number which had not been gathered in the autumn, many were at that time in a perfect state on the branches.

"Four feet is the most convenient width for the beds, but by passing the shoots under the path formed of peat earth, wherein they would root, other beds might soon be established on each side. From four to six inches depth of peat earth would be sufficient for such beds, and the paths should be level with them, it being desirable not to drain off the moisture.

"Dry heathy commons and wastes would produce a large supply of these fruits, with little labour or expense, either for the markets or for food for moor-game. A single plant would soon extend itself over a large space of ground, if turned up and kept clean till the runners had taken root; and as no manure is requisite, and little or no weeding wanted, the first trouble is all that would be necessary, except in situations where hares or rabbits abound: these animals are particularly fond of the young plants, and a temporary fence must be made to protect them from their depredations.

"Dung is peculiarly injurious to the cranberry: it absolutely destroys it, as I have proved by a variety of experiments, in which I found that all the plants completely failed which were planted in any compost of which garden mould or dung formed a part. Peat earth is the only soil in which they will flourish: nor can a supply of this very valuable fruit be expected except in situations where the plants will have a due enjoyment of sun and air."

The cuttings may be taken from any part of the old plants, for the old wood will root as well as the young branches.

Sweden produces abundance of cranberries, but they are only used for cleansing plate in that country.

A new species of cranberry is now cultivated in this kingdom, which has been called snowberry, on account of the colour of the fruit: it was brought from Nova

Scotia in the year 1760 by Mr. Jonathan Laycock, and is stated to be found in the swamps of Cyprus also. This berry has a perfumed taste, like *eau de noyau,* or bitter almonds: it is reared by Mr. Joseph Knight, of Little Chelsea, and several other nurserymen near the metropolis. Another variety was brought from Madeira in 1777, which requires the shelter of the green-house; and the Jamaica cranberry, which was introduced the following year, will not thrive in this country except in the stove.

Cranberries are of an astringent quality, and esteemed good to restore the appetite: they were formerly imagined efficacious in preventing pestilential diseases.

CUCUMBER.—CUCUMIS.

Natural order, Cucurbitaceæ. A genus of the Monœcia Syngenesia class.

The cucumber, which is one of the coldest fruits, is evidently a native of a warm climate; and by all the researches we have been able to make, we conclude it belongs to the soil of some parts of Asia and Africa. It seems to have been a common and favourite diet in Egypt in very early times; as among the murmurings of the Israelites when in the wilderness we find them regretting this vegetable.

The Hebrews called it קשא, from which the Greeks named it Κικυος, or Σικυος, of whom the Latins derived the word *Cucumis*, from which there is but little variation in any of the European languages.

We find cucumbers were cultivated by the Greeks, as their earliest writers on Natural History have mentioned them, and in particular recommend that the seeds should be steeped for two days in milk and honey before they are set, to make the fruit sweeter and pleasanter. Pliny mentions the great quantities that grew in some parts of Africa, and particularly in Barbary. All vegetables are so formed as to perpetuate themselves by seed in the climate where they originate; for if this were not the case, every species of plant that is not cultivated would soon cease to exist; and the cucumber has never been found to grow in the natural state in any part of Europe.

Columella is the oldest author who gives any direction for forwarding cucumbers by artificial means. "Those who wish for them early," says he, "should plant the seeds in well-dunged earth, put into osier baskets, that they may be carried out of the house, and placed in warm situations when the weather permits; and as soon as the season is advanced, the plants may be sunk in the earth with the baskets, or wheels may be put upon large vases, that they may be brought out with less labour. Notwithstanding they ought," continues he, "to be covered with *specularia*," which seem to have been transparent stones, that the Romans were in the habit of cutting thin, so as to admit light, and keep out the air, glass being unknown at that period.

It is related by Pliny, that Tiberius the emperor was so fond of cucumbers, that there was not a day throughout the year but he had them served up at his table. The beds and gardens wherein they grew, were made upon frames, so as to be removed every way with wheels; and in winter, during the cold and frosty days, they could be drawn back into certain high covered buildings, exposed to the sun, and there housed under roof. These appear to be the earliest accounts of the forcing of plants, of which we read. It is probable, also, that artificial heat was used; as we find, by the remains of their villas in this country, how perfectly the Romans were acquainted with the method of warming their rooms with flues.

Pliny says, "To make a delicate salad of cucumbers, boil them first, then peel them from the rind, and serve them up with oil, vinegar, and honey."

Mr. Aiton mentions the cucumber as being first cultivated here in the year 1573, in the reign of Queen Elizabeth. This appears to be an error, as cucumbers were very common in this country in the reign of Edward the

Third; but being unattended to during the wars of York and Lancaster, they soon after became entirely unknown, until the reign of Henry the Eighth, when they were again introduced to this kingdom. (*Gough's British Topography*, vol. I. p. 134.)

Gerard gives the earliest directions for making hot-beds for cucumbers in this country, when gardening was in its infant state. He directs, that they should be covered with mats over hoops, as glasses were not then known.

Lord Bacon says, "cucumbers will prove more tender and dainty if their seeds be steeped (little) in milk: the cause may be, for that the seed being mollified in milk, will be too weak to draw the grosser juices of the earth, but only the finer." He adds, "cucumbers will be less watery if the pit where you set them be filled up half-way with chaff or small sticks, and then pour earth upon them; for cucumbers, as it seemeth, do exceedingly affect moisture, and over-drink themselves, which this chaff or chips forbiddeth." This author also states, that "it hath been practised to cut off the stalks of cucumbers, immediately after bearing, close by the earth; and then to cast a pretty quantity of earth upon the plant that remaineth, and they will bear the next year fruit, long before the ordinary time. The cause may be, for that the sap goeth down the sooner, and is not spent in the stalk or leaf, which remaineth after the fruit; where note, that the dying in the winter of the roots of plants that are annual, seemeth to be partly caused by the over-expense of the sap into stalk and leaves; which being prevented, they will superannuate, if they stand warm." Miller informs us, that the cuttings of cucumbers, taken off about five or six inches long, from healthy plants in the summer crop, at the end of September or beginning of October, planted in pots of rich mould, plunged into the bark bed and shaded until they have struck, will produce fruit before Christmas. It is also recorded in Miller's Gardener's Dictionary, that Thomas Fowler, gardener to Sir Nathaniel Gould, at Stoke Newington, presented King George the First with a brace of well-grown cucumbers, on New Year's Day, 1721. The seeds from which they were raised were sown on the 25th of September.

His late revered Majesty had his table supplied with cucumbers, at all seasons of the year, by Mr. Aiton, under whose care the Royal Gardens of this kingdom have produced, in the highest perfection, nearly all the known fruits of the world.

Cucumbers are now grown with so much success by the aid of steam, that the London Markets have been regularly and abundantly supplied with them during the last winter. We have lately seen some pits for growing melons and cucumbers which have not only obviated the necessity of horse-dung, but by the more regular heat which the steam conveyed to the mould, the plants were kept in a more healthy state; and produced fruit so abundantly that one pit yielded about two hundred brace of fine cucumbers during the most uncongenial month of the year.

When cucumbers are thus raised earlier in the season than the bees leave their cells, or when the frames are kept too close to admit these little animals, the gardener should attentively observe the time when the anther bursts, and apply it to the stigma of the fertile flower, as the fruit is greatly assisted by being thus fecundated.

Mr. Martells is said to have lately cut from his garden at Southsea, Hants, a cucumber measuring five feet in length: we conclude it must have been the *Cucumis flexuosus*, snake melon.

The principal varieties of the cucumber are the Spring Grove, or early frame; Southgate, or late frame; Hot-house, or winter; Green turkey; White turkey.

Cucumbers are much less used in their natural state than formerly among wealthy families, but they are in great request for stews and made-dishes, and, when preserved, they are esteemed one of the most agreeable sweetmeats. As a pickle, girkins have been long admired; but whoever purchases them, should be careful to get them free from any substance that may have been used to colour them.

Lunan, in his account of the *sativus*, or cultivated cucumber, says, "although cucumbers are neither sweet nor acid, they are considerably acescent, and so produce flatulency, cholera, diarrhœa," &c. Their coldness and flatulency may be likewise in part attributed to the firmness of their texture.

They have been discharged, with little change, from the stomach, after having been detained there for forty-eight hours. By this means, therefore, their acidity is greatly increased; hence oil and pepper, the condiments commonly employed, are very useful to check their fermentation. Another condiment is sometimes used; viz. the skin of the cucumber, which is bitter, and may therefore supply the place of aromatics; but it should only be used when young.

Brookes states, that the cucumber is unfit for nourishment, and is generally offensive to the stomach, especially if not corrected with a good deal of pepper as well as vinegar. The seeds, he states, are reckoned among the four greater cold seeds: therefore emulsions of them have been prescribed in burning fevers, &c.

Frederic Murell, a physician at Berlin, informs us, that he cured a gentleman who was about twenty-one years of age, of a consumption, which succeeded a profuse spitting of blood, by keeping him some weeks on cucumbers, which he ate without any other preparation than peeling, and took no other diet, except a few biscuits and water.

Cowper has beautifully described the method

> To raise the prickly and green-coated gourd,
> So grateful to the palate; and when rare,
> So coveted; else base and disesteem'd,
> Food for the vulgar merely.

The Rev. Griffith Hughes, in his Natural History of Barbadoes, mentions the wild cucumber-vine as indigenous to that part of the world. It is called by Father Plumier *anguria fructu echinato eduli.* He describes the fruit as a small cucumber, whose surface is covered with many soft-pointed prickles: it is sometimes eaten; but is esteemed to be of too cold a nature to be wholesome.

Lunan, in his Hortus Jamaicensis, mentions the small wild cucumber as being a native of Jamaica, where it grows very plentifully, and is often used with other herbs in soups, and is a very agreeable ingredient: the rind is thickly beset with blunt prickles. Sloane mentions it as a pale green oval fruit, as big as a walnut, and says it is eaten very greedily by sheep and cattle.

The ancients used the wild cucumber as a sovereign remedy in various complaints. "The best kind," says Pliny, "was found in Arabia, and the next about Cyrene and Arcadia."

It was from the juice of these cucumbers that they procured the medicine called *elaterium,* which, Theophrastus states, could be kept good two hundred years; and for fifty years it would be so strong and full of virtue, that it would put out the light of a candle or lamp. Pliny says, "to try good elaterium, it is set near to a lighted candle, which it causes to sparkle upwards and downwards."

Elaterium was used not only as a purgative, but against

the sting of scorpions, and for the dropsy: with honey and oil, it was used for the quinsy and diseases of the windpipe. It was said to cure dimness and other imperfections of the eyes, the ringworm, tetter, &c. as well as the swelling kernels behind the ears.

The juice of wild cucumber-leaves dropped with vinegar into the ears, was thought a good remedy for deafness. A decoction of the fruit being sprinkled in any place, will drive away mice; it was also said to cure the gout, &c.: indeed, so many virtues were attributed to it by the ancients, that if we were to give credit to them, we must wonder that they had any complaint uncured.

The elaterium of the present day is so variously prepared, that it is to be met with in the shops from a cream colour, to nearly black. The lighter it is, generally the more active. The best is of a light grey colour, brittle, but with difficulty powdered, having no smell, and a bitter taste. As prepared by some chemists, a quarter of a grain will be a sufficiently active dose, while the same extract prepared by another, may be taken in doses of two or three grains, without acting more violently.

It produces a most copious secretion of serous fluid from the bowels, and by that means often gives the greatest relief to dropsical patients, where other medicines have been taken without any benefit. By some authors it is considered as a remedy which ought only to be resorted to in desperate cases; but we may confidently state, that when given with caution, it may often be employed in dropsical cases. It is advisable to give it in the form of powder, with some more mild medicine, as the sulphate, or supertartrate of potash.—*Medical Botany.*

The Romans had many superstitious opinions respecting these wild cucumbers. Wives who wished for children wore them tied round their bodies; and they were brought into houses by the midwife, but carried out, in the greatest haste, after child-birth.

Columella has recorded a variety of wonderful stories respecting the garden-cucumber; and some English authors of great celebrity have stated, that, when a cucumber-vine is growing, if you set a pot of water about five or six inches from it, it will shoot so much in twenty-four hours as to touch the pot; but that it will shrink from oil, and turn fairly away from it.

——— The gourd
And thirsty cucumber, when they perceive
Th' approaching olive, with resentment fly
Her fatty fibres, and with tendrils creep
Diverse, detesting contact.

Philips.

CURRANT-TREE.—RIBES.

Natural order, Pomaceæ. A genus of the Pentandria Monogynia class.

This agreeable and wholesome fruit is undoubtedly a native of our country: it was formerly found growing, in the wild state, in the woods and hedges of Yorkshire, Durham, and Westmorland, as well as on the banks of the Tay, and other parts of Scotland. The red currant grows naturally in Sweden and other northern parts of Europe. The white is only a variety of it, and was at first accidentally produced by culture. The salmon colour, or Champaigne currant, is evidently the offspring of accidental impregnation, and it has nothing but variety to recommend it.

The common black currant, *ribes nigrum*, is a distinct species of this kind of fruit, as is marked by its strong-scented leaves and berries, and of which even the wood partakes so sensibly, as to impart by its odour a correct idea of the flavour which the fruit gives to the palate. As a further proof of its being a northern fruit, we have no account of its having been at all known to the ancient Greeks or Romans, who have been very accurate in describing all the fruits known in their time. It seems not to have grown so far south as France; for the old French name of *groseilles d'outremer* evidently bespeaks it not to have been a native of that country, and even at the present time the French language has no appropriate name for it distinct from the gooseberry. The Dutch also acknowledge it not to have been indigenous to Holland, where it was called *besskins over zee.* Whether the Dutch first procured this fruit from Britain, or from any other northern countries, we must acknowledge ourselves indebted to the gardeners of that country for improving the size, if not the flavour, of this fruit.

The English name of currant seems to have been taken from the similitude of the fruit to that of the small Zante grapes, which we call currants, or Corinths, from Corinth, where this fruit formerly grew in great abundance, and which is so much used in this country for cakes, puddings, &c.

The Italians seem to have no other name for the currants than *uvette, little grapes.* At Geneva they are called *raisins de Mars.* The currant does not appear in the list of fruits published by Thomas Tusser in 1557, which we have transcribed to shew what fruits were cultivated in the latter part of Queen Mary's reign.

"Apples of all sorts, apricots, barberries; boollesse, black and white; cherries, red and black; chesnuts; cornet plums; damascens, white and black; filberts, red and white; gooseberries; grapes, white and red; green or grass plums; hurtil berries; medlers, or meles; mulberries; peaches, white and red; peeres of all sorts; peer plums, black and yellow; quince-trees; raspis; reisons; small nuts; strawberries, red and white; service trees; wardens, white and red; walnuts; wheat plums."

So little advance had horticulture made in this country even at that late period,

"That still, a stranger to our trees and flowers,
Knew not their name, their lineage, and their powers."

Currants were not distinguished from gooseberries by any particular name at that period; and even in Gerard's time they were considered as a species of the gooseberry.

He says, in his account of the latter fruit, "We have also in our London gardens another sort altogether without prickes, whose fruit is verie small, lesser by much than the common kinde, but of a perfect red colour, wherein it differeth from the rest of his kinde."

Lord Bacon, who wrote about fifty years after Tusser, has noticed them: he says, "the earliest fruits are strawberries, cherries, gooseberries, *corrans*, and after them early apples, early pears, apricots, rasps, and after them damisons, and most kinds of plums, peaches, &c.; and the latest are apples, wardens, grapes, nuts, quinces, almonds, sloes, brierberries, hops, medlers, services, cornelians, &c."

Worlidge speaks of the currant in his Vinetum Britannicum, which was published in the year 1675, wherein he says, "the English curran, once in esteem, but now cast out of all good gardens, as is the black, which was never worth any thing. The white curran was not long since in most esteem, until the red Dutch curran became native to our soil, which is also improved in some rich moist grounds, that it hath gained a higher name of the greatest red Dutch curran. These are the only fruits that are fit to be planted and propagated for wine, and for the conservatory."

Coles, the herbarist, tells us, that in his time, (1657) the white currant was called *Gozell* in Kent.

Currants are now a fruit of great importance in this country: they are so easily propagated, that every cottage gardener can rear them; they thrive in almost any soil and situation, even under the shade of orchard-trees, but the fruit is best when exposed to the open air, and upon a light loamy soil; and they are likewise so regular in bearing, that it is seldom they are injured by the weather. At the dessert, they are greatly esteemed, being found cooling and grateful to the stomach; and they are as much admired for their transparent beauty, as for their medicinal qualities, being moderately refrigerant, antiseptic, attenuant, and aperient. They may be used with advantage to allay thirst in most febrile complaints, to lessen an increased secretion of bile, and to correct a putrid and scorbutic state of the fluids, especially in sanguine temperaments: but, in constitutions of a contrary kind, they are apt to occasion flatulency and indigestion. Brookes says, they strengthen the stomach, excite appetite, and are good against vomiting.

Fruits in general are only wholesome when they have acquired their full maturity; and there are but few species of watery fruits that can be preserved, in their natural state, after they have arrived at perfection, for so long a time as the currant. The currant is a fruit that will ripen early, when planted in a warm situation, and may be retarded so as to be gathered in good condition in the month of November, when it is planted in a northern aspect, or protected by a mat to screen it from the heat of the sun. Thus, with care, a skilful gardener will furnish a dessert of this fruit for six months, without the aid of artificial heat.

Currants will keep for years in bottles, retaining all their qualities for tarts, &c. if they are gathered perfectly dry, and not too ripe. They only require to be kept from the air, and in a dry situation. We have found it an advantage to pack them in a chest, with the corks downwards; and, if the vacua be filled up with dry sand, it will insure their preservation.

The red currant gives the finest flavour for jelly.

The wine made from the white currants, if rich of the fruit, so as to require little sugar, is, when kept to a proper age, of a similar flavour to the Grave and Rhenish wines; and we have known it preferred as a summer table wine. Even in London this agreeable beverage may be made at less expense than moderate cider can be bought for. Diluted in water, this wine is an excellent drink in the hot season, particularly to those of feverish habits. It makes an excellent shrub; and the juice is a pleasant acid in punch, which, about thirty years back, was a favourite beverage in the coffee-houses in Paris.

The best English brandy we have tasted was distilled from weak currant wine, by a gentleman at Windsor; and there is no doubt but it could be made superior to the common brandies imported from France, were it encouraged, and certain restrictions taken from the distiller.

The black currants, which were formerly called *squinancy berries*, on account of their great use in quinsies, are natives of Sweden and the northern parts of Russia, as well as the northern counties of England, where they have been found in their natural state, growing in alder swamps, and in wet hedges by the banks of rivers. In some parts of Siberia, the black currants are said to grow to the size of hazel-nuts. A new variety of the black currant has lately been cultivated in Cambridgeshire, the fruit of which is so large, that a single berry weighed sixty-one grains, and measured two inches and a half in circumference. The inhabitants of Siberia make a drink of the leaves: in Russia a wine is made of the black currants, as well as in some parts of England.

The jelly made from these currants is recommended in most complaints of the throat: they are also esteemed cleansing, pellent, and diuretic: an infusion of the roots is useful in fevers of the eruptive kind.

The inner bark of all the species of the currant-tree, boiled in water, is a popular remedy in jaundice; and some medical men have recommended it in dropsical complaints.

The currant-tree that was brought from the isle of Zante, by our Levant traders, and first planted in England in the year 1533, we conclude was the vine that produces the small grapes which we call currants, and of which the English use more than all the rest of the world together. This fruit grows in great abundance in several places in the Archipelago. We have a factory at Zante, from whence we import them so closely pressed by treading, that they are often obliged to be dug out with an iron instrument, the natives thinking we use them as a dye.

In the grounds of the market gardeners near London, where great quantities of this fruit are grown to supply the metropolis, these shrubs are generally pruned soon after the fruit is gathered, when the ground is dug up between the rows, and planted with cabbages for spring use, by which means the ground is employed all the winter, without injuring the bushes. In hard winters these coleworts often escape the frost when those in more open situations are all destroyed; and as there is always a demand for greens in February and March, the grounds are generally cleared before the currants put out their leaves. We have observed that the most productive currant-bushes are those, which have been pruned to form a concave, as by this method the sun and air reaches the interior of the bush, aud the fruit becomes as much better tasted, as it does larger by keeping the shrub thin of wood, and shortening the strong shoots to about ten inches.

Currant-trees produce their fruit on small snags, that come out of the former year's wood: in pruning, care should be taken not to injure that part; but the shoots may be shortened or thinned as soon as the leaves are off. They require least room, and have a neat appearance in private gardens, when planted as espaliers; and the fruit of trees so managed is thought to ripen best.

DATE.—DACTYLUS.

Natural order, Palmæ or Palms.—Date Tree, Phœnix Dactylifera. A genus of the Diœcia Triandria class.

The Greeks called this tree Φοινιξ, from the red colour of the spathe. The fruit they called Δάκτυλος, whence we derive the name of date.

This species of the palm-tree is a native of the eastern countries, and has been known to grow in the deserts of Arabia and Syria from the earliest ages. Dates appear to have been the first food which the Israelites found in the wilderness of Shur. The ancients esteemed dates next to the vine and olive.

The palm-branch or palm-tree was anciently used as an emblem of victory, being carried before the conqueror in processions and rejoicings for having overthrown the enemy. It was also presented to the kings of Syria as a token of submission.

The palm-trees are very lucrative to the Arabs and other inhabitants of the desert, where the fruit forms a principal part of their food, particularly in all that part of the Zaara which is near Mount Atlas, where they grow but little corn, and chiefly depend on this fruit for subsistence. In this part of the world, forests of date-trees may be seen, some of which are several leagues in circumference. The Grecian and Roman authors have given full accounts of this fruit. It is related that Alexander's army having met with dates of a most delicious quality, many, who could not forbear eating too plentifully, died. There is one kind of date described by the ancient authors, that would inebriate and overturn the brain.

The Babylonian or royal dates were most esteemed: these, in ancient times, were reserved for the kings of Persia, and are said to have grown only in one orchard or park at Babylon, which was annexed to the Persian crown. The dates at Jericho, in Jewry, were also in high estimation with the ancients, who made both bread and wine of them. Pliny, who has written at great length upon this fruit, mentions forty-nine kinds of dates, varying according to the country where they grew; some of which were white, black, or brown, some were round, others in the shape of a finger, some very small, and others he describes as being as large as the pomegranate. One species of the date, the Lotus, was much cultivated in Italy, and is by some supposed to be the fruit by which the companions of Ulysses were enchanted and forgot their native country.

Gibbon, in noticing the natural productions of Assyria, says, that the face of the country was interspersed with groves of innumerable palm-trees: and the diligent natives celebrated, either in verse or prose, the three hundred and sixty uses to which the trunk, the branches, the leaves, the juice, and the fruit, were skilfully applied.

Italy and the coast of Spain have been renowned for palm-trees more than two thousand years; "but the dates," says Pliny, "never come to maturity or ripeness, nor were they ever known to grow without being planted:" this caused him to state that they were foreign trees.

In one part of Persia, as well as in Upper Egypt, many families subsist almost entirely upon this fruit, the gathering of which is a time of merriment in the desert, attended with the song and the dance.

"And still, when the merry date season is burning,
And calls to the palm-groves the young and the old,
The happiest there, from their pastime returning
At sunset, will weep when thy story is told."

T. Moore.

The Arabs eat dates without seasoning, for they have a very agreeable taste when they are fresh, and afford wholesome nourishment. These people dry and harden them in the sun, to reduce them to a kind of meal, which they preserve for food when they undertake long journeys across the deserts; and they will subsist a considerable time on this simple nourishment: pieces of the date-bread diluted in water afford a refreshing beverage. The Arabs likewise strip the bark and fibrous parts from the young date-trees, and eat the substance that is in the centre. It is very nourishing, and has a sweet taste, and they call it the marrow of the date-tree: they also eat the leaves when they are young and tender, mixed with lemon-juice, as a salad. The male flowers are also eaten, when tender, in the same manner. The fruit, before it is ripe, is somewhat astringent, but when thoroughly mature, is of the nature of the fig. A white liquor, known by the name of date-milk, is drawn from the palm-tree. To obtain it, all the branches are cut from the summit of one of these trees; and after several incisions have been made in it, they are covered with leaves, in order that the heat of the sun may not dry it: the sap then drops into a vessel placed to receive the liquor. The milk of the date-tree has an agreeable sweet taste when new: it is very refreshing, and is given even to sick people.

Even the stones of dates, though very hard, are not thrown away: they are bruised and laid in water to soften, when they become good food for sheep and camels. In Barbary, the Mahometans turn these stones, and form handsome beads for the pater-nosters of the Christians.

The Egyptians make an agreeable conserve of the fresh dates and sugar. The Arabs weave mats and other things of the same kind from the old leaves; and from the filaments which arise from the stumps of the branches, they fabricate both ropes and sails.

Among the trees of Egypt there is none more common than the date-tree, both on the sands and on the cultivated districts. It requires no attention, and is very profitable, the fruit being in great demand, particularly that in the neighbourhood of Rosetta, which is delicious. The branches are cut off with the dates upon them before they are thoroughly ripe, and thrust into baskets made for the purpose, which have no other aperture than a hole, through which the branches project. The dates thus packed up, ripen in succession, and boats are laden with them, and sent to Cairo.—Could they not be brought to England in this state?

The Mahometans, whose religion forbids their use of wine or spirituous liquors, extract from dates a strong beverage, to which they give a medicinal name, as we might say stomach or cholic water; and this is made more savoury with aromatic spices, according to the rank of those who thus endeavour to cheat their prophet. Apothecaries who are the venders of these comfortable draughts make large fortunes in Constantinople.

The Persians extract a most ardent spirit from this fruit. The nectar of the dates, as drunk by the sovereigns of Congo, is also a pure spirit obtained from the fermented dates.

The timber is so durable that it is thought incorruptible by the natives. It is used for making beams and implements of husbandry, as also for javelins; and the trees often grow to a hundred feet in height. There are but few trees which are used for so many valuable purposes, and we know of none where the sexual distinctions are so evident. It is the female tree which produces the fruit; but in order to obtain it the orientals, who live upon it, plant male trees also; and it is no uncommon practice for their enemies, in time of war, to cut down the male trees, which prevents the others from producing dates, and causes famine. The number of female trees cultivated in Asia is much greater than that of the males, the former being more profitable.

Before the Saracens were driven back to their original habitations on the Arabian and African sands, the environs of Reggio were adorned with stately groves of palm-trees. Many of these trees were felled by the Christians out of a whimsical hatred to the plant, as if it had been an appurtenance of Mahometanism. The infidels themselves, on their retreat, destroyed all the male-palms, except such as grew within the walls;—thus were destroyed:—

> " Those groups of lovely date-trees bending
> Languidly their leaf-crown'd heads,
> Like youthful maids, when sleep descending
> Warns them to their silken beds."
>
> *T. Moore.*

The sexual organs of the date-tree grow upon different stalks; and when they are in flower, the Arabs cut the male branches to impregnate the female blossoms. For this purpose, they make incisions in the trunk of each branch which they wish to produce fruit, and place in it a stalk of male flowers: without this precaution, the date-tree would produce only abortive fruit. In some parts the male branches are only shaken over the female blossoms.

This practice was known to the ancients, and is accurately described by Pliny, who says, "if the male tree be cut down, *his wives* will afterwards become barren, and bear no more dates, as if they were widows."

Linnæus, in his "Dissertation on the Sexes of Plants," speaking of the date-tree, says, "A female date-bearing palm flowered many years at Berlin without producing any seeds; but in the year 1749 the Berlin people taking care to have some of the blossoms of the male tree which was then flowering at Leipsic, sent them by the post, they obtained fruit by these means; and some dates, the offspring of this impregnation, being planted in my garden, sprang up, and to this day continue to grow vigorously."

Pére Labat, in his Account of America, mentions a tree which grew near a convent in Martinique, that produced a great quantity of fruit, which came to maturity enough for eating; and as there was no other tree of the kind in the island, it was desirable to propagate it, but none of the seeds would grow. He conjectures that the tree might probably be so far impregnated by some neighbouring palm-tree, as to render it capable of bearing fruit, but not sufficiently to make the seeds prolific.

M. Geoffrey cites a story from Jovicus Pontanus, who relates, "that, in his time, there were two palm-trees, the one a male, the other a female, in the woods of Otranto, fifteen leagues apart; that this latter was several years without bearing any fruit; till at length, rising above the other trees of the forest so as it might see," says the poet, "the male palm-tree at Brindisi, it then began to bear fruit in abundance." M. Geoffrey makes no doubt but that the tree then only began to bear fruit, because it was in a condition to catch on its branches the farina of the male brought thither by the wind.

It may appear to many persons almost incredible, that the pollen of the male flower should be conveyed to so great a distance; but that it should be attracted by a tree of its own species, will not so much create our wonder, when, with the least reflection, we must be satisfied that the glutinous moisture on the stigmata of flowers, has an attraction for the pollen of the anther of its kind only; else, when a variety of flowers were blossoming at the same time, we should have the rose impregnating the lily, and the wheat giving its generating powder to the poppy. All animals and insects, when left to nature, couple with their kinds. Vegetables do the same, although it is now clearly ascertained that it is possible to make the stigma of one blossom receive the pollen of another, if it is prevented from taking that of its own species; and thus we have within these last few years so great a variety of new flowers and fruits.

The date-tree grows very rapidly, and will produce fruit in some countries in the third year, while in others it is from four to six years before it begins to bear. When arrived at maturity, it makes no change, but remains in the same state for three generations, according to the account of the Arabs. Like most other fruits, the date requires cultivation to have it good, as the fruit which is produced from trees which have been raised from seed is poor and ill-tasted, while those trees which are reared from the shoots, give dates of a good quality.

The young shoots when taken from the male tree produce male plants, and the female suckers produce fruit-bearing trees.

When we observe the constant uniformity of nature in its productions, it is difficult to bring ourselves to a belief of what we read in the Memoirs of the Academy of Gottingen; that by planting the seed of the date in such a manner as that the side in which is the deepest incision be turned towards the heaven, a female tree will be produced, and if reversed, a male tree will be procured.

The flowers of both sexes come out in very long bunches from the trunk between the leaves, and are covered with a spatha which opens and withers: those of the male have six short stamina, with narrow four-cornered anthers filled with farina. The female flowers have no stamina.

Dates are imported into this country in a dried state, similar to dried figs: when in good condition, they are much esteemed and fetch a high price. At the present time they are sold for five shillings the pound, although inferior kinds may be bought much cheaper for medicinal purposes, for which they are principally used in England, being considered hard of digestion, and often causing the head-ache to those who eat them in quantities, and creating scorbutic complaints as well as the loss of teeth. In medicine the qualities of dates are to soften the asperities of the throat, to assuage all immoderate fluxes of the stomach, and to ease disorders of the reins, &c. The oil and phlegm render them moistening and good to assuage coughs. They stop vomitings and fluxes, and are good for the piles when taken in red wine. (*Barham.*)

They are principally brought from Africa, Egypt, and Syria, but the finest come from Tunis.

Near Elete, in Spain, there is a wood consisting of two hundred thousand palm-trees, bearing dates. These trees furnish a curious traffic: the branches of them are bound up in mats to bleach the leaves, which in time become white; they are then cut off, and sent in ship-loads to Genoa and other parts of Italy, for the grand procession of Palm Sunday. There is a great trade in them with Madrid also, where every house has its blessed palm-branch. The dates seldom ripen so thoroughly as to keep well.

Hughes, in his Natural History of Barbadoes, speaking of the date-tree, says, "The straightest and youngest branches, which grow near the summit of the tree, are much used here by the Jews, upon their Feast of Tabernacles: these they usually gild, and adorn with various flowers, and then carry them in procession to their synagogue." He adds, "whether this is the same kind of palm that was used by the Israelites, we know not; or whether it is not here succedaneously used as bearing the nearest resemblance to it."

ELDER.—SAMBUCUS.

Natural order, Dumosæ. In Botany, a genus of the Pentandria Trigynia class.

"Though lowly shrubs, and trees that shade the plain,
Delight not all."———

Boerhaave, the celebrated physician of Leyden, is said to have held this tree in so great veneration, that he seldom passed it without taking off his hat and paying reverence to it.

It appears that we have taken the word Elder from *Holder*, the Dutch name of this tree, as we learn from Turner that it was formerly called Bourtre in this country, and Coles tells us that the Scotch called it Boretree in his time, "perhaps," says this author, "because the pith being done forth, it seemeth as if it were bored."

The Greeks named it ἀκτῆ, as it delights to grow on the brinks and shadowy banks of rivers. The derivation of the Latin name is uncertain: some etymologists state, that it is called *Sambucus* from Sambyx, the person who is thought to have first noticed the plant; others think it should be called *Sabucus*, from the likeness that the musical instrument called *Sabuck*, or Sambuck, has to the hollow rods of the Elder when the pith is out.

The common elder-tree, *Sambucus nigra*, is a native of England, and is found also in most parts of Europe, as it will grow on any soil, and in situations where few other trees would live.

The elder thrives near wet ditches, and is often seen

growing on the ruins of old walls, or from the hollow of decayed trees: so hardy is this valuable and neglected tree, that it is found both in sheltered swamps and on the bleak tops of church towers.

The elder does not appear to have been used medicinally by the ancients, but the berries were employed by the Romans to dye the hair of the head black. If they be boiled in water, says Pliny, they are as good and wholesome to be eaten as other pot-herbs.

Sir J. E. Smith has remarked, that this tree is, as it were, a whole magazine of physic to rustic practitioners.

The bark, leaves, flowers, and berries, are said to have been used with advantage in medicine. The leaves are said to be purgative and emetic, and are applied externally for the hæmorrhoids and inflammations; an ointment is made also with them as well as the flowers: the latter are used inwardly as a carminative. Infusions made from the flowers while fresh, are gentle, laxative, and aperient; when dry, they are found to promote the cuticular secretion, and to be particularly serviceable in erysipelatous and eruptive disorders. Sydenham directs three handfuls of the inner bark to be boiled in a quart of milk and water, till only a pint remains, of which one half is to be taken at night and the other in the morning; and this repeated every day for those afflicted with the dropsy. Boerhaave recommends the expressed juice of the middle bark, given from a dram to half an ounce, as the best of hydragogues when the viscera are sound. It is said that if sheep that have the rot can get at the bark and young shoots of elder, they will soon cure themselves. It is an ingredient in the black dye.

Elder-flower water, the oil of elder, and elder syrup, are all used as medicines. The flowers are reported to be fatal to turkies, and the berries to poultry in general; we have observed that it seems the last thing which animals in general will browse upon. The whole plant has a narcotic smell, and it is thought not prudent to sleep under its shade. It is probable that this tree, particularly when in blossom, may inhale more impure air than many others of slower growth. This would naturally be exhaled in the night and possibly to the injury of those who continued to breathe the immediate air of the tree; but the author has resided in a cottage nearly surrounded with these trees without perceiving any ill effects, although his children were daily playing and sitting beneath their shade, at a time when the branches were covered with blossom. We shall, in a future work, notice how this tree may be made exceedingly ornamental in the shrubbery.

The berries are esteemed cordial, and useful in hysteric disorders; and are often put into gargarisms for sore mouths and throats.

The fungous excrescences, which are often found growing on the trunk of the elder-tree, bearing the resemblance of an ear, black in the inside and of a whitish colour on the outside, (called *auriculæ Judæorum*) are accounted good for inflammations and swellings of the tonsils, sore throats, and quinsies.

The wine made from elder-berries is too well known by families in the country to require any encomiums: it is the only wine the cottager can procure, and, when well made, is a most excellent and wholesome drink, taken warm before going to bed. It causes gentle perspiration, and is a mild opiate; and may be taken safely and with advantage, by those of costive habits.

If a rich syrup be made from ripe elder-berries and a few bitter almonds, when added to brandy it has all the flavour of the very best cherry-brandy.

The white elder-berries, when ripe, make wine much resembling rich grape-wine.

The buds and the young tender shoots are greatly admired as a pickle.

The leaves of the elder-tree are often put into the subterraneous paths of moles, to drive those noxious little animals from the garden. If fruit-trees, flowering shrubs, corn, or other vegetables, be whipped with the green leaves of the elder branches, it is said that insects will not attach to them. An infusion of these leaves in water is good to sprinkle over rose-buds, and other flowers subject to blights and the devastations of caterpillars.

The wood of old elder-trees is so hard, and takes so good a polish, that it is often used as a substitute for the box-tree. From its toughness, it is used for tops for fishing-rods; needles for weaving nets, butchers' skewers, &c. It was used by the Romans to make pipes and trumpets, as Pliny says, "the shepherds are thoroughly persuaded that the elder-tree, growing in a byplace out of the way, and where the crowing of cocks from any town cannot be heard, makes more shrill pipes and louder trumpets than any other." The parsley-leaved elder was thought, by Miller and others, to have been a distinct species of this tree; but experience teaches us that it is only a variety, as on sowing the seeds they have been found uniformly to produce only the common elder.

FIG.—FICUS.—CARICA.

Natural order, Scabridæ. A genus of the Poligamia Triœcia class.

———— "dark
Beneath his ample leaf, the luscious fig."

The generic name of this fruit seems to have been derived from the Hebrew, פג, although some etymological students derive it from *fœcundus*. From the little variation in all the European names for the fig, they have evidently been taken from the Latin.

The earliest mention of the fig-tree is in those passages of the Bible which relate to the creation and fall of man. "And they sewed fig-leaves together, and made themselves aprons." It is a fruit that appears to have been highly esteemed by the Israelites, who brought figs out of the land of Canaan, when they were sent by Moses to ascertain the produce and strength of that country.

The fig-tree is often mentioned, both in the Old and New Testament, in a manner to induce us to conclude that Figs formed a principal part of the food of the Syrian nation. When Abigail went to meet David, to appease him for the affront given by Nabal, her husband, she took with her, amongst other provisions, a present of two hundred cakes of figs.

When Lycurgus banished luxury from Sparta, and obliged the Spartan men to dine in one common hall, to enforce the practice of temperance and sobriety, every one was obliged to send thither his provisions monthly, which consisted of about one bushel of flour, eight measures of wine, five pounds of cheese, and two pounds and a half of figs.

The Athenians were so choice of their figs, that it was forbidden to export them out of Attica. Those who gave information of this fruit being sold contrary to law, were called *sykophantai*, from two Greek words signifying the discoverers of figs; and as they sometimes gave malicious information, the term was afterwards applied to all informers, parasites, liars, flatterers, impostors, &c. from whence the word *sycophant* is derived.

The story of Romulus and Remus being suckled by a wolf under a fig-tree, proves that this fruit must have been early known in Italy.

It was customary to carry a basket of figs next to the vessel of wine used in the Dionysia, or festivals in honour of Bacchus. The fig is related to have been the favourite fruit of Cleopatra, who was the most luxurious queen the world ever produced. The asp with which she terminated her life, was conveyed to her in a basket of figs.

Saturn, one of the Roman deities, was represented crowned with new figs; he being supposed to have first taught the use of agriculture in Italy. There was a temple in Rome dedicated to this god, before which grew a large fig-tree. The vestals, when they removed this tree (about the year of Rome 260) in order to build a chapel on the spot, offered an expiatory sacrifice.

The fig was a fruit much admired by the Romans, who brought it from most of the countries they conquered, and had so increased the varieties in Italy, by the commencement of the Christian era, that Pliny has furnished us with a description of twenty-nine sorts that were familiar to him. He says, " figs are restorative, and the best food that can be taken by those who are brought low by long sickness, and are on the recovery. They increase the strength of young people, preserve the elderly in better health, and make them look younger, and with fewer wrinkles. They are so nutritive, as to cause corpulency and strength: for this cause, professed wrestlers and champions were in times past fed with figs." This naturalist mentions the African figs as being admired; but says, "it is not long since they began to grow figs in Africa."—These appear to have been of an early kind; for we find when Cato wished to stimulate the senators to declare war against Carthage, he took an early African fig in his hand; then, addressing the assembly, he said, "I would demand of you how long it is since this fig was gathered from the tree?" and when they all agreed that it was fresh gathered, "Yes," answered Cato, "it is not yet three days since this fig was gathered at Carthage; and by it, see how near to the walls of our city we have a mortal enemy." With this argument he prevailed upon them to begin the third Punic war, in which Carthage, that had so long been a rival to Rome, was utterly destroyed. "The Lydian figs," says Pliny, "are of a reddish purple colour; the Rhodian, of a blackish hue; as is the Tiburtine, which ripens before others. The white figs are from Herculaneum, Albicerate, and Aratian; the Chelidonian figs are the latest, and ripen against the winter: some bear twice a-year, and some of the Chalcidian kind bear three times a-year." The Romans had figs from Chalcis and Chios, &c.; and many of their varieties, it appears, were named from those who first introduced or cultivated them in Italy. The Livian fig was so named after Livia, wife to the Emperor Augustus, who, it is said, made an unnatural use of it to poison her husband.

If the fig-tree was ever brought to this country by the Romans, it was, in all probability, confined to the southern counties; and, not being generally cultivated, was destroyed when their villas were demolished. It is generally supposed that it was not planted in England before the reign of Henry the Eighth, when luxury and the arts began to be encouraged, and noblemen's houses first put on the air of Italian magnificence. There are, at the present time, some fig-trees, of the white Marseilles kind, growing in the garden of the Episcopal Palace at Lambeth, which are said to have been planted by Cardinal Pole, who brought them from Italy during the reign of Henry the Eighth. There is also a fig-tree of the white sort at Mitcham, in the garden of the manor-house, formerly the private estate of Archbishop Cranmer; and it is confidently stated to have been planted by that prelate: the stem measures thirty inches in girth.

At Oxford, in the botanic garden of the Regius Professor of Hebrew, is a fig-tree, which was brought from the East and planted by Dr. Pocock, in the year 1648. Of this tree the following anecdote is related:—Dr. Kennicott, the celebrated Hebrew scholar, and compiler of the Polyglot Bible, was passionately fond of this fruit; and seeing a very fine fig on this tree that he wished to preserve, wrote on a label, "Dr. Kennicott's fig," which he tied to the fruit. An Oxonian wag, who had observed the transaction, watched the fruit daily, and when ripe, gathered it, and exchanged the label for one thus worded: —"A fig for Dr. Kennicott."

Dr. Turner has given us an ample account of the virtues of figs in the second part of his Herbal, which he dedicated to queen Elizabeth, and although he does not actually write that it was then cultivated in England, yet his saying "the figge-tree is so well knowen, that it nedith no farther description," would induce us to think that it was common in this country at that period.

We may conclude that the fig-trees, which are stated to have been planted in the time of Henry the Eighth, either had not fruited, or were but little known at that period;

as Tusser, who has furnished us with a list of the fruits which were grown in England in the succeeding reign, has not mentioned the fig-tree; and Lord Chancellor Bacon, who wrote still later, never mentions it as being cultivated in England, though, from the exalted situation he filled, and the circles in which he moved, he must have had great opportunities of knowing the earliest introduction of trees and plants, which occupied a part of his attention. The almond, which was not introduced until the days of Elizabeth, is particularly mentioned by him as one of our fruits; but the fig is not in his list. He says, "there be divers fruit-trees in the hot countries, which have blossoms, and young fruit, and ripe fruit, almost all the year, succeeding one another." And it is said, the orange has the like with us for a great part of summer; and so also has the fig."

The Hortus Kewensis informs us, that the fig-tree was planted in this country in 1548. Gerard says, in 1597, that "the fruit of the fig-tree never cometh to maturity with us, except the tree be planted under a hot wall." Parkinson also, in 1629, says, that "if you plant it not against a brick wall, it will not ripen so kindly;" but much must depend on the situation of the country. The same author says in his *Theatrum Botanicum*, 1640, "the blew figge is no doubt of the same operation with the white to all purposes, but the fruite commeth most to maturity with us, and is eaten with great pleasure with salt and pepper."

There is an orchard of fig-trees at Tarring, near Worthing, in Sussex, where the fruit grows on standard trees, and ripens as well as in any part of Spain; these trees are so regularly productive, as to form the principal support of a large family. Although the orchard does not exceed three-quarters of an acre, there are upwards of one hundred trees, that are about the size of large apple-trees, the branches extending near twenty feet each way from the trunk. Mr. Loud, the proprietor of this little figgery, informs us, that he gathers about one hundred dozen per day during the season, and that he averages the trees to produce him about twenty dozen each: the fruit ripens in August, September, and October, a part of the year when the neighbouring watering-places are frequented with fashionable company, that insures a ready sale for this agreeable fruit, at good prices. Figs were so abundant at Tarring one year, that the inhabitants made wine of them.

The second crop, we find, has occasionally ripened: the fruit, which, although smaller, is exceedingly sweet, is of the white and purple varieties. Two of these trees are now about seventy-five years old, having been planted in the year 1745 by John Long, who raised them from some old ones in an adjoining garden, near the ruins of the palace of Thomas-à-Becket in that town, who, tradition says, brought these trees from Italy, and planted them himself. The soil of the garden is a deep black loam on chalk.

The trees are but seldom and sparingly pruned, which we conclude is the cause of their being so prolific, as it is remarked that fig-trees rarely produce much fruit where the knife is regularly used. When they grow too luxuriantly, it has been found better to destroy a part of their roots, and to fill up the space with stones or broken bricks, than to prune the branches too much. There are also to be found at Tarring, in the garden of Mr. Edmonds, some large standard fig-trees, which produce a most delicious green fig. These trees are very old, but by whom or at what period they were planted, is unknown. One of them divides into two stems, each of which measures two feet ten inches round: it is probably the largest standard tree in England, being about forty feet in height.

In 1818 it ripened in August, and a second time in November. We have not met with this variety of the fig in any other garden in this country, which is not only the most rare, but the most exquisite in flavour, and quite a sweetmeat as to richness. The birds, particularly the white-throat, seek this fruit so greedily, that it is with difficulty preserved from them. These trees are regular bearers, and occasionally ripen the second crop. They are never pruned, nor do they receive dressing of any description. Mr. Knight, the president of the Horticultural Society, observes, that there cannot be a more defective manner of cultivating the fig-tree than that which is generally practised by gardeners,—of training them against walls, with their branches perpendicularly upwards; the wood, by this means, becomes too luxuriant to produce fruit. Where figs are trained to a wall, and pruning cannot be avoided, the autumn is the proper season, and it is better to cut the incumbering branches quite off, than to shorten them, as the fruit is always produced at the ends of the shoots. Those who protect their trees by glass shutters, or reeds made into pannels, may generally calculate on two crops in the year; and it has been lately proved, that by merely tying an old newspaper lightly over the branch, the fruit has been perfectly secured against the frost; but as standard trees are found much more productive than those trained against a wall, we should recommend them to be table-trained; that is, to keep the branches tied to stakes about two feet from the ground: they will then form a star from the trunk, and in winter the extremities of the branches may be untied and fastened to the bottom of the stakes, where they may be easily covered with straw or peashaum, &c. which may be confined down by spurs of wood, or slips of willow: it is advisable to put straw or some dry litter between the branches and the earth, to prevent the fruit from being injured by moisture. The branches should not be staked down too early in the winter, or uncovered too soon in the spring.

The ancients believed that there existed a sympathy between plants, and they therefore planted rue near their fig-trees, which was said to make the fruit sweeter; and that the rue not only grew more luxuriantly, but more bitter, by being thus neighboured by the fig-tree. We think this is very probable, without its having any thing to do with sympathy, as trees and plants will naturally draw juices from the earth most congenial to their nature: the rue may therefore exhaust the earth of those properties suitable for the nourishment of bitter plants, and leave the fig-tree to thrive from a soil which the former has qualified, by consuming the particles of the earth that are pernicious to sweet fruits. Shakspeare seems to have been of this opinion when he wrote—

> "And wholesome berries thrive, and ripen best,
> Neighbour'd by fruit of baser quality."

We have now in this country a great variety of this most delicious and wholesome fruit, which is, we believe, the only kind we possess that has sweetness, without acidity or oiliness. It is nourishing, easy of digestion, and grateful to the stomach; and is much esteemed in the countries where it is cultivated: but in England it seems to please only the refined palates of the higher order of society. In some parts of the coast of Sussex, where this fruit ripens in perfection, we have known it not only neglected by the middle and lower classes, but even mentioned with derision in their disputes.

The fig-tree is distinguished from all other trees we know of, by its bearing two successive and distinct crops of fruit in one year, each crop being produced on a distinct set of shoots. The juices of these shoots are excessively bitter, and so acrid, burning, and corrosive, that they curd milk, and dissolve that which is curded in the same way as vinegar. It is so powerful as to take the skin from the flesh, on which account some people use it to remove werts from their hands: it also forms one of the sympathetic inks, which are invisible till heated; but such are the wonderful proceedings of nature, that this very juice produces one of our most agreeable, cooling, sweet, and wholesome fruits.

Figs should not be eaten until quite ripe, as the milky juice is apt to cause dysenteries and fevers. Water is the proper beverage to drink after eating this fruit, as it dilutes the pulp, and corrects a certain inconvenient saliva. The author has found great relief in a nervous fever, from making fresh figs the principal of his diet.

The figs which grow in the province of Ghilan in Persia are very unwholesome and injurious, from the great moisture of the earth in that place. The most delicate figs are those which grow in Sicily, called the *Neapolitan fig*. It is a small black variety, that hangs on the tree till January.

At the Royal Gardens at Kew, there was a fig-house fifty feet in length, where, under the superintendence of Mr. Aiton, this fruit has been forced to the highest pitch of perfection: Mr. Aiton's chief reliance has been, we understand, on the second crop. In the year 1810, the royal tables were supplied with more than two hundred baskets of figs from that fig-house, fifty baskets of which were from the first crop, and one hundred and fifty baskets from the second. In one instance, Mr. Aiton had this fruit ripe in January, and sent excellent figs to the palace on the late Queen Charlotte's birth-day, the 18th of that month.

It is ascertained that housed figs prosper better where they are heated by steam than by dry heat; and we have seen them not only very productive when planted in boxes, but producing two crops more regularly than when planted on the outside and trained under cover, as, when the fruit is gathered, the trees are benefited by removing them into the air, which greatly refreshes them for a second forcing.

The maturity of the fig may be accelerated ten or twelve days by pricking the eye of the fruit with an ivory or bone pin dipped in olive oil, when about a third of their size; and although it does not make the fig fruitful like caprification, it adds much to its size and flavour. This simple process is particularly attended to by the cultivators of figs at Argenteuil, as well as at Naples. It is remarked, that figs growing near a dusty road ripen their fruit the best.

If the branches of these trees, just as they begin to shew the autumn fruit, be treated as we have already mentioned in describing the apple-tree, excepting that the mould should be more considerable, they may be cut off in the month of November, planted in a pot of good earth, and placed in a hot-house or a common green-house; the branch will ripen its fruit in the month of May, and which may be brought to table while growing.

The caprification of figs was practised by the ancients in the same manner as it is now attended to by the inhabitants of the Archipelago; and it is described by Theophrastus, Plutarch, Pliny, and other authors of antiquity. It is too curious a circumstance in the history of the fig-tree to be omitted, as it furnishes a convincing proof of the reality of the sexes of plants. The flowers of the fig-tree are situated within the pulpy receptacle, which we call the fruit. Of these receptacles in the wild fig-tree, some have male flowers only, and others have male and female.

In the cultivated fig, these are found to contain only

female flowers, that are fecundated by means of a kind of gnat bred in the fruit of the wild fig-trees, which pierces that of the cultivated, in order to deposit its eggs within; at the same time diffusing within the receptacle the farina of the male flowers: without this operation, the fruit may ripen, but no effective seeds are produced. Hence it is that we can raise no fig-trees from the fruit of our own gardens, having no wild figs to assist the seed. They are consequently raised by cuttings, or by layers.

In many parts of the Grecian islands, the inhabitants pay such attention to the caprification of the cultivated figs, that they attend daily for three months in the year to gather these little flies from the wild fig-trees, and to place them on the fig-trees in their gardens, by which means they not only get finer fruit, but from ten to twelve times the quantity: thus one of the most minute insects is, by the attention of man, made a principal cultivator of fruit.

It is a curious fact, that fresh-killed venison, or any other animal food, being hung up in a fig-tree for a single night, will become as tender, and as ready for dressing, as if kept for many days or weeks in the common manner. A gentleman, who lately made the experiment, assured the author that a haunch of venison which had lately been killed, was hung up in a fig-tree when the leaves were on, at about ten o'clock in the evening, and was removed before sun-rise in the morning, when it was found in a perfect state for cooking; and he added, that in a few hours more it would have been in a state of putrefaction.

In the neighbourhood of Argenteuil, near Paris, are immense fields covered with fig-trees: the inhabitants of the former town derive their chief support from the culture of this fruit; and we feel confident that there are many situations on the coast of Sussex, between the towns of Arundel and Shoreham, where

> "Upon the southern side of the slant hills,
> And where the woods fence off the northern blast,
> The season smiles, resigning all its rage,
> And has the warmth of May;"

and where, if figs were cultivated, the London markets could be amply supplied with this nutritious fruit.

The author of this work has frequently gathered in that neighbourhood the fruit of the second crop, which has stood the winter without any protection whatever, and ripened its figs about the end of June. These winter figs are much superior in flavour to what are matured in August and September; and were the ends of the bearing branches slightly covered with straw, or even oiled paper, for a few months in the winter, we have no hesitation in saying, that two crops might be regularly brought to market from the same trees.

The fig-tree, like the myrtle, delights in the sea air, where it is not too much exposed to the rude blast: would not the inhabitants of the coast do well to enlarge their fig plantations? The price of this fruit at the shops in London in September 1820, was from six to eight and twelve shillings per dozen. In the August following, the author bought them in Paris at sixpence and ninepence per dozen, even at their first coming to market; but they were smaller than those grown in the villages near Worthing, and by no means better in flavour.

We import the best dried figs from Turkey, Italy, Spain, and Provence. In the south of France, they are prepared by dipping them in scalding hot lye made of the ashes of the fig-tree, and then dried in the sun.

For medical purposes, figs are chiefly used in emollient cataplasms and pectoral decoctions.

The wood of the fig-tree is of a spongy texture, and, when charged with oil and emery, is much used on the continent by locksmiths, gunsmiths, and other artificers in iron and steel, to polish their work. This wood is considered almost indestructible, and on that account was formerly used in Egypt, and other eastern countries, for embalming bodies.

FILBERT.—CORYLUS.

Natural order, Amentaceæ. A genus of the Monœcia Polyandria class.

Filberts were originally brought out of Pontus into Natolia and Greece, and were therefore called Pontic nuts: from thence they were procured by the Romans, and brought into Italy, where they acquired the name of Abellan, or Avellan nuts, from Abella or Avella, a town of Campania, where the best were cultivated, (Pliny, b. xv. c. 22.) and from thence arose the French name Aveline.

When first known in this country, they were called nuts with full beards, to distinguish them from the common hazel nut, as it will be observed that the husk or covering of this nut resembles a man's full beard: this was first corrupted into filbeard and filberd, and from thence into filbert.

These nuts still continue to be cultivated in the neighbourhood of Avelino, and, according to Mr. Swinburn's account, the whole face of the neighbouring valley is covered with them, and which, in good years, brings in a profit of 60,000 ducats (11,250*l.*)

The inhabitants of Avelino refresh the roots of these trees with new earth, and prune off the straggling shoots with great attention. Evelyn tells us in his "Silva," that his family name was derived from Avelin: "I find (says he) some ancient records and deeds in my custody, where my ancestors' names were written Avelan, alias Evelin, generally."

It is supposed, that within a few miles round Maidstone in Kent, there are more filberts growing at the present time than in all England besides, there being several hundred acres planted with filbert-trees in the vicinity of that town. The London market is entirely supplied from thence with these nuts, which are excellent in quality, and, if quite ripe, will keep good for several years placed in a dry room.

Filberts are not only much more agreeable than the common nuts, but are esteemed wholesome and nourishing when taken with moderation. The cream of these nuts is good for the stone and heat of urine. Emulsions may also be made of them. The Romans used them with vinegar and wormwood-seed for the yellow jaundice.

They were formerly used in this country to eat after fish instead of cheese, to prevent the engendering of phlegm.

"Post pisces nuces, post carnes caseus adsit."

Filberts are not found to answer well but on very few soils: they seem to like a stony, sandy loam; for in rich soils they grow too luxuriantly to produce fruit, but much depends on skill and management in pruning these trees. In Kent, they are not suffered to grow above five or six feet high, and are kept with a short stem, like a gooseberry-bush, and very thin of wood, somewhat in the shape of a punch-bowl.

"E'en winter oft has seen it gay,
With fretted frost-work spangled o'er,
While pendants droop'd from every spray,
And crimson budlets told once more
That spring would all its charms restore!"

From the class in which the tree is ranged in botany, it will be observed, that the male and female flowers grow quite distinct. The male flower is a scaly catkin, resembling the bullion in fringe; it appears in autumn, and waits for the expansion of the female blossom in the spring, from whence the nut arises: this is very diminutive, but of a fine carmine colour; therefore the pruner should make himself acquainted with the wood that produces each blossom, and not destroy too many of the male flowers that will fall from the tree after they have discharged their pollen, to the benefit of the future fruit.

Although this tree is amongst the last that ripens its seed, it takes the lead of all our fruit-trees in its blossoms, which generally appear about the middle of January; the bud is carefully secured from frost by scales, which open but just sufficiently to let the red filaments escape to catch the farina of the elegantly drooping catkins.

To preserve filberts, they should be gathered quite ripe, and laid for some days on the floor of a room, where the sun can get in, to dry them effectually.

Columella states, that if nuts be steeped in water and honey before they are planted, they will grow more speedily, and produce sweeter fruit.

Filbert-trees are generally raised by suckers or layers, as in sowing the nuts there is a great uncertainty of keeping the fruit true to its kind; but we may conclude that those raised from seed might be improved by grafting as well as the walnut.

The produce of an acre planted with filberts has sometimes been sold for fifty pounds; yet we know of but one place in this island where they are cultivated to any extent for the market.

The Byzantium nut (*Corylus Colurna*), although much esteemed for its flavour and size, is but little cultivated in this country, and very rarely seen in our markets. This nut was brought from Constantinople, before Constantine had given his name to that city; and we are much inclined to think, that the Greeks procured it from more eastern countries. They were first cultivated in this country by Mr. John Ray, in 1665, and are generally called cobnuts.

Pliny informs us, that Vitellius brought the nuts, called *fistichs*, into Italy, a little before the death of Tiberius, and that Flaccus Pompeius, who served in the wars with Vitellius, carried them into Spain. Nuts are now grown in that country in such quantities, according to the account of Mr. Swinburn, that from a single wood, near Recus, sixty thousand bushels have been collected in one year, and shipped from Barcelona, whence they are called Barcelona nuts.

It was the custom among the Romans for the bridegroom, on the night of his marriage, to scatter nuts among the boys, intimating that he dropped boyish amusements, and thenceforth was to act as a man.

GOOSEBERRY.—GROSSULARIA.

Natural order, Pomaceæ. A genus of the Pentandria Monogynia class.

The gooseberry, which is now so much and so justly esteemed, is a native of Europe; and as it grew in the woods and hedges about Darlington, and in Cambridgeshire, Norfolk, and other counties, in the wild state, we consider it indigenous to this country, although Dr. Smith and Miller both entertained doubts of its being truly so. It appears not to have been known to the ancients, either in Greece or Rome, as their authors have made no mention of it; the generic name of *Grossularia* has been given to it by later writers, on account of its resembling the *Grossos*, small green figs; but it is noticed by the earliest naturalists who have written in this country, notwithstanding it was a fruit much neglected, according to Allioni's account, who says, "they are eatable, but somewhat astringent." Gerard says, "it is called *feaberry-bush*, in Cheshire, my native country," and we find that it had the same name in Lancashire and Yorkshire. In Norfolk it was abbreviated into *feabes*. It appears to have taken the name of *gooseberry*, from its being used as a sauce for young or green geese.

Culpepper, who was a Sussex author, tells us that they were called dewberries in that county, and in some places wineberry. We learn from Tusser, that this fruit had been cultivated as early as the time of Henry the Eighth, as in his hints for the September month, he says :—

> " The barbery, respis, and goosebery to,
> look now to be planted as other things do:
> The goosebery, respis, and roses al three,
> with strawberies vnder them, trimly agree."

Gerard says, "These plants do grow in our London gardens, and elsewhere, in great abundance. The fruit is used in divers sawces for meate: they are used in brothes insteade of verjuicé, which maketh the broth not onely pleasant to the taste, but is greatly profitable to such as are troubled with a hot burning ague." Parkinson says, that "the berries, whilst they are small, green, and hard, are much used to be boiled or scalded, to make sauce for fish or flesh of divers sorts." Green gooseberries are still continued to be used as a sauce for mackerel, in many parts of the country; and they are often mentioned by the French as *groseilles aux maquereaux*.

The gooseberry, which was but a small berry in the wild state, has, like the apple, been multiplied in its variety, and brought to its present size by the art and industry of the English and Dutch gardeners; and it is now deemed one of our most valuable fruits, being easily propagated, and regular in its production; furnishing our tables, at all seasons of the year, with a wholesome and agreeable diet. It is the earliest as well as one of the best fruits for spring tarts; and, when ripe, the gooseberry is regarded by all classes of society at the dessert, where it appears from July to November, with those who have well-regulated varieties; as some kinds ripen early, while others are not only later, but have the quality of hanging on the bushes until near Christmas. Among the last, the Warrington gooseberry is considered the best.

There is no fruit capable of more improvement, or that turns to more general advantage, or is attended with less expense in the cultivation, than the gooseberry; and, as it forms one of the most wholesome dishes of the *déjeuné* and the dessert, we shall point out the best mode of prolonging the enjoyment of so agreeable an addition to our table. The bushes which are intended to be covered should be kept pruned to a size suitable to the cases intended for them, which may be made similar in shape to the bee-hive, either of straw, rushes, or any substance that will effectually keep off the heat and light. These temporary covers should be placed over the bushes just as the fruit begins to turn towards ripening, but not before it has acquired its full size and combined all its acid, which is the first principle of saccharine matter. By thus defending the fruit from the dews, the heat of the sun, and the light—which contributes also to ripen it—the complete maturity is much retarded, and gooseberries may be gathered very fresh and ripe until near Christmas. The same bushes should not be covered the succeeding year, as it will naturally weaken the plants; and we would recommend the cover to be kept a few inches from the ground, so as not entirely to exclude the air, particularly towards the north.

We have not attempted to give even the names of all the varieties of this fruit, finding them so numerous: one nurseryman furnished us with his list, and obliged the author with a sight of 300 varieties, the largest of which in weight was equal to three guineas and a half.

"Mr. Stringer of Congleton, in Cheshire, produced at a gooseberry-show there, in 1821, the prize gooseberry, which measured five inches and one-eighth in circumference, and weighed twenty-one pennyweights and twelve grains."—*New Monthly Mag. Oct.* 1, 1821.

Gooseberries are preserved in the green state with little

trouble or expense, so as to retain their natural flavour for tarts or cream, &c.; and, when ripe, they make excellent jam, and a delicious and ornamental sweetmeat.

To procure gooseberries large for the table, it is desirable to cut off with a pair of scissors all the small berries, which are equally good for the purpose of tarts.

The wine made from green gooseberries, if properly managed, is but a shade inferior to champaign; and the black gooseberry, when ripe, affords a luscious wine.

When we can divest ourselves of the prejudices against all English wines, this fruit will be found covering our fields, as profitably as the vineyards of the south; for when we take into consideration how speedily the bushes are propagated, and how seldom the crop fails, it will be found that gooseberry-wine may be made cheaper than cider: let us then not despair of seeing wine presses and flowing vats in every corner of the kingdom.

——" in Nature's bounty rich,
In herbs and fruits; whatever greens the spring,
When heaven descends in show'rs: or bends the bough,
When summer reddens, and when autumn beams;
Or in the wintry glebe whatever lies
Conceal'd, and fattens with the richest sap."

Thomson.

The pale gooseberry was first brought from Flanders in the year that Henry the Eighth received the title of *Defender of the Faith.* This monarch, and his daughter Queen Elizabeth, seem to have encouraged the art of gardening, as during their reigns most of our best fruits and vegetables were first introduced and cultivated in this kingdom; but even during the reign of these sovereigns, gooseberry leaves were used as a salad by those who could not afford to send to Holland for a lettuce.

The gooseberry is but little esteemed on the contiuent,

for want of being more known; and foreigners seem astonished at the size and flavour of this fruit in England. It cannot be propagated with success in the warmer parts of the world; but in this happy island we procure, by the aid of stoves, the finest fruits of the hottest climes; we may therefore justly say with the poet—

"On foreign mountains may the sun refine
The grape's soft juice, and mellow it to wine:
With citron groves adorn a distant soil,
And the fat olive swell with floods of oil;
We envy not the warmer clime, that lies
In ten degrees of more indulgent skies."

It has been a question agitated among physicians, whether fruits be safer before or after meals. The answer to this seems to depend on a knowledge of the stomach. In a weak stomach, they are more apt to be noxious when empty, than when distended with animal food. Here likewise they cannot be taken in such quantity as to hurt. In strong stomachs there is little difference; there they would seem to promote appetite. In weak stomachs even when full, if taken in too great quantity, they may be very hurtful, by increasing the active fermentation of the whole. The ancients alleged, that the mild fruits should be taken before, and the acerb after meals, as being fitter to brace up the stomach, and promote digestion. (*Lectures on the Materia Medica.*)

The gooseberry-bush is propagated by cuttings or suckers; but the former way is preferable, as the roots are less likely to shoot out suckers. Straight shoots should be selected about eight inches long, and planted about half the length, in good mould or light earth. The best time for planting them is in the autumn, just before the leaves begin to fall. It is desirable to sow the seeds of ripe gooseberries, as by this means you have the chance of new varieties; and the bushes generally grow in a better shape than when produced either from cuttings or suckers.

In pruning these bushes, observe to keep the stem quite free from shoots; at least that from ten or twelve inches from the ground, there be but one regular stem. We have seen them trained on trellis work, where the fruit has grown and ripened well; and it is a most desirable method for small gardens, as they have a neat appearance, take but little room, and form a good background to borders of flowers which they protect from winds and embellish by their early and agreeably coloured foliage.

GOURD.—CUCURBITA.

Natural order, Cucurbitaceæ. A genus of the Monœcia Syngenesia class.

THE plants of this genus are very nearly allied to those of *cucumis;* and there is a great variety of them.

Gourds were more esteemed by the ancients than either melons or cucumbers. The Greeks called them Κολοκύνθα ἐδώδιμος, *Colocyntha Edulis,* to distinguish them from the wild or bitter gourd, called *Colocynthi* or *Coloquintida*; the Romans named it *Cucurbita,* because it will turn away or grow crooked, when it meets any thing in its passage.

Pliny has minutely described them as different from the pompion or cucumber. He says, "they are employed for more purposes, and are more useful than the former fruit. When properly dressed," he says, "they are a light, mild, and wholesome food. The young and tender stalks were dressed and served up to table as a good dish; and the fruit of those that climbed up trees, or walls, or on the frames of arbours, were better food than those which crept on the ground. They have of late been much used for pots and pitchers;" but long before, they had been used as barrels to keep wine in. Both the wild and the garden-gourd were much used in medicine by the Romans, who also employed the seeds as a charm to cure the ague. (Pliny, l. xx. c. 3.)

Gerard says, "the pulp, or meat of the gourd, used as a poultice, mitigates all hot swellings, and takes away the head-ache and the inflammation of the eyes"

The bottle-gourd (*lagenaria*) is called by the Arabians *Charrah.* The poor people eat it boiled with vinegar, or fill the shell with rice and meat, and thus make a kind of pudding of it. It grows in all parts of Egypt, and in Arabia, wherever the mountains are covered with rich soil: in many parts of the world it grows to near six feet long, and two feet thick. The rinds or shells are used by the negroes in the West-India islands as bottles, holding from one pint to many gallons. Barham speaks of one that held nine gallons; and the Rev. Mr. Griffith Hughes mentions them, in his History of Barbadoes, as holding twenty-two gallons. The shells are cleared of the pulp and seeds by the negroes in the following manner:—they make a hole at one end, into which they pour hot water, in order to dissolve the pulp, which afterwards is extracted with a stick, and the inside rinsed with sand and water, to loosen and clear away the fibres that remain; they are then dried and become fit for use, and will contain water or other liquids for a length of time.

Sloane mentions one of these gourds as large as the human body. Brown says, "the decoction of the leaves is recommended much in purging clysters, and the pulp of the fruit is often employed in resolutive poultices." He adds, that "it is bitter and purgative, and may be used instead of the common coloquintida." Sloane and Barham describe a sweet gourd, which, the latter says, "grows two or three feet long, as big as a man's thigh, is full of sweet pulp that makes a pleasant sort of sweetmeat or preserve." He says, "the distilled water is good in fevers, and the pulp applied to the eyes abates their inflammation." Sloane says, "the seeds are diuretic, and, made into emulsions, temper and take off the acrimony of urine."

Lunan describes the squash *(melopeps)*, a small gourd, not exceeding the size of a moderate fist, and which, he says, "when young and properly boiled and dressed with butter and black pepper, is a delicious vegetable.'' Louriero says, "this fruit is of great use in long voyages, as it may be kept several months fresh and sweet."

The Gourd, called Vegetable Marrow, is of a pale yellow colour. Those we have seen did not exceed from seven to nine inches in length. It has only been known a few years in this country; and, we believe, was not sold in the shops and markets before the summer of 1819; and although they are of so late an introduction, the accounts are very imperfect: but it seems most probable that the seeds were brought in some East-India ships, and perhaps originally from Persia, where it is called *cicader*. It is cultivated in the same manner as cucumbers, and is said by those who have grown it to be very productive. This fruit is used for culinary purposes in every stage of its growth. When very young, it is good fried with butter; when half-grown, it is said to be excellent, either plainly boiled, and served up sliced on toasted bread, as asparagus, or stewed with rice sauce, for which purpose it is likewise sliced. It is often sent to table mashed like turnips: when full grown, it is used for pies. It has been highly approved by many persons who have grown it, while others speak of it as but little superior to the pompion.

The author planted two seeds of this gourd in the month of May 1820, in a pot which was plunged into a hot bed. When the plants were about four inches high, a hole was dug wherein only one barrow of dung was put, which was covered with the common mould of the garden; into this the gourds were transplanted, and covered with a glass frame for about three weeks, which was then removed to give the plants room to display their natural beauty and propensity for climbing. They were planted between two plum-trees that were nine feet apart, and, as it were by instinct, each turned towards a tree, one taking a north-east direction, and the other a south-west course. By the middle of August, they had climbed about 16 feet in height, fixing their branches to those of the trees, so firmly by their cork-screw tendrils, as not to be disengaged without breaking. The leaves of these vines were exactly twelve inches long, and thirteen inches in the greatest breadth. With so much rapidity did these succulent plants draw juices from the earth, that the moisture in its passage was forced through the pores of the fibrous bark of the plant when, on meeting the air, it formed crystallised thorns, rather than a hairy substance. The flowers were exceedingly ornamental to the tree they had intruded on, being even larger than those of the pumpkin: the male blossoms were supported on stalks of about a foot in length, the female flowers were attached to the fruit in the same manner as all the tribe of gourds and cucumbers. The flowers generally withered ere mid-day, thus leaving but a few hours for the stigma of the fruit-blossoms to be supplied with the farina of the male flowers.

The stamen or column of the male flower, which supports the anther, is built on three piers, which rest on the bell, forming three arches over a bason that contains the ambrosial juice, which has been there formed as if to allure the bees to assist in the necessary impregnation: this nectar was devoured by those industrious insects with such eagerness as almost to persuade us that they were conscious of the short time nature had allowed them to revel in these golden bells. We observed with what impatient eagerness they thrust their tubes into the arches to pump up the sweets contained, regardless of the pollen which adhered to their downy legs and bodies; away they flew to the fruitful blossoms, which were less numerous, and in which the pistil and stigma are so formed that these busy insects could not collect the limpid treasure that floats around the style without resting thereon, when the prolific powder was taken from their sides, and detained by the glutinous moisture of the stigma. This operation was no sooner finished, than the calyx began to wither and wreath itself around the stigma, as if to protect it from other intruders.

In the garden of Dr. Crombey at Greenwich, we observed that where the vegetable marrow and cucumbers were growing on the same bed promiscuously, nearly one half of the former fruit had been impregnated by the pollen of the latter, and that it had so changed the nature of the fruit of the vegetable marrow, that it was scarcely to be distinguished from the cucumbers. On some of the vines we found perfect vegetable marrow, and other fruit between the two, which to us appears a convincing proof that the farina affects the fruit it inoculates, as well as the seed it impregnates. May not this account for the peach-tree often producing nectarines on the same branch?

We found the fruit of the vegetable marrow more porous than the flesh of either the cucumber or pumpkin, and when cut in slices like muffins, and fried in butter or oil, and served on rashers of bacon, it made an agreeable dish; we also admired it when stewed as cucumbers, but when plain boiled we found it rather insipid.

The great advantage of this vegetable is, that it is most productive in those hot summers when most other esculent vegetation is burnt up by heat.

GRAPE-VINE.—VITIS.

Natural order, Hederaceæ. A genus of the Pentandria Monogynia class.

"Great father Bacchus, to my song repair;
For clust'ring grapes are thy peculiar care:
For thee, large bunches load the bending vine,
And the last blessings of the year are thine.
To thee his joy the jolly Autumn owes,
When the fermenting juice the vat o'erflows.
Come strip with me, my god; come drench all o'er
Thy limbs in musk of wine, and drink at ev'ry pore."

THE generic name is derived from *vincire*, to bind.

The cultivation of the vine appears to have attracted the attention of man from the earliest times of which we have any account. Every part of the Scripture mentions the vine as being held in the highest estimation. "Noah planted vineyards, and made wine." Vines are mentioned among the blessings of the promised land, "a land of wheat, and barley, and vines," &c.

The patriarchs and prophets frequently represent in scripture the flourishing state of a nation, a tribe, or a family, under the emblem of a vine. "Thou hast brought a vine out of Egypt, thou hast cast out the heathen, and planted it; thou preparedst room before it, and didst cause it to take deep root, and it filled the land." Psalm lxxx.—Again the Psalmist mentions it, "Thy wife shall be as the fruitful vine, upon the walls of thine house."

The heathens, likewise, held the vine in the highest estimation. The Egyptians ascribed the invention of wine to Osiris, the Latins to Saturn; while Bacchus was elevated to the rank of a god, by the Greeks, for having taught men the use of the vine. As the god of vintage, of wine, and of drinkers, he is generally represented as crowned with the vine; and, according to Pliny, to have been the first who ever wore a crown,—

——— the grapy clusters spread
On his fair brows, and dangle on his head.

Ovid.

Bacchus was sometimes represented as an infant holding a cluster of grapes, with a horn; and he has often been depicted as an old man, whose head was encircled with the vine, to teach us that wine taken immoderately, will enervate us, consume our health, and render us loquacious and childish, like old men.

Juno's crown was also made of the vine. The vine, with grapes, is still selected as a proper ornament in all bacchanalian devices.

Wine was chiefly used by the ancient Romans in the worship of their gods. Young men under thirty, and women all their life-time, were forbidden to drink wine. Egnatius Macennius killed his wife with a cudgel, having caught her drinking wine out of a tun, for which he was tried by Romulus, and acquitted of murder. Fabius Pictor, in his annals, reports, that a Roman lady was starved to death by her own relations for opening a cupboard which contained the keys of the wine-cellar. Cato records, that the custom of kinsfolk kissing women when they met, was to know by their breath if they had been drinking wine; but these restrictions were removed when wine became more plentiful; and the use of it was then carried to such an excess, that even females would drink wine, and, by the aid of an emetic, throw it up again, in order to sharpen their appetites for supper.

Plato, who strictly restrains the use of wine, and severely censures the excess, says that "nothing more excellent or valuable than wine was ever granted by God to man."

Amphitryon is said by the Athenians to have been the first who diluted wine with water; and on this account the fable was invented of Bacchus having been struck by a thunderbolt, and cast, all inflamed, into the nymphs' bath to be extinguished.

At what exact period the vine was first cultivated in England is uncertain: but we conclude it was as early as about the tenth year A. D., as at that time the Romans had possession of great part of this island, and had introduced the luxuries of Italy wherever they settled. Augustus was then emperor, and it was common to send the sons of the British nobles to Rome to be educated: from this intercourse it seems unlikely that the culture of the vine should have been neglected at this time, though many authors are of opinion that the vine was not introduced into this country until about the year 280, when Probus, who greatly encouraged agricultural pursuits in all the provinces under Rome, was emperor.

It appears that license was granted to the provincials to plant vineyards about the year 280; and the Britons are expressly mentioned by Vopiscus among the nations who partook of it. From this we should certainly conclude, that the vine had been previously planted in this island.

Again, we are informed that the planting of vineyards in Italy had so much increased about A. D. 85, that agriculture was thereby neglected; on which account Domitian issued an edict prohibiting any new vineyards to be planted in Italy, and ordered at least one half of those in the provinces to be cut down. It therefore appears highly improbable that the vine should not have been planted in Britain previous to the year 280, when in 85 all the other Roman provinces were overrun with vineyards.

That we are indebted to the Romans for the first introduction of the vine, is generally allowed; although it is possible it might have been introduced at a much earlier period than we have stated, as the Phœnicians are said to have planted the vine in the isles of the Mediterranean sea, as well as in several parts of Europe and Africa; and as we have accounts of their trading to Britain for tin, they might have planted it on the English coast also: but this must remain a matter of conjecture, any farther than as it confirms the vine to have been originally brought from Palestine. In the Book of Numbers we find that the men whom Moses had sent to spy the land of Canaan, returned with a bunch of grapes, which they bare between two, upon a staff. The Damascus grapes, at the present time, are often found to weigh upwards of twenty-five pounds the bunch. In the accounts of Ægidius Van Egmont, envoy from the States to the king of Naples, and John Heyman, professor of the oriental languages in the university of Leyden, who have published their observations on the present state of Asia Minor, it is mentioned that, in the town called Sidonijah, which is four hours journey from Damascus, some of the grapes were as large as pigeons' eggs, and of a very exquisite taste. From these circumstances we may fairly conclude, that the vine is a native of Syria. That we do not hear more of the enormous clusters of grapes growing in the eastern parts, is owing to that country having been in the hands of the Saracens since the seventh century, when Abubeker overran it; and these people being Mahomedans, and prohibited the use of wine, it is natural to suppose that the management and culture of the vine would be greatly neglected by them.

Although wine is not made in Egypt, vines are much cultivated, and the grapes have a delicious perfume: the greater part of those which are eaten there, are of that species, of which the fruit contains only a single seed. The leaves of the vine are of great utility in the kitchens of Egypt: they serve to envelope large balls of hashed meat, one of the dishes most commonly presented at good tables. It is necessary that the leaves should be young: and they are frequently sold at a dearer rate than the grapes themselves. *(Sonnini's Travels in Egypt.)* In this country, vine-leaves are used in roasting those delicious little birds called *wheat-ears*.

Pliny concludes, that the vine was very rare in Italy in the time of Numa, who ordered that no libations of wine should be made at funerals; and to encourage the pruning of vines, he prohibited the use of any wines, in sacrifices to the gods, that were cut from vines which had not been pruned. The same author cites, from M. Varro, "that Mezentius, the king of Tuscany, aided the Rutilians of Ardea in their wars against the Latins, for no other hire but the wine and the vines which were in the territories of the Latins." He adds, "that wines did not come into much repute until six hundred years after the foundation of Rome."

Julius Cæsar found vines growing in Languedoc and Provence; but other parts of Gaul were totally without vines at that time. Strabo remarks, that Languedoc and Provence produced the same fruit as Italy; but it was not until about the year 270, that the vine was planted in the northern parts of Gaul, and about the rivers Rhine, Maine, and Moselle, and in Hungary.

The varieties of the grape-vine are very numerous; and we have accounts of some of them growing to an extraordinary size, and producing such fruit as appears almost incredible to our northern conception of grapes. Strabo, who lived in the reign of Augustus, testifies that the vines of Margiana, and in other places, were so big, that two men could scarcely compass them with their arms, and that they produced bunches of grapes two cubits, or a yard, in length. Columella states, that Seneca had a vine which produced him two thousand clusters of grapes in a year. Theophrastus mentions a vine that grew so large, that a statue of Jupiter, and the columns in Juno's temple, were made of it. The great doors of the cathedral at Ravenna are made of vine-tree planks, some of them twelve feet long and fifteen inches broad.

At Ecoan, at the Duke of Montmorency's house, is a table of large dimensions, made of vine planks. Pliny states, that vines in old times were, on account of their size, ranked among trees. Valerianus Cornelius mentions a vine of one stock that encompassed and surrounded a good farm-house with the branches. Upon the coast of Barbary, enormous vines are now growing, some of them being eight or nine feet in circumference; and in Persia there are some kinds of grapes so large, that a single one is a mouthful. From what we find in Huetius, Crete, Chios, and other islands in the Archipelago, afford bunches of grapes from ten to forty pounds weight each. Chios, now Scio, has long been celebrated for its vineyards, and Virgil has immortalized its wines by his pen.

> " The ritual feast shall overflow with wine,
> And Chios' richest nectar shall be thine:
> On the warm hearth, in winter's chilling hour,
> We'll sacrifice; at summer, in a bower."
>
> *Warton.*

Pliny mentions a vine, in his time, that was six hundred years old; and Miller states, that the vineyards in some parts of Italy hold good above three hundred years.

It is related, that Rhemnius Palæmon, who was a renowned Roman grammarian, bought a farm within ten miles of Rome, for which he gave six hundred thousand sesterces. By cultivation he so improved it, that the produce of his vines in one year sold for four hundred thousand sesterces. Pliny says, that many people ran to see the huge and mighty clusters of these grapes, which his idle neighbours attributed to his deep learning, while others accused him of using magic and the black art.

We have at the present time some remarkable vines in England; for since the introduction of stoves, no country has been able to rival us in the variety and perfection of this fruit, which has been so much increased since the introduction of steam into our vineries, that the last year, it is supposed, produced more fine grapes than had ever been gathered in any two preceding years. Several kinds of this fruit ripen well in the open air.

> "The vine, too, here, her curling tendrils shoots,
> Hangs out her clusters, glowing to the south,
> And scarcely wishes for a warmer sky."

The Duke of Portland has upwards of a hundred kinds of grape-vines at his seat at Welbeck; and in the year 1781, his Grace made a present to the Marquis of Rockingham of a bunch of grapes that grew in his vinery, which weighed nineteen pounds and a half: it was nineteen inches and a half in the greatest diameter, four feet and a half in circumference, and twenty-one inches and three quarters in length. It was conveyed to Wentworth House, a distance of twenty miles, by four labourers, who carried it suspended on a staff, in pairs, by turns.

In the year 1821, the Hon. F. G. Howard grew in his garden at Elford Hall, Staffordshire, a bunch of white grapes, which were of the extraordinary weight of fifteen pounds.

The vine at Hampton Court Palace, which was planted

in the year 1769, has a stem of thirteen inches in girth, and a principal branch one hundred and fourteen feet in length, which, in one year, produced two thousand and two hundred bunches of grapes, each weighing, on an average, a pound. His late revered Majesty enjoyed the fruit of this vine half a century. Fruit was the only luxury in which he indulged himself, and that was cultivated in the Royal Gardens to the highest perfection, and served at table in great abundance.

Mr. Eden planted a vine of the Black Hamburgh sort, at Valentine House, Essex, in the year 1758, which is the parent of the vine at Hampton-Court, and has extended itself to upwards of two hundred feet in length, being so productive that it ripened two thousand bunches of grapes in the year 1819.

Speechly describes a vine, which was growing in the open air at Northallerton, in Yorkshire, in 1789, that had once covered a space containing one hundred and thirty-seven square yards; and it was judged, that, had it been permitted, it would have extended to three or four times that space. The circumference of the stem, a little above the ground, is three feet eleven inches: it is supposed to have been planted 150 years.

In Jamaica, and some other of the West India islands, the vine produces two and often three crops a-year. Both Brown and Lunan observe, that grape-vines produce most abundantly in Jamaica, particularly the Muscadine, which ripens all its berries nearly at the same time, and has clusters of the fruit from eight to ten pounds weight; the pulp of which has been found less watery, and more fleshy, than the same fruit in the south of France, and yet the making of wine, even for the consumption of the island, has never been attempted.

Domesday book mentions, at Rageneia, in Essex, one park and six arpennies of vineyard, which, if successful, yielded twenty modii of wine. Vineyards are noticed in the Domesday book, as also by Bede, as early as the commencement of the eighth century.

That vineyards were common in this country, we have such numerous records in the early period of our history, as to place it beyond a doubt. Tacitus states that vineyards were planted by the Romans in Britain; and it is natural to suppose that the propagation of the vine would be first attempted in the southern parts of our island, both on account of the warmth, and its vicinity to Gaul. The neighbourhood of Winchester was so famous for vines, that it is supposed to have taken its name from that circumstance. Canterbury was celebrated for its vines. Somner tells us, that, in the year 1258, both the abbey and the priory of that city were plentifully furnished with vineyards. At Rochester, a large plot of ground contiguous to the city is still called the Vine; and at Halling near Rochester, the bishop of that see had formerly a vineyard; for when Edward the Second was at Bockinfeld, in 1316, bishop Hamson sent him thither, as Lambert tells us, "a present of his drinkes, and withal both wine and grapes of his own grouth in his vineyarde at Halling." Captain Nicholas Toke, of Godington, in Great Chart, in Kent, "hath so industriously and elegantly," says Philipot, "cultivated and improved our English vines, that the wine pressed and extracted out of their grapes, seems not only to parallel, but almost to outrival that of France." Of Sussex, Lambarde writes, "History doth mention that there was about that time (the Norman invasion) great store of vines at Santluc (near to Battle)."

The plot of ground called East Smithfield, was at one time converted into a vineyard, and held by four successive constables of the Tower in the reigns of Rufus, Henry, and Stephen, to their great emolument and profit.

Various parts of London, by their names, give evident proofs of their having been formerly planted with grapes, as Vine-streets in Hatton-garden, St. Giles's, and Piccadilly; the Vineyards by Houndsditch, and Coldbath-fields; and even within the walls of the City of London, there is a street called the Vineyard.

The Little Park at Windsor was appropriated as a vineyard for the use of the Castle, even so late as the reign of Richard the Second. Lambarde observes, that some part of the wine was spent in the king's household, and some sold for the king's profit. We also read that in different years of Henry the Second's reign, allowances were made to the officer who farmed Windsor of that prince, for wine, perry, and cider.

In Northamptonshire, Martin, abbot of Peterborough, in the time of King Stephen, is said, in the Saxon Chronicle, to have planted an extensive vineyard. Madox in his History of the Exchequer writes, that the sheriffs of Northamptonshire and Leicestershire were allowed in their account for the livery of the king's vine-dresser at Rockingham, and for necessaries for the vineyard.

The isle of Ely was expressly denominated the *isle of vines* by the Normans. The bishop of Ely, shortly after the Conquest, appears to have received at least three or four tuns of wine annually, as tithes from the vines in his diocese; and in his leases he made frequent reservations of a certain quantity of wine by way of rent: many of these wines were little inferior to the French wines in sweetness. Few ancient monasteries were without a vineyard attached to them.

In the archives of the church of Ely is the following register:—

Exitus Vineti . . .	2	15	3¼
Do. Vineæ	10	12	2¾

10 bushels of grapes from the vineyard	0	7	6
7 Dolia Musti from the vineyard, 12 Edw. II. . . .	15	1	0
Wine sold for . . .	1	12	0
Verjuice	1	7	0
One dolium, and one pipe filled with new wine, and supposed at Ely.			
For wine out of this vineyard .	1	2	2
For verjuice from thence . .	0	16	0
No wine, but verjuice made, 9 Edw. IV.			

From this it appears plainly, that at Ely grapes would sometimes ripen, and the convent made wine of them; and when they did not, they converted them into verjuice, which was much more used in diet formerly than at present.

William of Malmsbury mentions the county of Gloucester as excelling every other part of the country, in the twelfth century, in the number and richness of its vineyards. The first Earl of Salisbury planted a vineyard in his park adjoining Hatfield-house, Hertfordshire, which was in existence when Charles the First was conveyed there a prisoner to the army.

Evelyn says in his Diary, May 8, 1654:—"Returning from Hackney, I visited one Mr. Tomb's garden; it has a vineyard, planted in strawberry borders, staked at ten foot distances." On the 26th Sept. the following year, he observes, "I went to see Col. Blount's subterranean warren, and drank of the wine of his vineyard, which was good for little." He also writes, "23 Aug. 1670, went to Alburie to see how that garden proceeded. The canall was now digging and the vineyard planted." In some situations the very vines themselves tell us where our forefathers cultivated them. In a park near Berkeley, in Gloucestershire, tendrils of vines are found springing up yearly among the grass, from one of which a cutting is now flourishing in the garden of the late Sir Joseph Banks.

Historians and antiquaries appear remiss in not accounting for the total neglect of the British vineyards; but we may conclude, that as our intercourse increased with the continent, it was found more advantageous to import wine than to depend on the product of our own crop, which must have been an uncertain one, from the variableness of our climate. Again, the low price of foreign wines must have contributed much to the neglect of making it in England; as in the year 1342, according to Stow, the price of Gascon wines in London was fourpence, and that of Rhenish, sixpence per gallon; and, in 1389, the price of foreign wine was only twenty shillings per tun, for the best sort, and thirteen shillings and fourpence for the second quality, which was about three halfpence per dozen.

French wines would naturally be brought to this country in considerable quantities at the time we had so much command of that kingdom; and this would also operate to the neglect of our own vineyards. The advancement of agriculture must likewise have contributed to their being relinquished.

It is stated by several authors, that foreign wines were sold by apothecaries only, as a cordial, in the year 1300. I am of opinion, that it was Portugal wine only which the apothecaries sold, and not foreign wine in general; for about that time we find that the merchants of Gascoin were settled in London in great numbers; and that in the year 1317, an order was made to this effect, "That merchants, who are not of the freedom of the city, are not to sell, by retail, wines or other wares, within the city or suburbs. Witness the King, at York, the eighth day of June."

The suppression of all the monasteries in England must

also have contributed much towards the loss of our vineyards, as few of the greater religious foundations were without them; and the present high duties on wine could not have been anticipated by our forefathers, when they neglected their vines.

The first duty on wines was one penny per tun, which was in the year 1272, when wine gaugers were first appointed at London and the principal sea-ports. The new gauge duty at London alone amounted to fifteen pounds sixteen shillings and sevenpence, which makes the quantity imported amount to seven thousand five hundred and ninety-eight pipes. The principal customs for importation, at that period, seem to have been on wines chiefly French and Rhenish, as there is yet scarcely any mention of Spanish, or Portuguese, or Italian wine. *(Madox's History of the Exchequer.)*

In the year 1409, the duty on wine was three shillings per tun.

Grapes seem to have become rare about the year 1560. Strype, in his Life of Grindal, bishop of London, (who was one of the earliest encouragers of botany in this kingdom,) writes, that his grapes at Fulham "were esteemed of that value, and a fruit Queen Elizabeth stood so well affected to, and so early ripe, that the bishop used every year to send her Majesty a present of them."

The vintage is a season of mirth in all the wine countries, and seems to have been equally so in the earliest times. The prediction of Isaiah concerning Moab is particularly characteristic: "And gladness is taken away, and joy, out of the plentiful field; and in the vineyards there shall be no singing, neither shall there be any shouting: the treaders shall tread out no wine in their presses; I have made their vintage shouting to cease."

The various wines made from the juice of the grape are so numerous, that to give a short description of each would be to write a voluminous work, and could only be interesting to those who are in the wine trade. Pliny says, there were eighty kinds of the best wines in his days. The Grecians were renowned for their wines. Homer has celebrated several, particularly the kind called Maronean wine, which was made from grapes growing upon the coast of Africa; and also the Pramnian wine, which, according to Pliny's account, was made from one vineyard only in the neighbourhood of Smyrna, near to the temple of Cybele.

These wines were so rare and expensive in Rome, in the younger days of Lucullus, that only one draught was allowed at a repast, however sumptuous the feast was in other respects. "Lucullus," says Varro, "never saw at his father's board Greek wines served up but once at a meal; but when he returned from Asia, he gave to the people a largess of more than one hundred thousand gallons of this wine; and Hortensius, at his death, left above ten thousand barrels full of Greek wines to his heir."

We have selected the following lines of a poet, who wrote in the fourteenth century, to shew of what wines the English had knowledge:

"Ye shall have rumney and malespine,
Both ypocrasse and vernage wyne,
Mountrese and wyne of Greke,
Both algrade and despice eke;
Antioche and bastarde,
Pyment also, and garnarde,
Wyne of Greke and muscadell,
Both clare, pyment, and Rochell."

Some of these liquors, as ypocrasse, pyment, and clare, were compounded of wine, honey, and spices.

At the installation feast of George Neville, archbishop of York, and chancellor of England, amongst other liquors, is mentioned, "In ale, 300 tun; in wine, 100 tun; in ipocrasse, 1 pipe."

In the year 1311 we find Thomas earl of Leicester debited by his cofferer, or paymaster, Thomas Leicester, amongst other charges, with £104. 17*s.* 6*d.* for three hundred and sixty-nine pipes of red wine and two pipes of white, which is about 5*s.* 7¼*d.* per pipe. (*Stow's Survey of London.*)

In the year 1322, when the sentence of banishment against the Spencers was removed, the elder Spencer's petition to the King, setting forth the damage he had sustained, amongst other things enumerates forty tun of wine and ten tun of cider. From these circumstances we may fairly judge that wine was the principal beverage of the English nobility at that period.

Of all the productions of nature, wine is the thing most difficult to choose well; yet we scarce meet with an acquaintance that does not pride himself in possessing this quality, while at the same time we find the greatest connoisseurs often deceived in their judgment; and it is generally observed, that dealers in wine know less of its qualities than other people.

At the present time, the consumption of wine in these dominions is immense, notwithstanding the excessively high duties laid on foreign wines; and in the London Docks there are eleven large vaults for housing of wines until the duties are paid on them: one of these vaults often contains nearly thirty thousand pipes.

Portugal supplies us with both the red and the white port, which take their name from Oporto, from whence they are shipped; Lisbon, which is called after that city; and Bucellas, which is a wine made from the fruit of vines that have been brought from the Rhine, and planted in the neighbourhood of Lisbon, but where, if not often renewed, it degenerates, and becomes similar to the produce of Lisbon. No wine improves more by keeping than Bucellas, if good when bottled; and, excepting hock and the Grave wines, it is the most excellent dinner-wine we import. Port wine is imported in casks, containing one hundred and thirty-eight gallons, which is called a pipe, but often gauges two, or four gallons over: upon this the duty must be paid, although the merchant makes no charge for the extra quantity.

France has been long famous for her vineyards, and even exported wine to Italy in the reign of Vespasian. Our traffic with Bourdeaux for wine commenced about the year 1172; and we now obtain from France a great variety of delicate wines, among which are the red and white hermitage, burgundy, claret, champaigne of several sorts, frontignac, muscadel, lunel, barsac, langon, vin de grave, &c. &c. The generality of these wines do not require long keeping, and, without great care, burgundy and champaigne soon become ropy and spoiled. The most esteemed French wines are

> "The claret smooth,
> The mellow-tasted Burgundy, and quick,
> As is the wit it gives, the gay Champaigne."

From Switzerland we procure neufchâtel, velteline, la côte, reiff, &c. &c.

The borders of the Rhine furnish us with a variety of Rhenish wines, the most esteemed of which is called Hock, from Hockheim, the town where it is made. This wine cannot be kept too long, as it obtains both body and flavour, as well as colour, by age. Hock wine is given with the greatest advantage in cases of the typhus fever. About one-half of Germany can boast of having good vineyards, while the other half has none: all the wines of this country require long keeping.

The advantage of keeping particular wines was well known to the Romans.

> Est mihi nonum superantis annum,
> Plenus Albani cadus.
>
> *Hor.*

> " Phillis, this Alban cask is thine,
> Mellow'd by summers more than nine."

Pliny mentions having met with wines in his time that were made in the consulship of Opimius, which was almost two hundred years before. This author says, " there was a wine made at Vienna which sold the dearest: it had," says he, " the taste of pitch, and it is reputed cooler than other wines, and was therefore given to allay fever."

The Hungarian wines, if not sent to us in great quantities, are made up in quality, if we may judge by the price of tokay. At the sale of the Duke of Queensberry's wine, in 18—, the tokay sold for one hundred and fifty pounds per dozen, which is about a guinea a glass. The tokay made at Johanneski, in Poland, of the vintage of 1811, was sold on the spot for four thousand florins the cask of eight ohms, which is equal to twenty-seven shillings per gallon.

Spain furnishes us with sherry, paxeretta, mountain, tent, &c. Mr. Swinburn mentions, in his account of Spain, that in plentiful seasons the vineyards are so productive, that casks cannot be found to contain the wine; and that many vineyards remain ungathered, notwithstanding public notice being stuck on the church doors, that all who choose may gather, by paying a small acknowledgment. Those who are afflicted with bilious complaints should drink good sherry, in preference to all other wines, it being less likely to turn acid on the stomach.

The island of Madeira was planted with the vine from cuttings brought from Cyprus, by Prince Henry, son to John the First of Portugal, in the year 1420, when the island was first discovered; and it now affords about thirty thousand pipes of wine annually. The Rhenish vine has also been planted in Madeira, and produces a very superior wine, known by the name of Cerciel Madeira: this island also affords us a sweet wine, called Malmsey Madeira; but the genuine Malmsey wine is the produce of Malvisia, and is now very rare. The ancients sometimes ripened particular wines, by placing them in the smoke above a fire, or in an upper part of their houses; and it is well known to the moderns, who are curious in their Madeira wines, how much they improve by being kept in a garret, instead of a vaulted cellar. Good West-India Madeira, that has been exposed to the frost, as well as the heat of summer, will be found to have ripened as well as by a voyage to the East Indies.

The Teneriffe wine, when about three years old, can hardly be known from Madeira; but as it gets older, it becomes sweet and mellow, like Malaga. Formerly there was made at Teneriffe a great quantity of Canary sack, which the French call Vin de Malvesie, and we, corruptly after them, Malmsey, from Malvisia, a town in the Morea, famous for luscious wines.

The luscious red wine called Lachryma Christi, is produced from vineyards on Mount Vesuvius.

The Cape of Good Hope has been planted with vines from the Rhine, Persia, and other countries; and they have so increased, that there is scarcely a cottage without a vineyard in all the colony. It is from the Cape that we obtain those rich wines called Constantia, both red and white, which are made on one farm only, and the quantity does not exceed sixty pipes of red and 100 of the white per annum. We also receive from thence large quantities of the wine called Cape, which will be good when the growers know their interest better, and attend more to the quality and less to the quantity. There is another objection to this wine, which must be remedied before Cape can be agreeable, *viz.* that the vines, instead of being staked, as in other wine countries, are suffered to trail on the ground : it is natural, therefore, to conclude that those berries next the earth will rot, and a few unsound grapes will give an unpleasant flavour to a large quantity of wine.

"The juice of the ripe grape (says Dr. Darwin) is a nutritive and agreeable food, consisting chiefly of sugar and mucilage. The chemical process of fermentation converts the sugar into spirit; converts food into poison!" Yet the moderate use of wine has seldom been condemned by physicians; and in so moist and changeable a climate as England, a more plentiful draught may be allowed than in warmer countries.

Dr. Short recommends wine to be drunk in moist weather, and ale in dry weather.

Sentius, when he was prætor of Rome, said he never had any wine of Chios in his house before the physician prescribed it for the palpitation of the heart, a complaint he laboured under; which is a convincing proof of its having been used medicinally in those days. On the other hand, Androcydes, in his letter to Alexander the Great, says, (to correct his intemperate drinking of wine,) "My good lord, remember when you take your wine, that you drink the very blood of the earth; hemlock, you know, Sir, is poison to man, even so is wine to hemlock."

That an excess of this reviving beverage is pernicious to the health, no one will attempt to deny, any more than he would to excuse repeated intoxication. Wine is not so much used in this age to debase man as it was in times past. Those liquors least intoxicating are now preferred; and the quality of the wines given at table is at present more attended to than the quantity, which has introduced cheerfulness and good sense around the decanters, in exchange for boisterous disputes. In an age that has advanced so far towards refinement, there can be no need to set up the alarm of poison, or condemn all the wine-merchants as murderers, as has lately become the fashion of some authors, which can answer no other purpose than that of alarming the timid, and bringing a respectable body of men into contempt. We are surprised that any person should make so severe an accusation as that of stating to the world that poisonous drugs are employed by the wine-merchants, without giving one instance to make good the assertion. About the year 1426, when Sir John Rainwell was lord-mayor of London, he having received an information of the mal-practices of the Lombard merchants in adulterating their wines, to the great prejudice of the health of his Majesty's subjects, caused one hundred and fifty butts of that pernicious liquor to be seized in divers parts of the city, the heads whereof being knocked out, the wine, or putrid matter, ran into the street channels, and emitted such a very noxious smell, that it infected the air to a great degree. It will be observed that this was an imposition practised by foreign merchants; and we do not recollect having met with any instance where an English wine-merchant has been detected in this infamous practice, or of the charge of mixing his wine with perry (as has been stated to be often done), and thereby defrauding both the revenue and his customers. This latter charge can be refuted by the best of all possible reasons, *viz.*: it is against the interest of a wine-merchant so to do; for he has more difficulty in procuring superior wines, than he has in obtaining ready sales at high prices. The best wines are always the first sold, and afford the largest profit, whereas inferior wines are rarely disposed of without a loss. It is generally known, that, at the present time, the duty and other incidental charges on foreign wines form the greater part of the price, and that the worst pipe of Port or Madeira pays as much duty as the best: it is therefore a most material part of the business of a wine-merchant to import the best wines from the countries with which he trades. When the vintage proves rather unfavourable, or his importations are deficient in flavour, he pursues a very different course from adulteration: he is obliged to procure the richest wines he can obtain of the same kind to mix with them. This is often done at a great expense, because he has not the means of disposing of inferior wines, even at any price. It is not an uncommon practice to add Burgundy or Hermitage to improve Port wine: this cannot be deemed adulteration.

The fining of white wines is so simple a process, and attended with so little expense, that there can be no inducement to use poisonous drugs, as has been stated by a late publication to be a common practice. It is well known to every housekeeper, that isinglass, dissolved in Hock or Rhenish wine, will fine the most obstinate white wines. It is correctly stated, that there are persons who prepare finings for the wine-merchants at a cheap rate; but as this is publicly sold, any person has an opportunity to analyze it, and ascertain whether it consists of poisonous drugs: indeed it would have been more honourable to have analyzed the wines of any suspected person, and to have exposed them to the public, were they guilty of so injuring the constitutions of their benefactors. A wine-merchant seldom does more himself to the fining of his wines than to give directions to his cellar-man: were he to use pernicious finings, how often should we hear of his being betrayed by his discharged servants!

For red wines, the whites of eggs, with sometimes a part of the shells pulverized, are the universal and only finings used. A few years back, when there was so great a demand for pale sherry, the wine-merchants discharged the colour with the assistance of a small quantity of new milk. The folly of this fashion was no sooner seen, than good brown sherries returned into favour. The Africans of old used to mitigate and allay the tartness of their wines with a kind of lime plaster; while the Greeks of the same day quickened their's with clay and marble powdered, or with sea water. The Romans admired the flavour of pitch, which was often added to their wines. Thus we find it has ever been the study of the wine-merchant to suit the taste of the times, but at no period has it been found necessary to add baneful drugs.

Grapes furnish the French with another article of commerce, almost equal in importance to their wines; namely, brandy. It is computed that their exportation in this liquor is not less than 50,000 pipes or pieces per ann. which, at the average of five shillings per gallon, produces them nearly two millions sterling annually. The brandies imported into this country are principally from Bourdeaux, Rochelle, and Cogniac; but they are very inferior to those made in the neighbourhood of Nantes and Poictou, from whence private families in the city and suburbs of Paris supply themselves, and they are very careful to obtain the best quality of this spirit. All brandies are originally white, but by long keeping they naturally become a little stained by the cask; and to give this appearance of age to the brandies shipped for England, burnt sugar and other dyes are added to such an excess, as to destroy the natural flavour of the spirit.

Private families would do well to buy none but the best pale brandy, and the importation of bad brandies would then speedily cease.

The fruiterers of London have a considerable trade in preserved grapes, which are principally brought from Portugal in large earthen jars, closely cemented down: these grapes add considerably to the luxury of our winter desserts, as they are sold at moderate prices for so rare a fruit.

This art of preserving grapes was well known to the Romans. Columella gives a particular account of the manner in which they were preserved, both in his time, and in the time of his uncle Marcus Columella. He recommends them to be put into small jars that will only contain one bunch, and, that the fruit should be gathered quite dry, when the sun is on it, and after being cooled in the shade, to be suspended in the jars, and, the vacua to be filled up with oat chaff, after all the dust has been blown from it. The jars must be well baked or burned, and not such as imbibe moisture: the tops of the jars must be covered over, and pitched, to keep out the air.

The process of drying grapes into raisins is usually performed by tying two or three bunches together before they are cut from the vine, and dipping them into a hot lixivium of wood-ashes, with a little olive oil in it: they then shrivel, and partly dry; and in a few days they are cut from the vine, and dried in the sun. We procure the finest raisins from Damascus. Sun raisins are brought from Spain, and are so called to distinguish them from those that are scalded, or dried, in ovens. Large quantities are also imported from Malaga, Calabria, Muscadine, Smyrna, &c.

The vinous latitude is said to extend between the 25th and 51st degree in the northern hemisphere.

It has been observed, that all the vineyards in Germany, beyond the 51st degree, are dubious. This leaves the southern coast of England within the latitude for vines; and we have often been surprised that the culture of them should have been so little attended to, where the shelter of the hills, and the soil, seem to offer so promising a situation, and more particularly so as the vine does not require that depth of soil so necessary to ensure good crops of corn; for it is known to prosper best where the soil is not more than sixteen or eighteen inches above the chalk or gravel.

We read in the "Museum Rusticum," that there was in the year 1763, a noble vineyard attached to Arundel Castle in Sussex, a seat of the Duke of Norfolk's, and that it succeeded so well that it annually yielded a considerable quantity of wine. At that period there were above sixty pipes of this wine in his Grace's cellar at Arundel: it was a kind of Burgundy; and we are told that although it was not of quite so fine a flavour as the wines of Beaune, yet it much exceeded quantities of Burgundy wine annually imported into England, and most of what is consumed commonly in France.

Among the MS. notes of the late Peter Collinson is the following memorandum. "Oct. 18, 1765, I went to see Mr. Rogers's vineyard at Parson's Green, all of Burgundy grapes, and seemingly all perfectly ripe. I did not see a green grape in all this great quantity. He does not expect to make less than fourteen hogsheads of wine. The branches and fruit are remarkably large, and the vines very strong."

Bartholomew Rocque, of Walham Green, made wine for thirty years from a vineyard he had planted in a common field garden; and although the ground was flat, the wine was as good as that of Orleans or Auxerre.

"I have known," says Mr. Hanbury, "good wine made of grapes growing in England, and have drunk our Burgundy no way inferior, as my taste could find out, to that noted wine which we have constantly imported from that country."

Hales, in his "Practical Husbandry," says, "that he drank with Dr. Shaw wines made under his own care, from a little vineyard behind his garden at Kensington, which equalled many of the lighter wines of France; and while due care was taken of the vineyard at Hammersmith, much very good wine was obtained there for sale: yet neither of these were favourable spots. Mr. King's vineyard at Brompton was well known to the curious, as also that at Pain's Hill, near Cobham in Surrey."

Mr. Bradley says, he cannot help mentioning how poor soils might be improved by making of vineyards. If it could have answered in his time, how profitable must it be at the present, when wine sells at about four times the price it did at that period, and the nature of the vine is so much better understood.

There were lately several flourishing vineyards in Somersetshire: the late Sir William Basset, of that county, annually made some hogsheads of wine, which was palatable and well bodied. The idea that we cannot make good wine from the juice of our own grapes is erroneous: the author has found it quite equal to the Grave wines; and in some instances, when kept for eight or ten years, it has been drunk as Hock by the nicest judges: but those vitiated palates that have been so long accustomed to drink indifferent Port wines overloaded with bad brandy, think nothing good that is not black and strong, while others deem nothing worth planting that does not promise to return them immediate riches. Grapes that are not perfectly ripe, and even sour, will make good wine, but it will require longer keeping.

If a sweet wine be preferred, raisins should be used with the grapes; for sugar and water (the common addition to our country wines) can never produce a good beverage.

The following observations on the economical uses to

which the leaves and stalks of the vine may be applied, are taken from a letter in the Philosophical Magazine, No. 119, signed James Hall.

"From experiments which I have made, I find that, on being dried, which should be done in the shade, and infused in a tea-pot, the leaves of the vine make an excellent substitute for tea. I have also found, that on being cut small, bruised, and put into a vat or mashing-tub, and boiling water poured on them in the same way as is done with malt, the prunings of the vine produce liquor of a fine vinous quality, which, on being fermented, makes a very fine beverage, either strong or weak, as you please; and on being distilled, produces an excellent spirit of the nature of brandy. In the course of my experiments, I found that the fermented liquor from the prunings, particularly the tendrils, when allowed to pass the vinous, and to run into the acetous fermentation, makes uncommonly fine vinegar."

To this observation we beg to add, that we have lately tasted wine made from the summer prunings with a small addition of sugar, that was very superior to the common wine made in this country from *water, grapes, and sugar*; and that the vinegar made from the tendrils and prunings was of so excellent a quality, that it would sell for as high a price as most of the continental wines sell for from the press.

Vine-leaves, as well as the tendrils, have an astringent taste, and were formerly used in diarrhœas, hæmorrhages, and other disorders requiring refrigerant and styptic medicines. The juice or sap of the vine, called lachryma, has been recommended in calculous disorders, and is said to be an excellent application to weak eyes and specks of the cornea. The tendrils of the vine were eaten as a pickle by the Romans.

The expressed juice of the unripe fruit is called verjuice, and is considered a very useful external remedy for bruises.

The wood of the vine reduced to charcoal, is used by painters for drawing outlines, and is mentioned as good for tooth powder.

Although it forms no part of the plan of this work to enter fully upon the cultivation of trees, I cannot avoid giving a few remarks on a fruit of so much importance.

In the planting of vines, the first care should be to select cuttings of those kinds which are known to be good, and suitable to the situation and soil in which they are to be placed; and this cannot be better done than by consulting some of the most respectable nurserymen who are now so numerous in the vicinity of London, and other populous neighbourhoods: at the same time we consider it a duty to caution the planter against those advertising quacks who profess to ensure their trees to be invincible to all casualties, and with as much truth as the mountebank sends forth his nostrum to cure all diseases.

"The grafting of vines upon vines is not now in use," says Lord Bacon in his Natural History; and adds, "the ancients had it, and that three ways: the first was insition, which is the ordinary manner of grafting; the second was terebration through the middle of the stock, and putting in the scions there; and the third was paring of two vines, that grow together, to the marrow, and binding them close."

Speechly, in his work on the vine, says, "The grafting of grapes is but little attended to, although of so much importance; as a bad vine may be improved without loss of time;" and he states, that he has had fine grapes from the same year's grafts, which, if permitted, will run from thirty to forty feet the first summer. He mentions a vine of the Syrian kind, in a hot-house at Welbeck, that produced sixteen different sorts of grapes from as many graftings.

On this subject, Thomas Andrew Knight, Esq. says in a paper to the Horticultural Society, read the 18th of September, 1821, " I selected three cuttings of the black Hamburgh grape, each having at its base one joint of two years old wood. These were inserted in, or rather fitted to, branches of nearly the same size, but of greater age; and all succeeded most perfectly. The clay which surrounded the base of the grafts was kept constantly moist: and the moisture thus supplied to the grafts operated very beneficially, at least, if it was not essential to the success of the operation.

" A very skilful gardener in my vicinity, to whom I mentioned my intention of trying the foregoing experiment, was completely successful by a somewhat different method. He used grafts similar to mine; but his vine grew under the roof of the hot-house, in which situation he found it difficult to attach such a quantity of clay as would supply the requisite degree of moisture to the graft; and he therefore supported a pot under each graft, upon which he raised the mould in heaps sufficiently high to cover the grafts, and supply them with moisture."

While industry and ingenuity are so busily employed to forward the growth of this delightful fruit that we may taste of autumn ere summer has arrived, let it be our study to point out the most effectual way of retarding the maturity of the grape, and thus assist to join, as it were, the two ends of the year, and keep Bacchus's favourite clusters always on our board. King Stanislaus, to prolong the duration of grapes in an age that had not begun to forward them by steam, employed the ingenious device we are going to lay before the public, as an old Polish practice, that may be turned to many advantageous purposes in horticulture.

This Polish prince procured pots with notches on each side about half-way of the depth, into which was laid a young branch of the vine with fruit on it, having first been bent so as to make a small bruise in the branch, that the sap might escape to form a root in the pot, which was then filled up with suitable earth, and placed on the ground or a stool, according to the situation of the vine: it was kept regularly watered, and soon sent a root into the earth, which, although it supplied the young fruit with additional nourishment, and greatly enlarged the size, yet naturally kept back the ripening. When the frost was expected, the branch was cut off close to the pot, and removed into the house, where it continued to vegetate, the bend or slight section having produced the double effect of turning the descending sap to the profit of the fruit, as well as of forming fibres for a vine that could be planted out in the following spring.

These pots were brought to table when other grapes were gone, and had all the freshness required, with the autumnal beauty on the leaves. By this means grapes may be procured all the year, or until early varieties have been forced.

Vines have ever been found to thrive best on the banks of rivers, or where their roots can draw moisture in abundance, as is frequently remarked in scripture.

It has been stated, that the blood of animals, applied about the roots, greatly nourishes the vine: this must be owing to the quantity of saline particles which it contains.

Mr. Daws, of Slough, near Windsor, has made the experiment of painting one half of a wall, that was covered with a vine, black, and leaving the other half in its common state. That part of the vine which covered the black wall, ripened the grapes earlier, and yielded about three times the weight of fruit that the other half produced.

Gentlemen who prune their own vines should observe, that the fruit is always produced upon the shoots of the same year, which are thrown out of the buds of the last year's shoots; and that it is not the old wood that yields grapes. It is best to prune vines as soon as the fruit is gathered, as the bearing shoots for the following year cannot then be mistaken; and it is recommended to shorten them, so as to leave but four eyes, as by leaving too many, the vine is exhausted, and yields but poor small fruit. The shoots just above the fourth eye are to be cut, and the cutting to be sloped or cut in such a manner, that the water discharging from the shoot may not run on the bud to injure it. About the beginning of May, all vines should be looked over, and the shoots from the old wood should be rubbed off; and if one eye produces two shoots, the weakest must be removed. Vines require frequent examining, after this time, to rub off all dangling shoots; and about the latter end of June, the ends of the bearing branches are to be nipped off, but those intended for the next year's fruit, may go a month longer before they are topped.

The blossoms of the vine have an agreeable odour: the ancients used to put them into their wine, to give it this fragrance.

The Romans reared their vines by fastening them to certain trees, as the poplar and the elm, &c., whence these trees are said to be married to the vines, which gave rise to Ovid's elegant and entertaining story of Vertumnus and Pomona.

"If that fair elm," he cried, "alone should stand,
No grapes would glow with gold, and tempt the hand;
Or, if that vine without her elm should grow,
'Twould creep a poor neglected shrub below."

Pliny states that the vines in Italy would climb to the

very top, and even out-top the highest poplars; on which account the grape-gatherers, in time of vintage, put a clause in the covenant of their bargains when they were hired, that in case their foot should slip and their necks be broken, their masters should give orders for their funeral fire and tomb at their own expense.

This mode of culture is still continued in that country. Swinburne tells us in his "Travels in the two Sicilies," "The verse in Virgil—

Hinc altâ sub rupe canet frondator ad auras,
Ecl. 1.

The lopper shall sing to the winds under the lofty rock,

naturally occurs, when in our walks under the rocky cliffs of Posilipo, we see the peasant swinging from the top of a tree on a rope of twisted willows, trimming the poplar and the luxuriant tendrils of the vine, and hear him make the whole vale ring with his rustic ditty.

"A classical scholar cannot stroll under the groves of the plain without calling to mind Horace's

——Durus
Vindemiator et invictus, cui sæpe viator
Cessisset, magnâ compellans voce cucullum.

A rough and invincible vine-dresser, before whom the traveller often retired, calling him with a loud voice, 'Cuckoo,'

if he attend to the vine-dresser sitting among the boughs, lashing raw lads and bashful maidens as they return from market, with the same gross wit and rough jokes that gave such zest of old to the farces of Atella."

HAZEL.—CORYLUS;

OR, NUT TREE.

Natural order, Amentaceæ; a genus of the Monœcia Polyandria class.

The English word, Nut, is derived from the Latin, *Nux.* The common hazel-nut *(Nux silvestris)* is found growing wild in most parts of Europe, as also in every part of England. The ancients observed this tree with particular attention in the spring, as they drew from it a good or bad omen for the approaching harvest; and it has been well confirmed, that "a good nut year makes a good wheat year." It was a remark too conspicuous to escape the notice of Virgil, who writes—

> Contemplator item, cum se nux plurima sylvis
> Induet in florem, et ramos curvabit olentes:
> Si superant fœtus, pariter frumenta sequentur,
> Magnaque cum magno veniet tritura calore.
> At si luxuriâ foliorum exuberat umbra,
> Nequidquam pingues paleâ teret area culmos.

We do not find from what source the word Hazel was derived, but it seems to have been of long standing, and to have given names to several places where the dry, sandy, or stony soil suited its growth; as Haselmere, in Surrey, Hasulbury, in Wilts, Haslingfield, in Cambridgeshire, Haslinden, in Lancashire, &c. This tree is never cultivated for the sake of the nut, which is considered unwholesome, being hard of digestion, and causing shortness of breath and wheezing. Many young people have suffered by eating too freely of this fruit; and it has caused the death of several who have taken immoderately of it.

Nevertheless Culpepper, in his "Astrologo-Physical Discourse on Herbs," not only commends these nuts as a medicine for the lungs, but quaintly gives us his curious defence of nuts, which may be acceptable to idle boys, if not amusing to modern medical writers, to see how their brethren of 1681 indited.

"Why should the vulgar so familiarly affirm, that eating nuts causeth shortness of breath, than which nothing is falser? or, how can that which strengthens the lungs, cause shortness of breath? I confess the opinion is far elder than I am. I knew Tradition was a friend to errors before, but never that he was the father of slanders: or are men's tongues so given to slander one another, that they must slander nuts too, to keep their tongues in use? If any-thing of the hazel-nut be stopping, 'tis the husks and shells, and nobody is so mad as to eat them unless physically, and the red skin which covers the kernels, which you may easily pull off. And thus have I made an apology for nuts, which cannot speak for themselves."

We have already noticed the elegance of the pendant catkins of these trees in the history of the filbert, and it appears that they did not escape the notice of the rustic lasses of ancient Rome. Virgil makes Corydon say—

"With hazel Phyllis crowns her flowing hair;
And while she loves that common wreath to wear,
Nor bays, nor myrtle-boughs, with hazel shall compare."

The pleasure of nutting-parties is well known in this

country, and much enjoyed by the rustics; it is thus beautifully described by Thomson:—

" Ye swains, now hasten to the hazel bank,
Where down yon dale the wildly winding brook
Falls hoarse from steep to steep. In close array,
Fit for the thickets and the tangling shrub,
Ye virgins, come. For you their latest song
The woodlands raise; the clustering nuts for you
The lover finds amid the secret shade;
And where they burnish on the topmost bough,
With active vigour crushes down the tree;
Or shakes them ripe, from the resigning husk,
A glossy shower."

Evelyn tells us, that " these nuts, being fully ripe, and peeled in warm water, as they blanch almonds, make a pudding, very little, if at all, inferior to that our ladies make of almonds."

These nuts are not much used in medicine, but the cream of them is good for the stone, and heat of urine: emulsions made of them with mead, are recommended for old dry coughs.

Quercentan gave a dram of the powder of nut-shells, mixed with an equal quantity of prepared coral, in a glass of the water of carduus benedictus, or corn poppy, in the pleurisy.

The wood of the hazel-tree is used for making hoops for casks, hurdles, crates, springles to fasten down thatch, fishing-rods, &c.; it is also burnt for charcoal, and it was formerly much used for making gunpowder.

Plantis eduræ coryli nascuntur: Virgil.

" Hazels from sets and suckers take—"

from whence they thrive very well; but it is recommended to plant well-preserved nuts in the month of February, to obtain the finest hazel-trees.

In the country where yeast is scarce, they twist the slender branches of hazel together, and steep them in ale-yeast during its fermentation: they are then hung up to dry, and at the next brewing are put into the wort instead of yeast. The chips of this wood are used to fine wines.

In more superstitious times, divining-rods were made of hazel, which were supposed to have the property, when placed horizontally in the earth, of bending towards mines, springs of water, &c. They were even used by the magistrates of those credulous days to find out criminals guilty of murder, &c. by their inclining towards the person. We find that even the wisest and best men of those days could not entirely escape the infectious superstitions of their age. Lord Bacon confesses by his writings his belief of witches; and Evelyn, in his "Discourse of Forest Trees," says, under the article Hazel, "But now, after all, the most signal honour it was ever employed in, and which might deservedly exalt this humble and common plant above all the trees of the wood, is that of hurdles, especially the flexible white, the red, and brittle; not for that it is generally used for the folding of our innocent sheep, an emblem of the Church, but for making the walls of one of the first Christian Oratories in the world; and particularly in this island, that venerable and sacred fabrick at Glastonbury, founded by St. Joseph of Arimathea, which is storied to have been first composed out of a few small hazel-rods interwoven about certain stakes driven into the ground."

JUNIPER.—JUNIPERUS.

Natural order, Coniferæ. A genus of the Diœcia Monadelphia class.

"From lowest Juniper to Cedar tall."

Of this class of trees we reckon twelve different species and several varieties.

Etymologists are not agreed from what source the generic name of this tree is derived; some say *Juniperus, quod juniores et novellos fructus pariat*, because the new fruit is produced before the old is ripe, which is seldom matured until the second year; others give its derivation from πῦρ, *ignis*, from the pyramidical form of the leaves.

The earliest mention of the juniper-tree will be found in the first book of Kings, about 906 years before the Christian era, when the prophet Elijah took refuge in the wilderness of Beersheba, to avoid the persecution of King Ahab. "He went a day's journey into the wilderness, and came and sat down under a juniper-tree: And as he lay and slept under a juniper-tree, behold then an angel touched him, and said unto him, Arise and eat."

The juniper is also a native of most of the cold mountainous parts of Europe. Gerard says, "The common juniper-tree grows, in some parts of Kent, unto the bigness and stature of a fair great tree." It is found growing wild in considerable quantities on many parts of the Sussex and Surrey hills, from whence it is often transplanted into shrubberies. Being of a bluish evergreen, it contrasts well with the laurel and other shrubs of that nature. Evelyn tells us that his brother transplanted a juniper-bush of about two feet high, from a common into his garden, which in ten years had grown to such a size, that an arbour of seven feet square and eleven feet high, was cut out of it, and that it would have been much larger had it not been kept constantly shorn. The flowers of the juniper are herbaceous, and, if viewed with a microscope, would be found a most beautiful model, either for the jeweller, or the ornamental sculptor. The old English epicures had their spits, and spoons, made of juniper-wood, which we are told imparted a grateful relish to their food.

Juniper-berries, used by distillers to flavour their gin, are principally brought from Holland and Italy. These berries are carminative; but their most remarkable properties are in scouring the viscera, and particularly the reins and urinary passages, for which reason they are of great service in asthmas, cachexies, the jaundice, colic, the stone of the bladder and kidneys, as also crudities of the stomach. The oil of juniper-berries is a very stimulating diuretic: the decoction, inspissated to the consistency of a rob, or extract, has a pleasant, balsamic, sweet taste. This extract may be used with advantage, in catarrhs, debility of the stomach and intestines, and difficulties of the urinary excretions, in persons of advanced age.

Etmüller had a high opinion of juniper-berries. The rob, made of the expressed juice of the green berries, has been called by many *theriaca Germanorum*, so much are they esteemed by that nation for their alexipharmic qualities. The ripe berries, when dried, were formerly used in this country as pepper, before that spice was brought hither in such quantities. In many parts of Germany, they are still used as a culinary spice, and the flavour of these berries is esteemed in their sauer kraut. The heathcock of Germany is not eatable in the autumn, being so strongly flavoured with juniper-berries, on which this bird feeds. The wood of this shrub is also of use in physic, as it strengthens the stomach, clears the lungs, removes obstructions of the viscera, and is farther said to be sudorific, cephalic, and hysteric. So much is the flavour of the berries admired by the lower orders of Londoners, that it would be difficult to name any complaint, that they would not be afflicted with, for the sake of a plentiful supply of the cordial to which it is imparted.

In the hospitals on the continent both the wood and the berries of the juniper are burnt, to fumigate the rooms of the sick. Evelyn observes that the very chips render a wholesome perfume within doors as well as the dusty blossoms in spring without.

In Sweden, the juniper-berries are made into a conserve, and eaten at breakfast. The Swedes also prepare a beverage from them, which they consider useful as a medicine. In some places they are roasted, and used as a substitute for coffee.

Gerard says, in his third book, "Divers in Bohemia do take, instead of other drinke, the water wherein these berries have been steeped, who live in wonderful good health."

The wood of the juniper-tree is very hard, beautifully veined, susceptible of a very high polish, and is admired when used as veneering for cabinet furniture, being fragrant, and of a yellow colour. Pliny says, "the juniper has the same properties as the cedar," adding, "that it grew in Spain to a great size, but that wherever it grows, the heart is found more sound than cedar." This tree grows to a large size in some parts of Africa, and we see in one of the rooms in Chantilly, a slab of juniper-wood, nine inches in diameter, that was taken from a remarkably large tree, which grew at the top of one of the highest mountains in Switzerland. It has been said, that a coal of juniper-wood, covered with ashes of the same kind, will keep on fire a whole year. David alludes to the heat of these coals as a punishment to the false tongue:—"Sharp arrows of the mighty with coals of juniper." Psalm cxx. 4.

The juniper is propagated by sowing the seed as soon as ripe, on ground that has not been dunged; and the plants will grow in any soil, however dry or damp, but like other plants they resist the frost best in dry situations. If the under-branches are kept pruned, they will form trees of a considerable size in a few years, but they should not be pruned too much at any one time, particularly in the spring, as they are apt to discharge their resinous juice, which renders them weak and unhealthy. October is the best time for transplanting these shrubs, as well as for the pruning of them.

LEMON.—LIMON.—CITRUS.

Natural order, Bicornes. Of the class Polyadelphia Icosandria.

———— "Bear me, Pomona,
To where the lemon and the piercing lime,
With the deep orange, glowing through the green,
Their lighter glories blend."

THIS fruit derives its name from the Greek word λειμὼν, which signifies *a meadow*, because the leaves and the fruit, before they are ripe, are of the colour of a spring meadow.

The lemon and the citron-tree are natives of Asia, from whence they were brought into Greece and Italy. They appear to have been well known to the Romans in the days of Pliny, although they had failed in the cultivation of them; as that author informs us in his 13th book, chap. iii., where he says, speaking of foreign trees, "I will begin with that which is of all others the most wholesome, the citron-tree, called the Assyrian-tree, and by some the Median-apple: the fruit is a counterpoison, and singular antidote against all venom; the leaves," he says, "are like the arbutus, and it hath thorns. The pome citron is not good to be eaten as a fruit, but is very odoriferous, as are the leaves, which are used to be put in wardrobes among apparel, to give a perfume, and to keep off moths and spiders. This tree bears fruit at all times of the year, for, when some fall, others begin to mellow, and some to blossom. Many have tried to transplant the trees into their own country; and for this purpose they have had pots made, and enclosed them well with earth; but for all the care and pains taken about them, to make these trees grow in other countries, yet would they not forget Media and Persia, and, liking no other soil, would soon die."

Virgil, in his Second Georgic, has elegantly described this fruit, and its supposed medical powers against spells and poison.

> Media fert tristes succos tardumque saporem
> Felicis mali: quo non præsentius ullum
> (Pocula si quando sævæ infecêre novercæ,
> Miscueruntque herbas, et non innoxia verba)
> Auxilium venit, ac membris agit atra venena.
> Ipsa ingens arbos, faciemque simillima lauro:
> Et si non alium late jactaret odorem,
> Laurus erat: folia haud ullis labentia ventis:
> Flos apprime tenax: animas et olentia Medi
> Ora fovent illo, et senibus medicantur anhelis.

> " Sharp-tasted citron Median climes produce,
> Bitter the rind, but gen'rous is the juice;
> A cordial fruit, a present antidote
> Against the direful stepdame's deadly draught,
> Who, mixing wicked weeds with words impure,
> The fate of envied orphans would procure.
> Large is the plant, and like a laurel grows,
> And, did it not a diff'rent scent disclose,
> A laurel 'twere: the fragrant flow'rs contemn
> The stormy winds, tenacious of their stem;
> With this, the Medes to lab'ring age bequeath
> New lungs, and cure the sourness of the breath."
>
> *Dryden.*

Apicius, the celebrated Roman epicure, is said to have been the first that used lemons in food: he wrote a book on the pleasures and incitements of eating, in which he described the manner of dressing them. Galen was the first European physician that used lemons in medicine.

The lemon-tree appears to have been cultivated in this country as early as the reign of James the First, as Lord Bacon mentions the housing of hot-country plants, as lemons, oranges, and myrtles, to save them. It was cultivated in the Botanic Garden at Oxford, in 1648.

In some parts of Devonshire, lemon-trees are trained to the walls, and require no other care than to cover them with straw or mats during the winter. Earl Paulet presented some of these lemons to his late Majesty upwards of forty years ago, which grew in the garden of his sister, Lady Bridget Bastard, of Garston. The lemon-tree is of a much hardier nature than the orange: it is therefore brought to greater perfection in this country than the latter fruit. Lemons have long been propagated with success in Italy, Spain, Portugal, and the South of France, as well as in the West-India islands. The lemons of St. Helena are the most esteemed, growing larger, and of a milder flavour than other kinds, and, according to Browne, they frequently yield more than half-a-pint of juice.

A very superior kind of lemons is cultivated exclusively in the plain between Pisa and Leghorn, which, from their excellent quality, sell for fifty sous each in that place; but they are generally sent as presents to the various courts of Europe.

Lemons vary by cultivation and situation, like most other fruits. The sweet lemon is admired by many people, and is a desirable fruit for invalids, when oranges become too sweet.

This fruit is now become almost necessary in culinary purposes, as well as being an article of luxury in a variety of shapes: it makes an excellent sweetmeat when cleared of its pulp, and prepared with clarified syrup. Lemonade and lemon-ices are as well known in the present day as punch was in the last age. The yellow peel of the lemon is an agreeable aromatic; and, in cold phlegmatic constitutions it proves an excellent stomachic and carminative, warming the habit and strengthening the tone of the viscera.

Lemons are cooling and grateful to the stomach, allaying thirst, and increasing appetite; they are also useful in fevers, even malignant and pestilential. The juice, mixed with salt of wormwood, is an excellent medicine to stop vomiting, and to strengthen the stomach. The efficacy of lemon-juice in preventing the sea-scurvy, has long been recommended. Sir James Lancaster, in his voyage in 1601, carried with him several bottles of lemon-juice, and, by giving his sailors a few table-spoonsful in the morning, kept off this disorder.

In Captain Cook's voyages great benefit was derived from lemon and orange-juice, which were found in the sea-scurvy to be very efficacious.

Dr. Willich states, that the largest dose of opium may be checked in its narcotic effects, if a proper quantity of citric acid be taken with it; and that, with this adjunct, it induces cheerfulness instead of stupefaction, and is succeeded by gentle and refreshing sleep.

In Sicily, the juice of lemons forms an important article of commerce, it being considered the most valuable remedy for the scurvy in long voyages. It is also very extensively used by calico-printers, as a discharger of colour, to produce with more clearness and effect the white figured parts of coloured patterns, dyed with colours formed from iron.

When Gibraltar was besieged or blocked up in the autumn of 1780, vegetables had become so scarce, that a small cabbage sold for five shillings: hence the scurvy raged to a degree which threatened more fatal consequences than the gun-boats of the Spaniards. The women and children, as well as the officers, were equally affected with this dreadful disorder, when, happily, an antidote was procured by the capture of a Danish dogger, from Malaga, laden with lemons and oranges; these the governor immediately purchased for the use of the garrison, and distributed among them, which relieved them most wonderfully. The juice was given to those in the malignant state diluted with sugar, wine, or spirits. Various antiscorbutics had previously been used without success, such as acid of vitriol, sauer kraut, extract of malt, essence of spruce, &c.

As the juice of lemons and limes became in so much demand for medical use, as well as for the purposes of luxury, various modes of purifying and preserving it have been adopted by our ingenious chemists, who have succeeded in procuring the acid in a state of purity in crystals, called citric acid. Dr. James Lind gives the preference to oranges and lemons above all other medicine for scorbutic complaints, as these alone he considers a specific protection against the terrible effects of this distemper; but as the fruit is liable to spoil, and cannot always be procured, he proposes the following method of preserving its virtues for years in a convenient and small bulk; and which we shall transcribe for the benefit of those who prefer their own preparations in domestic purposes to those sold in the shops.

"Let the squeezed juice of these fruits be well cleared from the pulp, and depurated by standing for some time; then poured off from the gross sediment: or, to have it still purer, it may be filtrated. Then put it into a well-glazed earthen vessel, which should be wider at the top than the bottom, as a China basin or punch bowl, so that there may be the largest surface above, to favour the evaporation. This should be placed in a vessel of water over a clear fire. Let the water come almost to boil, and continue nearly in a state of boiling, for several hours, until the juice in the basin is become of the consistence of oil when warm, or of a syrup when cold. It is then to be corked up in bottles for use. Where it is desirable to preserve the perfect fragrance of the fruit, a very small quantity of the outer peel may be added to the extract a little before it is taken off the fire."

In making lemonade, or for any purpose requiring the flavour and fragrance of the peel, we should recollect that the essential oil is lodged in distinct cells on the surface of the peel; the best mode of obtaining this oil is by rubbing the peel with loaf sugar, and then sweetening the mixture with the sugar that has imbibed the essence; but where sweets are not required, it must be cut so thin as not to take off any part of the white rind.

The liquor called *shrub* is made with lemon and lime-juice added to rum.

The fruit of the Lime *(Lima)* resembles in acidity the lemon; and the tree, that of the orange, having winged leaves. It is much smaller than the common lemon, and is principally brought to this country from the West-India islands, where, says Lunan, "the negroes take the young fruit, soon after it is formed, or when about the size of a small hazel-nut, pare off the rind, which they beat into a fine pulp, and with a hair-pencil apply it carefully to the lids of sore eyes for a cure. It is supposed," continues Lunan, "this rawness of the eye-lids, accompanied with a humour, is generally caused by worms which lodge in it, and that this application destroys them."

Lime punch is more esteemed than that made from lemons, particularly for cold punch, which is a beverage greatly admired by turtle-eaters.

The author lately received from Portugal some fruit of

a variety of the lime, which is now growing in that country, the yellow rind of which has no other perfume or taste than that of burgamot: the juice is a weak acid, and by no means equal to the common lime or lemon: the fruit is nearly of a globular shape, and from ten to eleven inches in circumference.

The Citron is principally used as a sweetmeat.

The SHADDOCK-TREE; *Aurantium fructu maximo Indiæ Orientalis.*

This fruit is also a species of the *citrus,* and takes its name from Captain Shaddock, who first brought it from the East-Indies, where it is a native. It is now cultivated in the West-Indies, where the fruit often grows to the size of twenty inches in circumference, and is known to yield near half-a-pint of clear juice. It is described, in the Hortus Jamaicensis, as being often larger than a man's head. Shaddocks are preserved as a sweetmeat, and used in making punch, as well as limes and lemons.

LOCUST-TREE.—HYMENÆA.

Natural order, Lomentaceæ. A genus of the Decandria Monogynia class.

The generic name is derived from Hymen, the god of marriage.

This is a very large spreading tree, in shape resembling the beech. The flowers are produced in loose spikes at the end of the branches, and are succeeded by thick, fleshy, brown pods, shaped like those of the garden-bean, about six inches long, and two and a half broad, wherein there are three or four round, flat, blackish beans or stones, bigger than those of the tamarind, enclosed in a whitish substance of fine filaments, as sweet as sugar or honey. The wild bees are fond of building their nests in these trees: we may therefore justly conclude that St. John found both the locust and wild honey on the same trees, and that it was this fruit on which he fed, and not on insects called locusts, as some authors have stated.

The Indians eat this fruit with great avidity, though it is apt to purge when fresh gathered, but loses that quality as it grows older.

The juice, or decoction of the leaves, is carminative, and eases the colic pain. The inward bark destroys worms. Between the principal roots of the tree exudes a fine transparent resin, which is collected in large lumps; it is called *gum animi*, and makes the finest varnish that is known, superior even to the Chinese lacca.

The tree is now well known in the West Indies; and when old, the timber is in request to make wheel-work for various machines.

As this tree becomes interesting to us from the mention made of it in Scripture, we shall be justified in giving some particulars from the Botanical Manuscript of Mr. Anthony Robinson, who writes thus:

"On the 8th July, 1759, I had the pleasure of seeing the perfect flower of the hymenæa of Linnæus expanded, from which I took this description: the receptacle of the cup was bell-shaped, permanent; the perianth consisted of four ovate, coriaceous, thick leaves, almost equal, placed scalewise, which, for the most part, dropped as soon as the petals were expanded. The leaves of the cup were placed on the margin of the receptacle. The petals were white, five in number, ovate, erect, patent, and almost equal, as long as the cup; the stamina were ten, subulated, erect, patent filaments, one fourth longer than the petals; the germen was placed on a receptacle, arising out of a hole in the centre of the receptacle, compressed and small; the style subulate, and somewhat longer than the stamens; the stigma coronated; the anthers were large, oblong, and the flower has nothing of a pyramid in its form. There was great difficulty in getting a complete flower, for the leaves of the cup dropped off with the least motion. The petals were considerably permanent, but the stamens more so. Linnæus has described the blossoms erroneously."

This tree was first cultivated in England, in the year 1688. (*Hortus Kewensis.*)

LOVE-APPLE.—SOLANUM LYCOPERSICUM;

OR, TOMATO-BERRY.

Natural order, Luridæ. A genus of the Pentandria Monogynia class.

The love-apple, or tomato, is the fruit of the lycopersion, an herbaceous branching plant, or vine, with a hairy stem, and a rank smell; on which account it was formerly called *Malum Aureum odore fœtido,* the stinking golden apple. It was also called the wolf's peach, from lycopersion.

It is a native of South America, and, in all probability, of Mexico; from whence it appears to have been brought by the Spaniards, who, as Barham observes, use it in their sauces and gravies; because the juice, as they say, is as good as any gravy, and so by its richness warms the blood.

Dodoens, in his Pemptades, published at Antwerp in 1583, describes it as growing at that time in the continental gardens, and says, that its fruit was eaten dressed with pepper, salt, and oil.

Parkinson, whose works were published in 1656, mentions it as being cultivated in England for ornament and curiosity only. Even at the present time they are grown in many gardens in the country, merely for the singularity of their appearance, varying very much in size and shape as well as colour; some being of a bright yellow, and others of a fine red. It appears, by the Hortus Kewensis, to have been cultivated in England as early as the year 1596; but we conclude it was introduced several years previous to that date, as Gerard mentions it in the early part of his voluminous work, as growing in his garden. This author calls it *pomum amoris;* and says, "apples of love do growe in Spaine, Italie, and such hot countries, from whence myself have received seedes for my garden, where they do increase and prosper."

"There hath happened unto my handes another sort," says this author, "agreeing very notablie with the former, onely the fruite heereof was yellow of colour." (Now this work, which was published in 1597, must have taken some years in compiling and printing, &c. as it contains several thousand wood plates.)

Miller says, in the sixth edition of his Gardener's Dictionary, "the Italians and Spaniards eat love-apples as we do cucumbers, with pepper, oil, and salt, as well as for sauces.

The Portuguese call this fruit *tomato,* and eat it either raw or stewed.

Lunan says of this fruit, "I have eaten five or six raw at a time: they are full of a pulpy juice, and of small seeds, which you swallow with the pulp, and have something of a gravy taste. The juice is cooling, and very proper for defluxions of hot humours in the eyes, which may occasion a glaucoma, if not prevented: they are also good in the St. Anthony's fire, and all inflammations; and a cataplasm of them is very proper for burns." Miller also says, that the love-apple was used as a medicine in his time.

This fruit has long been used by the wealthy Jewish families in this country: and within these last few years it has come into great use with all our best cooks, as it possesses in itself an agreeable acid, a very unusual quality in ripe vegetables, and which makes it quite distinct from all garden vegetables that are used for culinary purposes in this country. It makes a good pickle, and is preserved in various ways for winter use, and is made into a kind of ketchup also. When boiled in soups and sauces, it imparts an acid of a most agreeable flavour: it is also served at table boiled or roasted, and sometimes fried with eggs. Love-apples are now to be seen in great abundance at all our vegetable markets; but I do not find that they are used by the middle or lower classes of English families, who have yet to learn the art of improving their dishes with vegetables.

Mr. John Wilmot, of Isleworth, states, that in 1819 he gathered, from six hundred plants, four hundred half sieves, which is about equal to one hundred and thirty-three bushels, and that he then had many to spare. He adds, that the plants produced from twenty to forty pounds weight each, and that some of the apples measured twelve inches in circumference.

Mr. Wilmot recommends them to be planted against a bank, as being more congenial to their nature than a wall. There are several varieties of the tomato; and that which produces fruit about the size of a cherry is the most acid, therefore the most desirable kind for private gardens, although not so profitable for market.

A new species of this fruit, *Solanum deurens*, has been introduced by Mr Anderson, of the Apothecaries' Garden, Chelsea, who received the seeds from Germany; it is said to be a native of the Isle of France, while others consider it to be indigenous to South America. The fruit is about the size of a cherry, and of an orange colour, and is used in food like the common sort; it has prospered in the greenhouse, but succeeds better in the bark bed of the stove.

MEDLAR.—MESPILUS.

Natural order, Pomaceæ. A genus of the Icosandria Pentagynia class.

"——Medlar-fruit, delicious in decay."

THIS fruit was known to the ancient Greeks, as it is mentioned by Theophrastus: but it appears not to have been cultivated in Italy in Cato's days. Pliny mentions three kinds: the Anthedon, the Setanian medlar, which he describes as the largest and palest in colour, and the Gallicum, or Bastard French Medlar.

Some authors affirm it to have been originally a German fruit; but the name Anthedon was doubtless given to it from its being brought from a city of that name in Greece; while the Gallicum is declared by Pliny to have come from France: the Setanian seems to have derived its name from its growing near the marshes of Setia. The Medlar appears also to have been indigenous to this country, as it is mentioned by all our early writers. Tusser calls the fruit Medlers or Meles. Gerard says, "The medlar-tree oftentimes grows in hedges among briars and brambles: being grafted on a white-thorn, it prospers and produces fruit three times as large as those which are not grafted at all, and almost the size of small apples. We have," says he, "divers sorts of them in our orchards." He mentions the Neapolitan Medlar, with leaves like the hawthorn; and the Dwarf, growing naturally upon the Alps, and hills of Narbonne and Verona.

The Dutch Medlar, which is much larger and finer-flavoured than the common sort, is the only kind now in request for planting in the garden or orchard. This fruit cannot be eaten when fresh gathered, being too harsh for the palate; but after it has been laid up for a few weeks, and undergone a putrefactive fermentation, it becomes quite soft, and is an agreeable fruit for the desserts in November and December.

This fruit is cooling, drying, and binding, especially before it is ripe, and is useful in all kinds of fluxes. The *lapilli*, or hard seeds, are accounted good for the stone and gravel; they are an ingredient in the *syrupus myrtinus*. *(Miller's Bot. Off.)*

The medlar-tree is propagated by budding or grafting on the hawthorn, as has been noticed by Philips:

> "Men have gather'd from the hawthorn's branch
> Large medlars, imitating regal crowns."

It will also take upon the quince or pear stock, and both these will take upon the medlar, which shews they have great affinity to each other; but it is more productive when grafted on the hawthorn.

The pruner must observe not to shorten any of the branches, as the fruit is always produced at the extremities of the boughs.

The medlar-tree is very ornamental when in blossom, and forms a beautiful shrub for the pleasure ground, particularly when looked down upon from higher grounds.

MELON.—MELO.—CUCUMIS.

Natural order, Cucurbitaceæ. A genus of the Monæcia Syngenesia class.

The melon most esteemed in every part of Europe, is the Cantaleupe, which takes its name from a town so called, about fifteen miles from Rome, where it has been cultivated since the Mithridatic war, being one of the fruits brought from Armenia, by Lucullus. It grows, says Miller, in that part of Armenia which borders on Persia, in such plenty, that a horse-load is sold for a French crown. The flesh of this melon, when in perfection, is delicious, and does not offend the most tender stomach, but may be eaten with safety: its outer coat is full of knobs and protuberances; it is of a middle size, rather round than long: that with an orange-coloured flesh is the best.

The Musk Melon appears to be a native of Tartary, where it is found growing wild; these and the water melon, form a principal part of the food of the Nayay Tartars. It has lately been found in great abundance on the sandy plains in the neighbourhood of Jeypoor. This kind of melon has long been cultivated in Italy, from whence we conclude it was brought to England, as it was first introduced into this country in the year 1520: and from Gerard's account it appears to have been nearly confined to the Royal Gardens: he had not grown it himself, but says, "They delight in hot regions, notwithstanding I have seen, at the Queen's house at St. James's, very many of this sort ripe, through the diligent and curious nourishing of them by a skilful gentleman, the keeper of the said house, called Master Fowle; and in other places neere unto the Right Honourable the Lord of Sussex house, of Bermondsey, by London, where from yeere to yeere there is verie great plenty, especially if the weather be any thing temperate." "It hath," adds Gerard, "the smell of musk, and from which account it is called the Musk Melon."

It is stated in Gough's British Topography, that melons were common in this country as early as the time of Edward the Third, but were entirely lost, as well as the cucumber, during the wars of York and Lancaster.

Miller justly remarks, that, in this country, there are too many melons produced of no value by those who supply the market, who, endeavouring to enlarge their size, render the fruit of no value, and unworthy the trouble and expense, being more fit for the dunghill than the table. In warmer countries, the melon is raised with little or no trouble, and the fruit attains a peculiarly fine flavour; but in this climate it requires great attention and expense to rear it, therefore—

"Grudge not, ye rich, (since luxury must have
His dainties, and the world's more numerous half
Lives by contriving delicacies for you,)
Grudge not the cost. Ye little know the cares,
The vigilance, the labour, and the skill,
That day and night are exercised, and hang
Upon the ticklish balance of suspense,
That ye may garnish your profuse regales
With summer fruits brought forth by wintry suns:
Ten thousand dangers lie in wait to thwart
The process."

Cowper.

No country has a greater variety of melons than England; yet it is so rare to find them good in the market, that the demand for them in London, compared to that in Paris, cannot be more than in the proportion of one to a thousand.

From the attention now paid to horticultural pursuits, and the advantage of steam-pits instead of stable-dung for growing this fruit, we may hope not only to equal our continental neighbours in quantity, but to excel them in quality, which is already done in private gardens. A melon of the large netted cantelope, was cut on the 10th of September 1821, at Denby Grange, the seat of Sir J. L. Kaye, Bart. which weighed eighteen pounds: the circumference was two feet six inches, and measured lengthways two feet ten inches and a half; the eatable depth of the slice was full two inches and a half, and the flavour of a very superior quality.

The Spanish winter-melon has lately been introduced in our gardens, and it is a great addition to our desserts, as it possesses the quality of keeping sound until February. The author partook of one of these melons in the middle of January last, that had retained its firmness and flavour, although it had been cut in the month of September.

Among the numerous varieties of melons we have lately seen introduced, is the *Green-fleshed Egyptian.* The flesh is semi-transparent, green next the skin, and becoming white in the centre; it is perfectly melting, rich, sweet, and high-flavoured, and is said to be an abundant bearer, and generally of a size from two to three pounds each; and, like all the green melons, the flesh of this is more digestible than that of the red varieties, and this variety in particular is considered as having that quality more remarkably than any other. It has also the merit of ripening its flesh very close up to its skin, and consequently of affording a much larger eatable portion, for its weight, than is usual to most melons.

We have observed, in other parts of this work, that the French have particular places where they cultivate peculiar fruits only: this is the case with melons; and where they are grown in such abundance as entirely to occupy the attention of whole villages, the culture must necessarily be better understood than in our gardens, where the same persons have to cultivate every kind of fruit or vegetable: the mind being thus divided between so many varieties, that none can be so thoroughly understood. Another great disadvantage arises in the common mode of growing melons in this country, that is, by planting them near to cucumbers, and sometimes quite surrounded by them, and often by gourds, which, it is well known, will, by their incestuous intercourse, not only affect the seeds for future plants, but change the nature of the fruit, which becomes polluted by the farina of other species of the *cucurbitaceæ*.

When a melon is perfectly fine, it is full without any vacuity: this is known by knocking upon it; and, when cut, the flesh should be dry, no water running out, only a little dew, which should be of a fine red colour. This fruit is principally used at desserts in England, and eaten with sugar, ginger, pepper, or salt, agreeably to the taste; while in France it is chiefly served up at dinner, as a sauce for boiled meats. Miller says, "the seeds should not be sown before they are three years old, but not older than six;" although we read, in the Philosophical Transactions, of melons being raised from seeds that were forty-three years old. Melon-seeds are cooling and diuretic: they are anodyne, and were formerly used to take off stranguries occasioned by blisters; but sweet almonds are now preferred.

Pliny writes, that "melons, being eaten as meat, cool the body, and make it soluble: the fleshy substance of them applied to the eyes assuages pain, and restraineth the waterish and rheumatic flux. The root heals wens or ulcers; and being dried, stops vomits:" it was also used by the Romans in washing-balls and soap, as a good scourer.

The water-melon, or *cucurbita citullus*, is a fruit greatly appreciated in Egypt, China, the East Indies, and other hot climates, where it is extensively cultivated on account of its grateful coolness and delicious flavour; the flesh of it is so succulent, that it melts in the mouth, and its central pulp is fluid, like the cocoa-nut, and may be sucked, or poured out, through a hole in the rind, being a most refreshing beverage to the inhabitants of warm countries.

In same parts of Upper Egypt, whole districts are covered with water-melons. They are sown in the sand, on the banks of rivers: and it is in this situation, where the burning heat co-operates with the freshness of the water, which moistens the stalks, that this fruit acquires its agreeable pulp. The Egyptians esteem it equally wholesome and agreeable. Sonnini says, their own melons are not so good as those grown in Europe.

In so enlightened an age, we may venture occasionally to speak as theorists, practical gardeners being now generally too well informed to put speculative plans into practice without previously considering well the effects likely to be produced. The author is of opinion that by the assistance of steam-pits water-melons could now be grown in sea-sand only, which, while it retains its heat, would also nourish by its nitrous particles.

The water-melon is allowed to be eaten in fevers and

inflammatory complaints. One kind of the water-melon is pickled like gherkins, and much used by the French cooks in their fricassees; and they are sometimes baked in sweet wine. Gerard mentions, that the surgeons who belonged to the fleet, brought home many kinds of melons and pompions from the shores of the Mediterranean sea; but they could not have been ripened well in this country, before glasses were used for that purpose; and Parkinson seems to have been the earliest English author who gives directions for making hot-beds for melons, and covering them with bell glasses, which was in 1629.

We have already observed that, the perfumed fruits should be gathered from twenty-four to forty-eight hours before they have acquired the last degree of their maturity, but which must be regulated according to their nature and the heat of the season. The quality and flavour of the melon depend more upon the time of gathering and treatment when gathered than any other fruit; we shall, therefore, translate what Mons. Cadet de Vaux remarks in "Le Ménage des Fruits:" "When melons are not ripe, or unequally so, the portion of flesh next to the stalk is of an intolerable bitterness; a bitterness destined to be converted into a sugared principle. But break it off from the branch and let it acquire a secondary maturity, partly on the hot bed and partly in the hot-house, or, if the weather is very hot, in a cool place, when it will become excellent; whilst if ripened on the vine it would not be half so valuable. When the fruit has acquired all its perfume, it is savoury, melting and juicy, because its acid and its water are not yet perfectly combined; the digestion will be easier, and nothing is to be feared from a slight excess that we may indulge in with fruits thus perfectioned by time, by a mild fermentation, which is only the intestine movement which the frequent alternative of temperature excites: thus sensuality is here found, which is not very common, perfectly agreeing with health."

Madame de Genlis relates, that "the master of Lockman, the famous fabulist, who was a slave, having given him a bitter melon, was astonished to see him eat the whole of it; and, on naming his surprise, received this answer: 'I have experienced so many benefits from you,' said Lockman, 'that it cannot be strange that I should have eaten without complaint the first bitter fruit which you ever presented me with.' This answer so affected his master, that he gave Lockman his liberty."

MULBERRY.—MORUS.

Natural order, Scabridæ. A genus of the Monœcia Tetandria class.

" The mulberry-tree was hung with blooming wreaths;
The mulberry-tree stood centre of the dance;
The mulberry-tree was hymn'd with dulcet airs;
And from his touchwood trunk the mulberry-tree
Supplied such relics as devotion holds
Still sacred, and preserves with pious care."

Cowper.

In the Persian language this tree is called *Tút* (توت). The Greeks called the tree *Μορεα*, and the fruit *Μορον*, hence the Latin name *Morus*. The Dutch call it *Maulberham*, from whence probably the English name. The derivation of the generic name seems most probably from *μωρος*, *stultus, per antiphrasin;* the mulberry-tree being reputed the wisest of trees, in not budding till cold weather is fully past. Pliny says, if you want a sign that the winter is past, and all the cold entirely gone, when you see the mulberry-tree bud and put out leaves, fear no more frost nor hard weather, to do harm for that year.

" This fruit, in Heraldry, is an hieroglyphic of wisdom, whose property is to speak and to do all things in opportune season."—*Guillim.*

The mulberry-tree is mentioned in the 2nd book of Samuel, where we read that David came upon the Philistines, and smote them "over against the mulberry-trees." Again, in the Psalms we read, "He destroyed their vines with hailstones, and their mulberry-trees with frost."

This fruit was first brought from Persia into Greece and Rome, and was more esteemed by the Romans, even in their most luxurious days, than any other fruit.

Ovid has celebrated this tree in his story of Pyramus and Thisbe:—

> "The berries, stain'd with blood, began to shew
> A dark complexion, and forget their snow;
> While, fatten'd with a flowing gore, the root
> Was doom'd for ever to a purple fruit.
> The pray'r which, dying, Thisbe had preferr'd,
> Both gods and parents with compassion heard:
> The whiteness of the mulberry soon fled,
> And, ripening, sadden'd in a dusky red."

Pliny observes (book xv. c. 24), that "there is no other tree that was so neglected by the wit of man, either by grafting, or in giving it names, except that of making the fruit large and fair." "At Rome," he continues, "we make a difference between the mulberries of Ostia and those of Tusculum." This author observes, in his xvith book, c. 25, that "of all the cultivated trees, the mulberry is the last that buds, and which it never does until the cold weather is past; and was therefore called the wisest of all trees: but when it begins to put forth buds, it dispatches the business in one night, and that with so much force, that their breaking forth may be evidently heard."

Martyn tells us in his edition of Miller, that the silkworm was unknown to Theophrastus and Pliny; but this able compiler must have overlooked the 22d chapter of the 11th book of the world's greatest naturalist, where Pliny says, "The silkworm in Assyria is called *Bombyx*, when a fly; it afterwards grows to a *Bombylius*, and then to a *Necydalus*: of which, in six months after, come the silk-worms, *Bombyces*. These worms spin the silk of which our expensive ladies form their costly garments and superfluous apparel, which we call *Bombycina*. The first that devised the means to unwind these webs of the silkworm, and to weave the same again, was a woman in Coos, named Pamphila, daughter of Latous; and we must not," says this author, "defraud her of due honour and praise for the invention of those fine transparent silk fabricks, which, instead of apparel to cover and hide, shew the person through them."

In the following chapter he describes the silkworms of Coos in a manner that convinces us that their introduction to Europe was earlier than has been generally supposed. After describing the worm, he says, "they enwrap and enfold themselves in a round ball of the thread; they are then taken and put into earthen pots, and covered with bran to keep them warm. He tells us farther, that these balls are put into some moisture before they are unwound by a spindle made of some light reed, and from this (says he, satirically,) is made that fine silk cloth which even men are not now ashamed to put on and use in the summer, that they may go thinly clad. How could they carry armour on their backs, their common clothing being now too heavy?"

The mulberry was much used in medicine by the Romans, particularly for the diseases of the mouth, the windpipe, the uvula, and the stomach. The leaves and the roots were also used medicinally by them.—(*Pliny*, *b*. xxiii. *c*. 17.)

The mulberry-tree is stated to have been introduced into this country in the year 1548, and it is said that it was first planted at Sion House, where the original trees still thrive, and which we have seen since the first part of this work has been put to press. The interior of these trees is so entirely decayed, that the timber has so far returned to its native earth, that it will crumble in the hand; yet its branches, that are supported by props, are so well nourished by means of the bark, that the fruit and the foliage appear as luxuriant as those of the youngest trees: a strong proof of the durability of the mulberry-tree in this country. The first Duke of Northumberland said he could trace these trees back three centuries.

This fruit is mentioned by Tusser, in 1557, and by Gerard in 1597, who notices both the white and the black mulberry, and says they grow in sundry gardens in England: he adds, "that in Italy they do maintain great woods and groves of them, that their silk-worms may feed thereon."

The planting of mulberry-trees was much encouraged by King James the First, about the year 1600; but parties running so high at that period, the attention of the nation was occupied on political affairs; and the procuring of silk in England was neglected, and has never since been attempted, although the mulberry-tree has been found to thrive exceedingly well, and the silk-worms to spin as well as in any other part of the world. The mulberry-trees are now alive, and bearing fruit in many parts of the country, that were planted in the time of James the First; which is a proof of their durability. The author has lately seen a mulberry-tree, of the Nigra species, which is supposed to be one of the oldest in England, in the garden of the Rev. Dr. Crombie, adjoining Greenwich Park; and, notwithstanding its neglected and dilapidated state, it is one of the greatest curiosities he has ever seen in the shape of a fruit-tree in this country. It throws out ten large branches so near the earth, that it has the appearance of half a score of large trees rather than of one; and notwithstanding many of the projecting branches have been sawed off, still it completely covers a circumference of one hundred and fifty feet; and although the elder-trees have fixed their abode in some parts of the trunk, and other parts are covered with ivy, yet it continues to give shoots as vigorous as the youngest tree, and produces the finest mulberries in England. It is a regular bearer; and the gardener assured him that he gathered more than eighty quarts a week during the season.

We have noticed in the History of Cultivated Vegetables that the City of London petitioned the Parliament to prevent the use of hops in beer, and Newcastle coals as fuel; we are now going to prove that it was from the ignorance of the City merchants in asking, and the weakness of king James's ministers in granting, that England does not at this time abound in mulberry-trees, and that our unemployed cottagers are not profitably occupied at the present moment in winding and weaving the silks of our own country, instead of pressing so heavily on the parochial purse as to endanger the prosperity of the agriculturist.

"King James did," says Evelyn, "with extraordinary care, recommend it (the planting of mulberry-trees) to this nation by a book of directions, acts of council, and all other princely assistance."

In the year 1600, we find that by the special order of that monarch, the first mulberry garden known in England was planted at Charlton Park, near Blackheath, Kent, by Mons. Vetron from Picardy, and Matthew Stellendge, Esq. to whom a patent royal was granted to plant mulberry-trees in all parts of England. The motive was a hope that Britain, in a few years, might be able to keep the silk markets with her neighbours; and the scheme for a while succeeded; and so sedulous were the King and his whole royal family in feeding silkworms and preparing thread, that the Queen had silk enough of her own winding to make many yards of taffeta, which being wrought into proper garments, her Majesty, on the King's birthday, appeared at Court in a complete suit, all the effect of her Majesty's own industry. The prosperity of the royal scheme was beyond expectation; but upon a warm representation of the merchants respecting the impolicy of checking the imports, and other causes likely to arise, the pursuit declined as rapidly as it had advanced, and in a very short time not a public silk-work was to be seen, except at this place where they had their commencement. These identical trees were cut down, and sold by auction in 1821, and the timber was in fine preservation, although of two centuries vegetation.

Buckingham House is said to be built on the site of the old mulberry garden which adjoined to St. James's Park; others suppose it was situated where Arlington Street now is, as the piece of ground called Mulberry Garden was granted by Charles II. in 1672, to Henry earl of Arlington. These gardens were the rendezvous of fashion in the time of the commonwealth. Evelyn says in his Diary, May 10, 1654, " My Lady Gerrard treated us at Mulberry Garden, now y[e] onely place of refreshment about the towne for persons of y[e] best quality to be exceedingly cheated at, Cromwell and his partizans having shut up and seized on Spring Garden, w[ch] till now had been y[e] usual rendezvous for ladys and gallants at this season."

The mulberry-tree planted by Shakspeare afterwards became an object of veneration; and when cut down by an avaricious proprietor, the wood was made into various utensils, which sold for a high price, and were preserved with more than common affection. Mrs. Garrick has an arm-chair made from this tree, which the inimitable actor, her husband, greatly valued.

Henry the Fourth of France was equally unsuccessful with James of England in his attempt to introduce the mulberry-tree and the making of silk in his kingdom, although he filled the gardens, parks, and highways, with these trees, beginning in his own garden as an example. Louis the Fourteenth, by the indefatigable diligence of Mons. Colbert, superintendant of that monarch's manufactures, so successfully revived it, that it soon produced an incredible revenue to that nation.

Mons. Cadet de Vaux says, "Oliver de Serres has been called the Xenophon of France, principally from his pointing out the best mode of cultivating the mulberry-tree, a tree to which France is so much indebted."

Evelyn says, "It is demonstrable that mulberries in four or five years may be made to spread all over this land." Every later writer tells us, that in the south of England they would be sure to succeed; yet from the mouth of the Thames to that of the Severn, you will find ten thousand useless laurels cultivated without a purpose, or affording a single benefit excepting only their indifferent ornament, to one of these trees, which by their leaves would employ the people and enrich the country,—while their fruit would greatly assist to counteract the scorbutic complaints of our villagers, and afford us, by its juice, a wine little inferior to that produced from the grape—to say nothing about the beauty of the tree, or the value of the timber.

In speaking of the benefit derived from these trees, Evelyn says, "that they are frequently let to farm for vast sums; so as one sole tree has yielded the proprietor a rent of twenty shillings per annum for the leaves only, and six or seven pounds of silk, worth as many pounds sterling, in five or six weeks, to those who kept the worms.

We have already proved the longevity of these trees, we shall presently shew that they will thrive in barren or in rich land; but we are now going to give the important remarks of an ingenious writer on rural economy, who says, "I am acquainted with but one tree of any growth or beauty, that seems to have the least capability of resisting the malign influence of the sea atmosphere; and that is the mulberry. From two or three grand specimens of this beautiful tree, of which I have had long knowledge, standing in the most exposed situations of the north-east coast of England, it seems not only to defy the enemy, but to delight in its situation, throwing out its noble limbs in all directions, and assuming a foliage rich, full, and tufted to its topmost boughs. One of these specimens to which I allude is of great magnitude, even though some of its vast limbs have been torn from it; but it is still in vigour, and in point of richness of effect, the oak itself is scarcely superior.

"These trees are also abundantly prolific, and in all good seasons the fruit arrives at perfection. Is it not singular, therefore, that the cultivation of this beautiful and useful species should have been so long neglected? It might be supposed, that one single flourishing specimen, in a situation where all other trees fail, would have been an inducement to the trial of others. The slow growth of the mulberry-tree may be urged as an objection; but, on the other hand, it appears to be a tree of great longevity, which is no small recommendation."

Let us not, therefore, obstinately persist in keeping this tree so great a stranger to our shores, but impress upon the minds of those who have estates on the eastern coast of Sussex, how much they would benefit posterity by forming plantations of mulberry-trees in many parts of the South Downs, particularly in the vicinity of Brighton, where more is wanting, and less is done, by way of embellishing the neighbourhood by planting, than in any other spot in the kingdom.

Should a few spirited land-proprietors make the experiment of grubbing up their hedge-rows, and planting fences of mulberry-trees, we have no doubt but that in a few years they would reap as great a profit from their hedges as from their corn. It would find immediate employ for many labourers, and would in time require the assistance of thousands of the lower classes to gather the leaves, and attend to the breeding and feeding of the silkworms, the winding of the silk, &c.; indeed, the whole process is calculated as an employ for the aged and the infirm, who, being unable to do laborious work, must now, of necessity, add to the weight of the parochial taxes. The author is fully of opinion that it would be the foundation of a permanent reduction in the poor-rates, which must continue to augment, unless employ be found equal to the increase of the population. It is worthy of notice that the trees which are planted for the feeding of the silkworms, are seldom suffered to grow to a height to injure the land; but they are kept as shrubs or espaliers. The great nurseries of mulberry plants in the plain of Valencia, in Spain, are produced from seeds obtained by rubbing a rope of esparts with ripe mulberries, and then burying the rope two inches under ground. As the young plants come up, they are drawn and transplanted; the trees are afterwards set out in rows in the fields, and pruned once in two years.

It is supposed that this plan could be advantageously carried into effect without the loss of a single year; as many persons whom we have consulted on the subject are of opinion, that the young plants from the seeds would be as good to feed the worm as those of older trees. Father Loureiro states, that in Cochin China they root up the plants every third year, and make fresh plantations of the cuttings, because the young shoots afford a more delicate food for the worms, and produce a finer silk.

At Genoa, and other countries where the silkworms

spin, even the coverings of the chrysalis are turned to profit, as from these the most valuable and beautiful artificial flowers are made, which greatly excel those made in Paris from cambric.

Let us now notice what remarks have been made by ingenious travellers and men of science and observation on these valuable trees. Hanway tells us that "Ghilan is a part of Persia where the silk flourishes, and particularly the mulberry-tree, although the moisture of the earth is so great as to be unwholesome; and in the year 1741, the snow fell in such quantities, that in some places it was said to be seven feet in depth.

M. de Goyne observes, that those mulberry-trees that grow on light sandy barren grounds, that have little moisture, will produce the finest and strongest silk, while those which are produced in fertile fat land, abounding in juice, yield a coarser and weaker silk; that young trees from six to twelve years old will not produce so fine or good silk as trees of eighteen to twenty years old. He tells us, that a closet twelve feet square and ten feet high, will contain eighteen thousand worms, and that one hundred and fifty balls ought to produce one ounce of silk, and a shed of the size described, seven pounds and a half.

Swinburn says, "The fertile plains of Reggio contain avenues of mulberry-trees. On each side of the road are houses erected for the accommodation of silkworms, upon a particular plan of construction. The windows are long, and not above six inches wide. This narrowness prevents too great a quantity of air being admitted at a time, which would overpower the tender insects. When the eggs are on the point of being hatched, these holes are shut, and a moderate fire is kept up in the rooms. The worms, as soon as they come out, are placed upon beds of reeds, and there fed with leaves of the mulberry-tree, which in this district is invariably of the red sort. It is preferred to the white fruited kind, as being a later shooter, and better adapted to the periods of the worms' life, which would be endangered from late changes of weather, if forced out of its shell at the time the white mulberry produces its leaves: besides, it is the opinion of silk-workers, that worms fed with the red mulberry produce a more compact heavy silk, than those that live upon the leaves of the white one. I am apt to think this a vulgar prejudice, unwarranted by experience, as the Chinese, Piedmontese, and Languedocians, prefer the white sort. In order to provide food for them in cases of a blight among mulberry-trees, other leaves have been tried, and bramble-tops have been found the best succedaneum. In the management of this produce, the Calabrese are much inferior to the Tuscans, who, though many degrees farther north, contrive to have two hatchings or seasons in a year. These silkworm-houses are the property of respectable families in Reggio, who furnish rooms, leaves, eggs, and every necessary implement; take two-thirds of the profit, and leave the other for the attendants. A succession of eggs is imported from Leghorn, and other places, to renew the breed, and by frequent changes keep up the quality of the silk. Lizards are great enemies to the silkworms in Italy; this, and the tyranny exercised by lords in that country, would not be felt in England. A tax, also, has been laid on every mulberry-tree, which caused many hundred to be cut down."

Nievhoff says, in his "History of China," that "in the province of Chekiang are several woods consisting of mulberry-trees, which the inhabitants cut every year, that so they may not grow up to any largeness; for they find by experience, that the leaves of the lower trees make the best silk: so that by this only means, all that keep silkworms know very well how to distinguish the first spinning of the silk from the second, because the first is the product of the soft and tender leaves which shoot forth in the spring, and are then eaten by the worm; but the hard and sowre summer leaves make the second spinning; which alteration of the same food does occasion so great a difference in the work of these small creatures. And such is the infinite abundance of silk in this province, that ten suits of silk may be bought cheaper than one of cloth in Europe."

About the year 877, all the mulberry-trees in China were cut down by the revolters under an officer of the name of *Baichu*, on which account the silk-trade failed for some years, to the great distress of the inhabitants.

Not to dwell longer on the subject of the trees, let us next take a review of the silk-trade, and follow it from Persia to our own island, in which we shall not omit to notice the exertions made by Queen Elizabeth to secure a part of this valuable trade to the people she governed, and the dangers and difficulties that attended the procuring raw silk, in an age that had not contemplated the possibility of procuring it from our own fields.

The mulberry must have been a most valuable tree to the Persians and Chinese in ancient times, as it enabled them exclusively to supply all the known world with silk, the price of which, in Europe, was an equal weight of pure gold, even as late as Justinian's time, A.D. 526. Madame de Genlis gives the invention of silks to the Chinese: she relates in her work (La Botanique, Historique et Littéraire), that the Empress Siling Chi, wife to Hoamti, was desired by that emperor to examine the silkworms, and endeavour to turn their web to some useful purpose, which she did, after various trials and experiments; and by feeding them with mulberry-leaves, she discovered the means of winding the silks, and the making of silk-stuffs, which she embroidered with flowers and birds. Voltaire states, that the valuable insect that produces the silk, is originally from China, from whence it was carried into Persia, though not until very late, together with the art of weaving the down in which it is enveloped.

It is now 2143 years since wrought silks were first introduced into Greece from Persia; and about forty-nine years afterwards the Grecians obtained them from India.

In Rome a law was passed by the senate in the reign of Tiberius, forbidding men to debase themselves by wearing silk, as being fit only for women.

Heliogabalus was the first Roman that wore a garment all silk, which must have been about the year 220, A.D. The Emperor Aurelianus, who died in 275, denied his empress a robe of silk, because it was too dear. In the year 555 some monks, who had been in India, brought some eggs of the silkworm to Constantinople, where, in time, they produced raw silk, which was manufactured at Athens, Thebes, Corinth, &c.

Charlemagne sent Offa, king of Mercia, a present of a belt, and two silken vests, in the year 780, which is the earliest account we have of silk being seen in this country.

In 1130 the Sicilians were taught to breed silkworms, and to spin and weave silk; from whence the art was carried to Italy, Spain, and the south of France. Some noblemen's ladies wore silk mantles at a ball given at Kenilworth Castle, in Warwickshire, in 1286; and it was worn by the English clergy in 1534.

Stockings made of silk were first worn by Henry the Second, of France, in 1543; and in 1549 mulberry-trees were propagated through all France; and the breeding of silkworms was much encouraged by Henry the Fourth of that country.

Henry the Eighth of England received a few pair of

silk stockings from Spain; but knit silk stockings were not known until they were made by Mrs. Montague, who presented the first pair to Queen Elizabeth. Thus silk has gradually come into use; and it is now so common in this country, that it would be diffioult to find a female servant in the streets of London, or any part of the kingdom, who had not some portion of her dress composed of silk.

Anthonie Jenkinson obtained the assistance of Queen Elizabeth, at the commencement of her reign, to enable him to trade with Persia in raw silk; but his journey thither was attended with very little success beyond an introduction obtained by the Queen's letter, which ran thus:—

"To the right mightie, and right victorious prince, the great Sophie, emperor of the Persians, Medes, Parthians, Hyrcanes, &c. &c. desiring safe pasports for the purpose of making merchandize, &c. dated the 25th day of Aprill, in the yeere of the creation of the world 5523, and of our Lord Jesus Christ 1561, and of our raigne the third."

In 1579 Christopher Burrough went into Persia, and returned home in 1581. He built a vessel on the Volga at Niezanovogorode, in which he transported several kinds of merchandize as far as Baku. At Niezabad his vessel was stranded and great part of his cargo lost. At Derbend he sold a part of his cargo to the Turks, and bought another vessel to bring home his returns of raw silk; but either through want of experience, or constrained by necessity, he came to Russia so late in the season as November, which occasioned his ship being cut to pieces by the ice: the cargo, however, was saved in a boat, which floating out to sea with the ice, and being in great danger of perishing, was at length frozen up. The crew left the boat and her cargo, and went in search of assistance; but, losing their way, their lives were much endangered by hunger, as well as by a shower of arrows from a flying party of Nagai Tartars. At length they had the good fortune to bring their cargo safe to Astrachan, and thus ended the British Caspian commerce.

However, Monsieur de Thou remarks, that the English made immense profits by their trade with Persia, by reason that in Queen Elizabeth's reign they had the exclusive privilege of importing all manner of foreign commodities into Russia. By this privilege they were encouraged to visit more carefully the several provinces of that vast empire.

In 1626 Sir Robert Shirley was sent embassador from the English court to Abas the Great, king of Persia; when this king promised that he would deliver in Gambroon ten thousand bales of silk, (supposed to mean bales of seven batmans of twelve pounds and one-fifth English, not twenty-five batmans, as now usually shipped on the Caspian,) and take the value in English cloth: his object seemed to be to deprive the Turks of this trade, which greatly enriched them.

We have already proved that the breeding of silkworms was known in the Archipelago as early as the first century, which makes the monkish tale of the missionaries a few centuries too late. The story goes, that about the year 551 two Persian monks, employed as missionaries in some of the Christian churches established in India, penetrated into the country of the Seres, or China. There they observed the labours of the silkworm, and became acquainted with the art of working up its productions into a variety of elegant fabrics. They explained to the Greek Emperor at Constantinople these mysteries, hitherto unknown in Europe; and undertook to bring to the capital a sufficient number of these wonderful insects. This they accomplished by conveying the eggs of the silk worm in a hollow cane.

Soon after the conquest of Constantinople by the Venetians in 1204, they attempted the establishment of the silk manufacture in their dominions; and in a short time the silk fabricks of Venice vied with those of Greece and Sicily; for a monarch of the latter country, who had travelled into Greece, brought back with him people who could nourish silkworms and manufacture silk. Thus it travelled by degrees through all Italy, which, with Constantinople, for some ages supplied the northern parts of the world. The Spaniards, laying a heavy tax upon raw silk, were the first cause that induced the French monarch to attempt the manufacture in his country; and we now find that the wealthy families of Italy get their silks from France. England had this manufactory first established through the want of policy and good government of France, whose industrious artizans being driven from their homes through difference in religious opinions, settled themselves in Spitalfields, where to this day many of their posterity continue to manufacture silks.

In 1661, Evelyn says, "I went to ye wonderfull engine for weaving silk stockings, said to have been ye invention of an Oxford scholler forty years since."

A machine had been erected in Savoy for weaving silks, of which, notwithstanding the punishment of immediate death decreed against those who should make any description of it, Sir Thomas Lombe contrived to get a model; and in the year 1714, he erected a machine at Derby, for which, in 1718, he obtained a patent. This machine contained 26,726 wheels, and 97,746 movements, which worked 73,726 yards of silk thread every time the water-wheel went round, which it did three times in one minute; one water-wheel gave motion to all the rest of the wheels and movements, of which any one could be stopped separately; one fire-engine conveyed warm air to every individual part of the machine; and one regulator governed the whole work.

On the 3d April, 1732, we find his Majesty gave his assent to the bill for granting fourteen thousand pounds to Sir Thomas Lombe, as a recompense for his introducing this machine for working silk.

Having thus obtained artists and machinery, let us no longer neglect the cultivation of the tree that is to employ them.

It is observed in Evelyn's Sylva, that this tree possesses the peculiar property of breeding no vermin, neither does it harbour any caterpillar except the silkworm. The fruit when ripe stains the hands; but, when unripe, is a good cleanser.

It is one of the latest trees to blossom, and one of the earliest to ripen its fruit; which, when ripe, is of a cooling aperient nature, but quite of an opposite quality when unripe, being a strong astringent.

The root of the mulberry-tree has an acrid bitter taste: it is powerful in its effects; and has been used with great advantage against worms, particularly the tape-worm. The juice of this fruit, mixed with cider, is esteemed the best of all the English vinous liquors.

Miller mentions eight varieties of this agreeable fruit; which appears to be again duly appreciated at the dessert, as we find it is cultivated in a hot-house belonging to T. A. Knight, Esq., who, we believe, is the first person that has attempted to force this excellent berry. In the garden of Thos. Wm. Coke, Esq. M. P., at Holkham-hall, Norfolk, there are two mulberry-trees trained to a trellis, upon a south wall. These trees are about sixteen feet high, and the lateral extent of the branches of one of them is upwards of ninety-four feet, and the other exceeds ninety-seven feet. They have been planted about thirty years; and it is found that the fruit is much larger than that produced on standard trees, their time of maturity much earlier, and that they afford an abundant succession from the middle of July until October. They are pruned twice a-year, leaving spurs of two inches long, which, at the winter pruning, are shortened to about an inch in length. It is both a common and a bad practice to make grass-plats under mulberry-trees, by this means retarding the ripening of the fruit by the coolness of the grass; whereas the heat reflected from the earth would greatly promote the ripening.

The Alba, or white mulberry, is a native of China.

The Nigra, or black mulberry, is the tree of the largest size, and the fruit is of a blackish red colour, and from it a good wine is made: this variety is a native of Persia.

The Rubra, or red mulberry, is a native of Virginia.

The Japan mulberry-tree is called *Papyrifera*, from the bark, of which a kind of paper is made.

The fact that the mulberry-tree seldom produces fruit until it has arrived at a considerable age, has been much against its cultivation; but it is now discovered, that by grafting it from the aged trees, or, to use a common phrase, putting an old head on young shoulders, it soon becomes fruitful.

It is said that these trees, as standards, never require pruning; but a friend who pruned his trees by the recommendation of the author, according to the plan practised at Holkham Hall, found that his mulberry-trees made more wood, and greater progress the following year, than they had done altogether in the six former years.

NECTARINE.—AMYGDALUS, NUCIPERSICA.

Natural order, Pomaceæ. A genus of the Icosandria Monogynia class.

"Blushing like youthful cheeks: the nectarine full
Of lavish juice."

This fruit is thought to have derived its name from the Nectar of the heathen gods. Matthiolus and Cæsalpinus call it *Nucipersica,* because it resembles the smoothness of the outer skin of the walnut.

It is a native of Persia, and was brought into this country with the peach, about the year 1524. It does not appear at that time to have been distinguished by any name distinct from other peaches, of which it is a species, as Gerard was living when it was first obtained, and published his History of Plants about thirty-five years later, wherein he describes four kinds of peaches, and says, "they are set and planted in gardens and vineyards: I have them all in my garden," continues he, "with many other sorts," which shews there was a variety when first introduced. He mentions one kind of peach which appears to have been the Nectarine, *Persica rubra.* "The fruit or peaches," says Gerard, "of this sort, be round, of a red colour on the outside: the meat likewise about the stone is of a gallant red colour. These kinds of peaches are very like to wine in taste, and therefore marvellous pleasant."

Pliny says, of all the peaches, the one most admired

in Rome is that named Duracina, from the solid substance of the meat; which seems to agree with the quality of the nectarine, the principal distinction of which, from other peaches, consists in the firmness and fineness of its pulp, its superior flavour, and smooth skin.

There have been many instances of nectarines having grown not only on peach trees, but on branches bearing both peaches and nectarines, without either budding or grafting. Whether this is owing to its being so nearly allied to the peach, or by the pollen of the nectarine being conveyed by the bees or the wind, we have not yet been able to ascertain, although this circumstance has occurred in the gardens of persons eminent for their knowledge of fruits, as Mr. Wilmot, of Isleworth; James Wyatt, Esq., Hounslow; William Gilpin, Esq., East Sheen; and in the garden of the Earl of Lanesborough, Yorkshire. Having, however, observed that the fruit of the vegetable marrow has been changed in the same manner when growing with cucumbers, we are confirmed in the opinion that it is owing to the accidental impregnation of the blossom. This fruit is generally esteemed more wholesome than the peach, as it is more delicious in flavour, but like other watery fruits is best before meals.

Thomson has beautifully distinguished it from the common peach in his Seasons :—

————As I steal along the sunny wall,
Where autumn basks with fruit empurpled deep,
My pleasing theme continual prompts my thought;
Presents the downy peach, the shining plum,
The ruddy, fragrant nectarine: and, dark
Beneath his ample leaf, the luscious fig.

But it is only when in fruit that the tree can well be distinguished from the peach, of which it is evidently only a variety. The favourite kinds of nectarines are *Fairchild's early nectarine*, which is the earliest: it is a round fruit not larger than the nutmeg peach, of a beautiful red colour, and ripens about the end of July or beginning of August.

The Newington nectarine is esteemed the finest flavoured of all the varieties; and when thoroughly ripe, it is thought by many persons not to be second to any fruit. It has a beautiful red colour next the sun, and a bright yellow towards the wall. The Scarlet, the Brugnon, the Roman red, the Golden, and several other varieties, are all more or less admired as they are suited with soil and situation to ripen. The latest ripe is the Peterborough, or late green nectarine, which generally ripens about the middle of October.

The flowers have an aromatic bitter taste, and, when fresh, an infusion of half an ounce in water, or a dram when dry, and sweetened with sugar, is a useful laxative for children. (*Brookes*, vol. 6.)

We particularly recommend these trees to be protected in the spring by sliding shutters of glass or oiled paper; the richness of the fruit when at the dessert will well repay the small expense, and a more regular crop may be anticipated, for, as Speechly justly remarks, "The decay of peach and nectarine trees almost uniformly commences on the upperside of the large branches: the cause of this defect, as I have constantly observed, is brought on by snow being permitted to lodge on the horizontal branches during the winter and spring months, but more particularly at the time of the rising of the sap in the spring. Snow lodging on the branches during that period, generally proves highly detrimental to them. In a severe season, the snow goes off by slow degrees, and what is dissolved by the rays of the sun by day, is constantly congealed into ice by the frost at night. Now, the capillary vessels which are thus exposed, being surcharged with moisture in the evening, the frost which comes on at night freezes the sap in the vessels which contain it, and causing it to expand, thus tears the vessels asunder, and brings on a decay of that part of the branch."

This particularly points out the necessity of protecting these trees in the spring; but where it is not convenient to do so, the snow should be removed from the branches by a pair of kitchen bellows, as by using a brush there would be danger of injuring the buds.

Where these trees are grown in tubs for the purpose of forcing, we should recommend the square-shaped box with a divided door on each side, which would give an opportunity of refreshing the roots with new mould, without removing the plants, and this should be done some time before they are removed into the hot-house. By this means of conveying nourishment, most large housed trees may be kept in a vigorous state.

OLIVE.—OLEA.

Natural order, Sepiariæ. A genus of the Diandria Monogynia class.

"I bear these peaceful branches in my hand."

THE generic name is derived from the Greek Ελαια, from λειος, *lævis*, smooth. *Olea* is generally put for the tree, *Oliva* for the fruit, and *Oleum* for the juice.

Of this tree we have very ancient mention, since it is related in the book of Genesis, that the dove which Noah sent out of the ark, returned with an olive-leaf in its mouth, by which he knew that the waters of the Deluge had abated. Since this time the olive-branch has been used as an emblem of peace by all civilized nations; and it is observed that a green bough answers the same purpose amongst the most savage people in every part of the world.

"High on the stern Æneas took his stand,
And held a branch of olive in his hand.
—Now suppliants, from Laurentum sent, demand
A truce, with olive branches in their hand."

Virgil.

"As the young olive, in some silvan scene,
Crown'd by fresh fountains with eternal green,
Lifts the gay head, in snowy flow'rets fair,
And plays and dances to the gentle air."

The olive-tree is said to have been transported from Egypt into Attica by the care of Cecrops, about one thousand five hundred and fifty-six years before the Christian era. In the fabulous histories of Greece, we are informed, that the gods having been called on to settle a dispute between Neptune and Minerva, arising from the desire of each of them to give name to the new city of Cecrops; they determined to give the preference to the one who should produce the most beneficial gift to mankind. Neptune, striking the ground with his trident, created a horse; but Minerva, by causing an olive-tree to spring from the earth, gained her point; and from her the city was called Athenæ, now Athens; since the olive, the emblem of peace or agriculture, was much preferable to the horse, the symbol of war and bloodshed. Minerva and the Graces are also represented as crowned with olive-branches.

A contribution of olives was given by all the Grecians who attended the Panathenæa, a festival held at Athens in honour of Minerva. Those who excelled in any of the games during this festival, were crowned with a wreath of olives, which grew in the grove of Academus, a place near the city, with spacious and shady walks, belonging to a man of that name. Plato having here opened a school of philosophy, all places of learning have been since called Academies.

As to the soil of the olive-tree, we may conclude, from several passages in Scripture, that it grew naturally in Syria; but particularly near Jerusalem, if we may judge by the Mount of Olives, so often mentioned in the New Testament. It was first planted in Italy in the thirteenth year of the reign of Servius Tullius, the sixth king of Rome.

The olive seems to have been highly appreciated by the Romans; as Pliny says, except the vine, there is not a tree bearing fruit of so great account as the olive. "Fenestella informs us," says this author, "that during the reign of Tarquinius Priscus, which was about the

183d year from the foundation of Rome, there were no olive-trees either in Italy, Spain, or Africa, which is a strong presumption that they grew originally only in Syria." Theophrastus states, that in the 440th year of the city, there were no olive-trees in Italy, but on the coast, and within forty miles of the sea; but Pliny says, in his time, they were to be found in the very heart of Spain and France, but that the olives of Syria, although smaller, produced the best oil. Virgil mentions but three kinds of olives: Columella mentions ten varieties, but says he believes they were much more numerous. The olive-tree is cultivated with great assiduity by the peasants, on the banks of the river Kizilasan in Persia.

The olive-tree was first introduced into England in the year 1570; but there is little inducement for us to cultivate it, since it is by no means handsome, and we have no desire for its ripe fruit. Besides, the climate in general is not sufficiently warm to assure us of a crop, though we have no doubt but it would flourish in many situations on the south side of the Sussex Downs, where the fig-tree thrives: indeed, in some parts of Devonshire it is found as a standard tree, and is seldom injured by the frost.

Several olive-trees were planted against a warm wall at Camden House near Kensington, which succeeded very well till their tops advanced above the wall; after which they were generally cut down to the top of the wall in winter. These in 1719 produced a good quantity of fruit, which grew so large as to be fit for pickling.

According to Columella, this tree flourishes best in dry hills that are full of white clay; for in moist and fat fields it produces plenty of leaves, but no fruit. Though this author contradicts the opinion that the olive will not grow sixty miles from the sea, he states, that where an oak has stood, it cannot be raised.

The olive-tree requires but little care in the cultivation, but it seldom produces fruit oftener than once in two years. Signor Battiloro describes a singular variety of olive-tree, which deviates so much from the general habit of the tree, that it produces four or five crops of fruit in the year, according to the temperature of the season, the olives being small and black, but affording delicious oil. The same intelligent observer has related the following anecdote:

"Francesco Longuano, a person known in Italy by his proficiency in literature, happening one day to converse with me concerning the olive-tree, mentioned that he had read in the writings of an ancient Greek author, whose name had escaped his recollection, that in the city of Coriolanum, near that of Venasso, there was an olive-tree which put forth blossoms every month, and that this Greek noticed the circumstance as a prodigy. That city, at present a village, called Ciurnalo, being at a little distance from my castle, I repaired to it, for the purpose of tracing, if possible, the remains of such a tree; and fortunately, owing to the kind attention of the priest, I actually encountered five of them; and on returning to the same spot in September, I found on them four different kinds of olives, and the recent blossoms of a fifth crop. The inhabitants call them *Olive d'ogni mese.*"

This fruit the modern Greeks during Lent eat in its ripe state, without any preparation, but a little pepper, or salt and oil.

The sweet olives in the south of Italy are of a large size, and eaten annually in October, when pulled from the trees; or if neglected by the inhabitants, they are greedily devoured by birds.

We receive the olive from the south of France, from Spain, and Portugal, pickled in the following manner: it is gathered unripe, and suffered to steep in water some days, and afterwards put into a ley of water and barilla, or kali, with the ashes of olive-stones calcined, or with lime. It is then bottled or barrelled with salt and water, and in this state do we meet with it at the desserts of our most wealthy tables, where fashion has done much in having introduced and given a fondness for olives, which seems to be an acquired taste: however, they are grateful to the stomach, and are considered good to promote digestion and appetite.

But olives are chiefly cultivated for the sake of the oil that they produce, which is not only a profitable article of commerce, but forms a principal one of food to the inhabitants of the places where these trees are found. This oil is contained in the pulp only, whereas other fruits have it in the nut or kernel. It is obtained by simple pressure, in the following manner: the olives are first bruised by a mill-stone, and afterwards put into the trough of a press, which, by means of turning a strong screw, forces all the liquor out, which is called *virgin oil.* A coarser kind is obtained afterwards, by adding hot water to the bruised fruit.

Oil is the main support of commerce in some provinces of Italy. It forms the great trade of the Gallipolitans. It appears by the books of their custom-house, that in 1766, eleven thousand four hundred and fifty-nine salme were shipped off for national markets, and thirty-four thousand four hundred and ninety-three salme for foreign ones. This quantity cannot be valued at less than a million of ducats. The exportation of oil brings into Calabria-ultra half a million of ducats annually.

The olive-tree is attended to with the nicest care near Naples, and no trouble spared to increase its fruitfulness, or revive prolific vigour in plants that begin to feel the decay of age; at one time they manure or water the roots; in winter the peasants bare the roots of the old trees, lay upon them a thin coat of litter, and leave them thus, during four months, to imbibe the restorative salts of the atmosphere. Few of them have any principal bole; for all predominant shoots are early cut out, that every part may derive equal benefit from the influence of the sun. The fruit in some places is suffered to hang till it falls through ripeness.

Aristæus, son of Apollo by Cyrene, was regarded as a rural deity for having taught mankind to extract olive oil, and also to make honey, cheese, and butter. The wrestlers were anointed with it; and it was made a substitute for butter, which among the Romans was used as a medicine.

We find in the book of Leviticus, that oil formed a principal part of the meat-offerings, which the Israelites presented to the Lord.

Pliny informs us, that in the 500th year of the city, when Appius Claudius and L. Junius were consuls together, a pound of oil was sold for twelve asses; but that in the year 680, ten pounds of oil sold for one ass, and that, in twenty-two years after that time, Italy was able to furnish the provinces with oil; and it was much used at their baths, having, as they supposed, the property of warming the body, and defending it against the cold.

The best olive-oil at present is obtained from Provence.

Although the greater number of the English eat but very little olive-oil, yet oil in some shape forms a considerable part of our food, both animal and vegetable, and affords much nourishment: but with some, oily substances do not unite with the contents of the stomach, especially where acids abound.

Dr. A. Hunter was decidedly of opinion, that all plants receive their principal nourishment from oily particles incorporated with water, by means of an alkaline salt, or absorbent earth. Till oil is made miscible, it is unable to enter the radical vessels of vegetables; and on that account, Providence has bountifully supplied all natural soils with chalky or other absorbent particles.

Olive-oil is esteemed good for the breast and lungs; it tempers the sharp choleric humours in the bowels, is useful against all corrosive mineral poisons, as arsenic, &c.; opens the urinary passages; and is good for the stone and gravel. Olive-oil congeals at 38° of Fahrenheit.

The wood of the olive-tree is used by cabinet-makers, from its being beautifully veined, and admitting an excellent polish.

These trees may be obtained from those Italian houses which import orange-trees; they require nearly the same treatment; but when they have taken good root, they may be taken from the pots, and planted in a warm situation.

ORANGE.—CITRUS.—AURANTIUM.

Natural order, Bicornes. A genus of the Polyadelphia Icosandria class.

"Here orange-trees with blooms and pendants shine,
And vernal honours to their autumn join;
Exceed their promise in the ripen'd store,
Yet in the rising blossom promise more.

Pope.

The derivation of the generic name of this fruit is uncertain. Some say it is from a place in Asia so called. Vossius states the Latins derived it from Africa, while others affirm that it is an Arabic word.

The China, or sweet oranges, with which this country is now so amply supplied, and at such moderate prices, that all classes of society enjoy them as perfectly as if they had been indigenous to the climate, were not known to the ancient Europeans. They were first brought into Europe by Juan de Castro, a celebrated Portuguese warrior, who made them a present to the Condé Mellor, the king of Portugal's prime minister, who was only able to raise one plant from a great number that were brought to Europe. This tree, which was planted in 1548, and from which all the European orange-trees of this sort were produced, is said to be now alive at Lisbon, in the garden of Count S. Laurent.

The Romans had endeavoured to cultivate the citrus before the Christian era, for the beauty of the tree and its medicinal qualities; but, as it has already been observed in the history of the lemon, they could not succeed in the time of Pliny, who says, (Book xvi. c. 32) "The Assyrian pome-citron-tree will not bear fruit out of Syria." The same author, in his 12th book, c. 3, informs us that the Romans were acquainted with the Persian and Median pome-citron; but he never mentions it as a fruit to be eaten: the kernels, he states, were in particular employed by the Parthians, to sweeten the breath. In his 13th book, chap. 15, we are informed, that the Romans had tables made of the citron wood, which they procured from Mauritania and Cyrenaica, in Africa.

Some authors are of opinion, that the orange was the golden apple of the Hesperides; which, as the ancient Europeans could not propagate it, was said to have been taken back by Minerva. The fable states, that Hercules, to obtain information of this garden, seized Nereus, god of the sea, in his sleep, who directed him to Africa. If he had to cross the deserts of that country to obtain this fruit, the allusion of its being guarded by a dragon, is both natural and just; the fruit was therefore called *Aurea mala Hesperidum.*

About the eleventh or twelfth century several varieties of the orange were cultivated in the neighbourhood of Reggio, from whence they were extended over Italy, and from hence they were taken to Spain and Portugal, being found much hardier than was at first expected; therefore the sweet orange, soon after it was introduced, became plentiful in these countries, where there were already abundance of stocks to graft on. Gerard notices in his work, which was published in 1597, that orange and lemon-trees grew on the coast of Italy, and in the islands of the Adriatic; and on the coast of Spain they were, says he, in great quantities, as well as in certain provinces of France, which lie upon the midland coast.

At the present time, these trees are cultivated in Italy to so great an extent, that there are almost forests of them. Prince Antonio Borghese, at his palace near Rome, has upwards of seventy sorts of orange and lemon-trees, among which are some very rare kinds: it is a fruit so much esteemed in Italy, where it thrives well, that apples, pears, and cherries, have almost become extinct in that country.

Lord Lyttelton says:—

"In the soft bosom of Campania's vale,
When now the wintry tempests all are fled,
And genial summer breathes her gentle gale,
The verdant orange lifts its beauteous head;
From every branch the balmy flow'rets rise,
On every bough the golden fruits are seen;
With odours sweet it fills the smiling skies;
But, in the midst of all its blooming pride,
A sudden blast from Apenninus blows,
Cold with perpetual snows;
The tender blighted plant shrinks up its leaves, and dies."

The delightful perfume of an orange-grove is such as to scent the air for miles; and the tree gives a succession of flowers during the whole summer on which account it is cultivated in all green-houses.

Cotton observes:—

"The orange, with a vernal face,
Wears ev'ry rich autumnal grace,
While the young blossoms here unfold,
There shines the fruit like pendant gold;
Citrons their balmy sweets exhale,
And triumph in the distant gale."

Large orangeries have been built for the express purpose of housing these trees: the most magnificent one is that of Versailles, built by Louis the Fourteenth.

Oranges were known in this country in the time of Henry the Eighth, but I find no account of the orange-tree being cultivated in England prior to Queen Elizabeth's reign. The Seville orange-tree appears to have been first planted the year before the East India Company was incorporated, and two years previous to the return of Sir Francis Drake, our first circumnavigator. It is said to have been introduced by Sir Francis Carew, and first planted at his seat at Beddington in Surrey. Evelyn says, in his Diary, 27th September 1658, "I went to Beddington, (Surry,) that ancient seat of the Carews, famous for the first-orange gardens in England, being now overgrown trees planted in ye ground, and secured in winter with a wooden tabernacle and stoves." In September 1700, the same author notes, that he again visited Beddington, and that "the orange-trees, which had then been standing 120 years, large and goodly trees, and laden with fruit, were now in decay, the estate being fallen to a child under age, and kept only by a servant or two from utter dilapidation." This would make the introduction of orange-trees to this country about the year 1580.

These trees were entirely killed by the great frost in 1739–40. They had been enclosed by a permanent building only the year before, and it is supposed that the dampness of the new building, or the want of a sufficient air and light, might have assisted in destroying these venerable trees, which, according to the account of Mr. Henry Day, the gardener, were about fourteen feet high, and the girth of the stem twenty-nine inches, with branches that spread from ten to twelve feet each way.

Lord Bacon, mentions the housing of orange and lemon-trees in this country to keep them in the winter. He also states, that if the seeds of oranges be sown in April, they produce an agreeable salad.

Henrietta Maria, queen of Charles the First, had an orange-house and orange-garden at her mansion, Wimbleton Hall, in the parish of Wimbleton, in the county of Surrey; and by an estimate and survey which was made in the month of November 1649, for the sale of that property, by order of the Parliament, we find how highly orange-trees were estimated even in those turbulent days. It is described as follows:—

"In the north side of which sayd oringe-garden, there stands one large garden-house; the outwalls of brick, fitted for the keepinge of oringe-trees, neatly covered with blue slate, and ridged and guttered with lead; the materials of which house, with the greate doores, and the iron thereof, with a certeine stone pavement lying before these doores, in nature of a little walke, four foote broad, and seventy-nine foote long, wee valew to bee worth 66*l.* 13*s.* 4*d.*

"In which sayd garden-house there are now standing, in squared boxes fitted for that purpose, fortie-two oringe trees bearing fayre and large oringes, which trees, with the boxes, and the earth and materials therein feeding the same, wee valew at ten poundes a tree, one tree with another, in toto, amounting unto 420*l.*

"In the sayd garden-house there now allsoe is one lemon-tree, bearing greate and very large lemons, which, together with the box that it grows in, and the earth and materialls therein feeding the same, wee valew at 20*l.*

"In the sayd garden-house there now allsoe is one pome-citron-tree, which, togeather with the box that it growes in, and the earth and materialls feeding the same, wee valew at 10*l.*

"There are also belonginge to the said oringe-garden six pomegranet-trees, bearing faire and large fruits, which, togeather with the square boxes they growe in, and the earth and materialls therein feeding the same, wee valew at three poundes a tree, one with another, in toto, 18*l*."

There were also eighteen orange-trees that had not borne fruit, which, with their boxes, were valued at 5*l*. a tree, one with another, 90*l*.

A white marble fountain, with a statue of Diana upon it, and " a fayer led cestern belonging to it, and a chanelled pavement," were esteemed to be worth 7*l*.

" Another fountain of white marble, with a statue of a mermaid, with the cestern, &c." were valued at 10*l*.

Evelyn notes, in his Diary, 25th September 1679. " Mr. Slingsby and Sig. Verris came to dine with me, to whom I gave China oranges off my owne trees, as good, I think, as ever were eaten." He also notes, " March 24, 1687, went to Kew to visit Sir Henry Capell's, whose Orangerie and Myrtelum are most beautiful and perfectly well kept. He was contriving very high palisados of reeds to shade his oranges during the summer, and painting those reeds in oil."

Orange-trees have been grown in the southern parts of Devonshire for more than 100 years past. When trained to walls, they produce large, handsome fruit, but not of equal value to the lemons grown in the same situation. Most of these were raised in this country from seeds, and they are thought to be more hardy than trees imported; but the orange-trees which are brought every year from Italy, and sold principally at the Italian warehouses in London, are as large as those of our own growth would be in twenty years. With proper care, these trees will have good heads, and produce fruit in about three years.

The Mandarin orange, *(citrus nobilis,)* which is so called in China on account of its superiority to other oranges, was first introduced to this country by Sir

Abraham Hume, in the year 1805. It has not yet been cultivated in the countries that supply us with oranges, but we may hope to meet with it in our markets ere many years, as this variety of the orange appears as hardy as other kinds; and from those that have been ripened by the late Sir Joseph Banks, and other gentlemen in this country, the fruit has been found to be most delicious. The rind is of a deep saffron colour, or rather between an orange-colour and scarlet: the large variety often measures five inches in diameter; but the Chinese greatly prefer the smaller variety of this orange, which the Botanical Register states to be an entirely distinct species from the common China orange, *Citrus Aurantium*. It is a native of Cochin China, and is cultivated at Canton.

We have lately seen orange-trees imported from the south of France, which have arrived in small tubs; and so well packed, that the fruit and blossoms remained on the trees when they reached the neighbourhood of London.

In the Philosophical Transactions, No. 114, there is a very remarkable account of a tree standing in a grove near Florence, having an orange stock, which had been so grafted on, that it became in its branches, leaves, flowers, and fruit, three-formed; some emulating the orange, some the lemon or citron, and some partaking of both forms in one. These mixed fruits never produce any perfect seeds: sometimes there are no seeds at all in them, and sometimes only a few empty ones.

Oranges require the same attention as apples or peaches in grafting; for in the most favourable climates, if suffered to grow wild, the fruit is flat, and rather bitter.

The Maltese graft their orange-trees on the pomegranate stock, which causes the juice to be of a red colour, and the flavour to be more esteemed. The Rev. Mr. Hughes, in his Natural History of Barbadoes, mentions the golden orange as growing in that island. He describes the fruit as a large fine orange, of a deep colour within, from whence it derives the name Golden Orange. He adds, "This fruit is neither of the Seville nor China kind, though it partakes of both, having the sweetness of the China mixed with the agreeable bitterness and flavour of the Seville orange."

Oranges may be eaten without injury to the health, even when a person is overheated; but in the evening or at night, they are not thought so wholesome.

The juice of oranges is a pleasing acid, and good in inflammatory and putrid disorders, both acute and chronical. The juice contains an essential acid salt, mixed with much mucilage. The salt may be obtained in crystals, by diluting the juice, clarifying it with whites of eggs, and using evaporation. In this way a saline extract may be made, capable of being preserved, and possessed of the same medicinal qualities as the juice, which is said to be very powerful in the scurvy. When Commodore Anson sailed round the world, his men, who were afflicted with the scurvy, were surprisingly recovered from that disorder by the oranges they found in the island of Tinian.

Orangeade, an agreeable drink made of orange-juice, water, and sugar, may be given, says Lemery, to people in the height of a fever.

The Seville orange is esteemed far preferable for medicinal purposes, and the blossoms of this species are the most odoriferous: the leaves are also used in medicine. The yellow rind of these oranges, separated from the white fungous matter under it, is a grateful, warm, aromatic bitter, often used as a stomachic and corroborant. It is warmer than the peel of lemons, of a more durable flavour, abounds more with a light, fragrant, essential oil, which is lodged in distinct cells on the surface of the peel. The rind of the China orange has a weak smell, and is seldom employed for medicinal purposes. Seville oranges also produce the best marmalade, and the richest wine: it is from the flowers of this kind of orange, that orange-flower water is distilled. These oranges are often preserved whole as a sweetmeat, and are justly admired.

The seeds of the orange kind will be found, on nice examination, different from the seed of any other fruit. They have been anatomized by the curious, and, with the aid of a good microscope, are found to be almost as wonderful, in their formation, as the human frame when dissected.

When these trees are removed from the conservatory, they should be so placed as to receive the morning and evening sun, but not the full tide of the meridian rays, from which they are best sheltered by trees, provided the drip is avoided. If laurels are well arranged in the planting, so as partly to form a back-ground, and occasionally to admit room for an orange-tub, a small number of these trees may be contrived to make a fine appearance in the windings of the shrubbery.

Oranges and lemons may be preserved in the highest perfection by freezing, and placing them in an ice-house. When intended to be used, they should be previously put into a vessel of cold water till they are thawed. Those who have not the advantage of ice vaults, may keep them for a considerable time, by choosing such as are not quite ripe, and procuring some fine dry sand, which should be heated in the sun, or over a fire; when cold, put it in a large earthen vessel, and then a layer of oranges or lemons with their stalk-ends downwards, observing they do not touch each other; cover them with sand, and form another layer in the same manner, until the vessel is full; then cover them two or three inches deep with sand, and place them in a cold and dry room.

PEACH.—PERSICA, OR AMYGDALUS.

Natural order, Pomaceæ. A genus of the Icosandria Monogynia class.

"Myself will search our planted grounds at home,
For downy peaches and the glossy plum."

Virgil.

THE Greeks called this fruit Ἀμυγάλη and Ἀμύγδαλον; from the lines or furrows on the stone, from which the Latins derived the name of *Amygdalus.*

The Italians call this fruit *Persiche,* the French Peche, from which the English name seems derived.

All the ancient authors agree that the peach-tree is a native of Persia; and it appears that the fruit was thought to be of a poisonous nature. It is evident that there had formerly been traditionary tales of this fruit having been sent into Egypt to poison the inhabitants. Columella says, in his 10th book :—

"And apples, which most barbarous Persia sent,
With native poison arm'd (as fame relates):
But now they've lost their pow'r to kill, and yield
Ambrosial juice, and have forgot to hurt;
And of their country still retain the name."

The peaches which grow in the province of Ghilan in Persia, are still said to be very unwholesome and injurious, from the great moisture of the earth.

Pliny, in his 15th book, chap. 13, mentions, that they had been stated to possess venomous qualities; and that it had been asserted that this fruit was sent into Egypt by the kings of Persia, by way of revenge, to plague the natives; but he treats this story as a mere fable, adding, that the name Persica evidently bespeaks them a Persian fruit. Cato has not mentioned them; and Pliny adds, that it was not long since peaches were known in Rome, and there was great difficulty in rearing them. He informs us they were brought from Egypt to the isle of Rhodes, where they could never be made to produce fruit; and from thence to Italy. He says, moreover, that it was not a common fruit in Greece or in Natolia. This author states again, in book 23, chap. 7, that he considered it the most harmless fruit in the world; that it had the most juice with the least smell of any fruit, and yet caused thirst in those who ate of it.

Peaches were evidently cultivated in France at an early period, as Columella continues his account of this fruit, by stating,—

> "Those of small size to ripen make great haste;
> Such as great Gaul bestows observe due time
> And season, not too early, nor too late."

Pliny says, book 15, chap. 12, "as for the French and Asiatic peaches, they bear the name of the regions and nations from whence they come."

It is stated that the peach-tree was not cultivated in England before the year 1562; and by whom it was first introduced, or from what country it was procured, we have no authentic account, although in Gerard's work (1597) he describes the white peach, the red peach, the yellow peach, and the d'avant peach, and adds, "I have them all in my garden, with many other sorts."

The peach-tree, he continues, "soone commeth vp; it beareth fruit the third or fourth yeer after it is planted, and it soone decaieth; and is not of long continuance,"

From this account, and finding it in the list of fruits, published in the year 1557, by Thomas Tusser, who mentions peaches, white and red, there can be little doubt but that it was introduced as early as the reign of Henry the Eighth. We are decidedly of opinion that it was brought into England, from Italy, by Wolf, the king's gardener, in the year 1524, as at this time we find that he brought the apricot from the latter country.

Of this deliciously melting fruit we have now a great variety, from the small nutmeg peach, which ripens in July, to the large October peach, which is more agreeable to the sight than to the palate. This fruit has been almost equally multiplied in its varieties with the apple, by sowing the stones, and lately by the ingenious method of impregnating the blossoms. T. A. Knight, Esq. President of the Horticultural Society, has procured a new peach by this operation: he impregnated the pistillum of the blossom on an almond-tree, with the pollen of the peach-flower; and this almond, when planted, produced a peach-tree instead of one of its own kind, and has since ripened peaches.

The peach varies so much in quality, that many sorts are not worth the growing: it is therefore to be hoped that we shall soon have them exploded, and the better varieties cultivated in situations most congenial to their tender nature. At Montreuil, a village near Paris, the whole population is exclusively employed in the cultivation of peaches, which has maintained the inhabitants for several ages; and the consequence is, that they raise better peaches there than any other part of France affords.

We have often observed, that the finest-flavoured peaches have been gathered from trees of the greatest age; and we have met with many instances of these trees bearing amply when they have been from forty to sixty years old. These trees generally yield a crop, when younger ones fail.

Father Hennepin, a religious missionary, who first described the regions of Louisiana in his voyage down the Mississippi, gives an account of the numerous peach-trees which he observed in every direction in that part of America; and as the latitude is the same as that part of Asia, of which these trees are the natural production, there can be no doubt but they are indigenous to Louisiana as well as to Persia, although in many parts of America the peach is regarded as a foreign fruit, it having been introduced from Europe before Louisiana had been explored.

This fruit is now cultivated with such success in some parts of North America, that it is not uncommon to see orchards containing one thousand standard peach-trees, which are so productive, that the fruit is used to fatten swine: from a single orchard have been procured, after the pulp is fermented and distilled, one hundred barrels of peach brandy.

Peaches grow so rapidly in New South Wales, that if a stone is set, in three years an abundant crop is produced.

Peaches are forced with considerable success. These, of necessity, must bear a high price in the market, so long as glass continues an object of heavy taxation. The expense of fuel, it appears, will not be so excessive, since the heating of flues by steam promises to answer.

Mr. Kirk, of Old Brompton, has lately introduced an entire new variety of the peach, which he obtained from Java. It was ripened in the summer of 1820, by John Braddick, Esq. of Thames Ditton, and it proves to be the Chinese *Flat Peach*. The fruit is of a singular form, being quite flat, and the eye large, and bearing the appearance of the crown of a medlar, of a yellow colour, speckled with red on the part exposed to the sun, and covered with a fine down. The flesh is pale yellow, having a beautiful radiated circle of fine red surrounding the stone, and extending far into the fruit, which is of a good flavour, and both sweet and juicy.

The *Rosanne Peach*, which is a variety of the Yellow Alberge, but of a superior flavour, is thought to be the best for standard trees, as, when planted in favourable situations, it ripens its fruit well, and acquires a fine colour.

It is observed, that the best peaches of every kind are red next the sun, and of a yellowish cast towards the wall: the pulp should also be of a yellowish tint, and juicy; the skin thin, and the stone small. To have them in perfection, they should not be gathered until they will fall into the hand by the slightest touch of the finger.

This is one of the fruits in particular which is recommended to be eaten in the morning, in preference to the usual time of dessert. Brookes says, "peaches agree well with persons of hot constitutions and costive habits, especially if they are eaten in a morning fasting."

The flowers of the peach-tree are used in medicine: when made into a syrup, they are given as an aperient to children, and are recommended as a great destroyer of worms.

It should be observed not to get the flowers from those peach-trees that have been grafted upon almond-stocks, as the flowers partake of the property of the stock, which greatly alters their virtue. The plum is a purgative, the almond not at all so.

Gerard also says, "the leaves of the peach-tree boiled in milk, will destroy the worms in young children."

The young leaves are used by cooks to flavour blancmange, custards, puddings, &c.; and a liquor resembling noyau is made by steeping peach-leaves in white brandy, and, when sweetened with sugar-candy, and fined with milk, it is difficult to distinguish it from the flavoured cordial of Martinique.

Michaelmas is the time recommended for the winter pruning of the nectarine, as well as the peach-tree, when, with little attention, the blossom-buds will be known from the wood-buds; the latter being less turgid, longer, and narrower, than the blossom-buds. In shortening the branches, observe to leave a wood-bud at the end instead of the fruit-bud. Care should be taken to nip off the ends of the strong shoots in the month of May, which will cause them to throw out new boughs in every part of the tree, as it produces its fruit from the young wood, either of the same, or at the most of the former year's shoot.

Peach-trees are often injured by a desire to retain too full a crop on the branches, which not only prevents the present fruit from coming to maturity, but, by exhausting the tree, prevents its fruiting in future years. When the peach has attained the size of a small gooseberry, the trees should be carefully thinned, leaving the fruit not nearer than from four to six inches to each other.

In dry summers, when the branches are well set with fruit, these trees necessarily require moisture. We observe, in general, too little attention paid to the watering of fruit-trees: we recommend trenches to be thrown up round the stems, and these trenches to be filled up with bean-stalks, half-decayed leaves, sticks, or any litter of that nature that will break the fall of the water, and keep the ground moist for a longer period.

From the wood of the peach-tree the colour called rose-pink is procured.

PEAR.—PYRUS.

Natural order, Pomaceæ. A genus of the Icosandria Pentagynia class.

"Now let me graft my pears, and prune the vine;
The fruit is theirs, the labour only mine."

Virgil.

The Latin name is supposed to be from πυρ, fire, and which we consider was given it from the growth of the tree, which is generally in the shape of a flame, and not from the pyramidical form of the fruit, as is commonly stated.

The accounts we have of this fruit are of great antiquity, as the pear-tree was consecrated to Minerva previously to the olive.

The earliest writers mention it as a fruit growing abundantly in Syria and Egypt, as well as in Greece; and it appears to have been brought into Italy from these places about the time that Sylla made himself master of the latter country, although there is no doubt but the Romans had several kinds of this fruit before that time. Virgil speaks of pears which he had from Cato; and Columella mentions a considerable variety of pears. Pliny writes of them in his 15th book, chap. 2, as being then exceedingly numerous in Italy: "some have," says he, "no other name than the country from whence they came, as the

Syrian, the Alexandrine, the Numidian, the Grecian, the Picentine, the Numantine, &c. &c.:" but of all the pears, he mentions the Crustumine as the most delicate and agreeable; next to that the Falernian pear was esteemed, and so called for the abundance of juice it produced, which he compares to wine. The Tiberian pears were so named because they were the sort Tiberius the emperor preferred; others were named after the persons who had introduced or cultivated them; some from the season when they ripened, as the barley-pear, &c.; and many from their odour, as the aromatic and laurel-pears. "Some are reproached," says he, "with the name of proud pears, because they are earliest ripe, and will not keep:" there were winter-pears, and pears for baking, &c. "Both pears and apples," continues this author, "have the properties of wine, on which account physicians are careful how they give them to their patients; but when sodden in wine and water, they are esteemed wholesome." Again he states, book xxiii. chap. 7, "all pears whatsoever are but a heavy meat, even to those in good health, and the sick are debarred from eating of them; and yet, if they are well boiled or baked, they are exceedingly pleasant, and moderately wholesome: when sodden or baked with honey, they agree with the stomach."

Some pears were used as a counterpoison against the venomous mushrooms; the ashes of the pear-tree wood are also used for the same medicinal purpose.

The arms of the city of Worcester are, Argent, a Fess between three Pears Sable. This, in all probability, alludes to the early cultivation of this fruit in that neighbourhood.

"This fruit," says Guillim, in his Display of Heraldry, "was ordained for the comfort of man; but as the devil made use of the apple to the destruction of man, so did the devil's imps use the pear to a wicked end, when the monks of Swinsted, inviting King John to a banquet, poisoned him in a dish of pears, though others write it was in a cup of ale."

From this traditionary tale it may be concluded that pears had been cultivated prior to the time of King John, as the wild pear never could have been a dish for the table of a monarch or a monk.

In an account-book of Henry the Eighth, now remaining in the Exchequer, there are the following charges among others:—

	l.	*s.*	*d.*
"For Medlars and Wardens (Pears) .	0	3	4
"Item, to a woman who gaff the Kyng Peres	0	0	2

The wild pear-tree, as well as the crab-apple, appears also to be a native of this country, where it is often found growing, particularly in Somersetshire and Sussex. The latter county gave names to several varieties that were esteemed in Worlidge's time (1675), as the Petworth pear, and the Arundel pear; but the kinds are now either lost, or have received new names.

At what period the cultivated pear was first brought into this country we have no account; but we may surmise that the Romans did not neglect the propagation of this fruit when they were masters of Britain. The pear is mentioned by all our early writers. Swinburn says, the waste lands near the plains of Puglia, are covered with wild pear-trees. Gerard says in his time, to write of pears and apples would require a particular volume: "every country," says he, "hath his peculiar fruit; myselfe knowe some one curious, who hath in one peece of ground, at the point of three score sundrie sorts of pears, and those exceeding good; not doubting but, if his minde had been to seek after multitudes, he might have gotten togither the like number of those of worsse kindes.

Master Richard Pointer," he says, "has them all growing in his ground at Twicknam, near London, who is a most cunning and curious grafter and planter of all manner of rare fruits; and also in the ground of an excellent grafter and painful planter, Master Henry Banbury, of Touthill-street, neere vnto Westminster; and likewise in the ground of a diligent and most affectionate louer of plants, Master Warner, neere Hornsey Down, by London; and in divers other grounds about London."

Miller mentions eighty varieties of the pear in his day, and, at the present time, they are so much increased, that Mr. Lee, of Hammersmith, assured the author that he possessed two hundred and thirteen kinds of pear-trees. At the close of the seventeenth century the French gardeners reckoned about seven hundred different sorts: of which, however, scarcely more than fifty were of superior quality. Thus, few trees, under the guidance of man, have exhibited so many varieties; and we trust that, while the Horticultural Society are seeking for new kinds, those of established fame will not be neglected. It is desirable to have our orchards planted with a variety, that we may have some for all seasons and for various purposes; but it is equally to be wished that the best of each sort should be selected, not only of the dessert kinds, but those for baking and preserving, as well as those for making perry, which is one of the justly-admired British beverages.

"And taste revived,
The breath of orchard big with bending fruit
Obedient to the breeze and beaten ray,
From the deep-loaded bough a mellow shower
Incessant melts away. The juicy pear
Lies, in a soft profusion, scattered round.
A various sweetness swells the gentle race,

By Nature's all-refining hand prepared,
Of tempered sun, and water, earth, and air,
In ever-changing composition mixed."

Thomson.

Perry is considered the best liquor that can be drunk after a surfeit of mushrooms. An agreeable wine is made from the wild pears and crab-apples.

In general pears are thought windy, and improper for weak stomachs; those are best that are quite ripe, and have a sweet juice, and then they are seldom noxious, unless eaten to excess.—*(Brooks.)*

We know of no fruit that varies in quality more than the pear, for while some of the kinds are so unpalatable as not only to be refused by the swine, but even rejected by idle boys, others are of so delicious a flavour that we see most of the autumnal fruits give place to them at the dessert. We shall, therefore, with a hope of meeting good pears in greater abundance, give such hints as may lead to their increase, first observing that a bad pear is injurious to health and brings no price in the market, while a rich melting pear is eagerly sought after even at six times the price of oranges or many other imported fruits, and we never recollect hearing of any person being injured by eating such pears. Those, therefore, who have discovered their trees to produce a worthless fruit, should lose no time in grafting them with a known variety, that both themselves and future generations may be benefited.

The author having witnessed the advantage of taking off a ring of bark from the branches of unfruitful pear trees, particularly recommends the practice, as it has not been found to injure the trees at Hampton Court Palace, where it has been repeated for several successive years. Many persons object to the experiment, fearing to injure the branches; but what is the value of unproductive branches? Michael Morrah, Esq. of Worthing, made a most satisfactory proof of the utility of ring barking, having a large pear-tree in his garden which had never even produced blossom. In the month of June 1820, he took a ring of the bark from two principal branches, the one of which extended to the east, the other to the west. In the following spring these two branches were covered with flowers, although no other part of the tree gave out a single blossom. The author saw this tree in the autumn, and counted thirty fine grown pears on one of the ringed branches. Some gardeners have rejected the plan as being unnatural, as if it was more unnatural to make a tree fruitful by stopping the circulation of the sap, than to make it productive by grafting.

We have already noticed the necessity of watering fruit-trees, and particularly recommend it to pear-trees that have large crops on them, as it will both prevent their falling off, and assist greatly in their size, for the crops of standard trees cannot well be thinned. Worlidge observes, that

> " The pear, when it has room enough to spread,
> Where it has warmth sufficient over head,
> If it be seconded by the wet ground,
> With blossoms and swelling fruit will be crown'd."

The wet summer of 1821, alone would convince us how much these trees are assisted in their crops by moisture. The author had a trench thrown round a standard pear-tree in his garden at Bayswater, for the purpose of giving it water, but the season turning out rainy made it unnecessary, and as the trench remained it received a double portion, the result was that the tree ripened a full crop, about half-matured a second crop, and had its branches covered with white blossoms for the third time in the month of November.

In the same summer, a pear-tree of the brown Bury kind at the White Swan, in Hyde-Street, in the suburbs of Winchester, blossomed in May, again in June, a third time in July, and a fourth time in August; in the month of October the four progressive crops were hanging on the branches.

Mr. Worlidge notices a pear-tree that was growing near Ross in Herefordshire, in 1675, that was, he says, " as wide in the circumference as three men could encompass with their extended arms, and of so large a head that the fruit of it yielded seven hogsheads of perry in one year.

Mr. John Wheeler of Horsham has favoured us with the particulars of a pear-tree, which he planted at Hill's Place, near that town, about thirty-eight years back, and which has been in general very productive; the tree is about ten feet in height, and the branches extend fifty-eight feet, and are only prevented by other trees from a still greater extension. The pear is of the jargonelle kind, and the fruit sells in the country at three shillings per dozen; a price that ought to induce a farther cultivation of pear-trees: besides which, we have often observed, that pear-trees are productive in years when apples fail.

When we reflect on the labours of the horticulturists who have, by cultivation, made the pear-tree forget its natural thorns, and instead of an acerb berry produce us a fruit so fair and nectareous, we find our warmest gratitude an insufficient return; while from the nurserymen, whose study it is to bring to our shores the improved grafts of every clime to cheer the sense and glad the heart, our warmest support and fullest approbation cannot be withheld. Let us hope that those who have a still greater charge, that of the cultivation of the mind of the rising generation, will be equally assiduous in engrafting their young stocks with principles that must ensure good fruits, "and give a god-like joy," to the world at large.

> " Catch then, oh catch, the transient hour,
> Improve each moment as it flies:
> Life's a short summer, man a flower;
> He dies; alas! how soon he dies."
>
> *Johnson.*

The pear-tree is liable to be much injured, if pruned by those who do not understand the nature of it. The blossoms are commonly produced from buds at the extremity of the last year's shoots, and, as these are often cut off by the unskilful pruner, it prevents their producing fruit, and causes the boughs to send out new branches, which overfill the tree with wood. The summer is the best time to look over pear-trees, and to remove all superfluous and foreright shoots, which would too much shade the fruit. If this be carefully done, they will require but little pruning in the autumn.

Pears that are to be kept for winter use, should hang as long on the trees as the state of the weather will allow. They should then be put in a heap, in an open and dry situation, for about ten days; then wiped dry with a woollen cloth, and packed close from the air and moisture. But to keep this fruit in its greatest perfection, small earthen jars should be selected, about the size of the pear, which should be packed separately in clean oat chaff, and tied down with skin, or brown paper cemented with pitch. These jars should then be packed in a chest, or dry closet, with the bottom upwards. Pears are found more generally productive when grafted on quince stocks, than upon those of their own kind or the white thorn.

The timber of the pear-tree is of a yellowish colour, and is used for making carpenters' tools, measuring rulers, picture-frames, and a variety of purposes. Gerard says, " the timber of the wild pear is very firm and solid, and good to be cut into moulds." The plates in his book were cut out of this wood, as were, says he, "breast-plates for English gentlewomen." Sir William Ouseley tells us that the Persians make their beautiful *Káshúks*, or spoons, from this wood; the Mahometan religion prohibiting them from using at their meals, spoons, or any part of the table-service, made of gold or silver. This injunction of their prophet is most religiously observed; but for this privation they fully compensate themselves in the luxurious and splendid equipage of their coffee; it being no uncommon thing to see their zarph (an outer cup in which the china cup containing the coffee is put) of enamelled gold, ornamented with diamonds to the value of from ten thousand to thirty thousand piastres.

PINE-APPLE PLANT.—ANANAS.

Natural order, Coronariæ. A species of the Bromelia, and of the class Hexandria Monogynia.

" What Nature, alas! has denied
  To the delicate growth of our isle,
Art has in a measure supplied;
  E'en winter is deck'd with a smile."

Cowper.

THESE species of plants were named Bromelia in memory of Olaus Bromel, a Swedish author of the seventeenth century.

The Brazilians call this delicious fruit Nana, from which the generic name has been formed.

It takes its name of pine-apple from the resemblance it bears to the cones of the pine-tree. It is considered the king of fruits, being second to none in flavour, and always appearing at table with a crown.

The Ananas is an herbaceous plant, with leaves somewhat resembling those of the aloe. It grows wild, in vast abundance, in many parts of Africa and South America; and is cultivated in the hotter islands of the West Indies, where it requires but little attention to procure this elegant fruit in perfection and plenty.

That the history of a fruit of so exquisite a flavour, and so late an introduction, should be so little known to us, appears extraordinary; by various ingenious devices, its cultivation has reached a degree of perfection that could never have been anticipated by the first growers of the Ananas in this country. It is said already to have been brought to a higher state of perfection here than in its natural soil; to what farther degree of excellence it may arrive, under the skilful treatment of the British horticulturist, time alone will shew. We consider the principal cause of the ease with which this fruit is now grown amongst us, is the liberal and spirited manner by which the growers have, from time to time, laid their improved plans before the public by their well-directed pens. The only return we can make for these national benefits, is to compile from authentic sources the most accurate information respecting this delicacy of the Torrid Zone.

It appears to us to have been indigenous to the new world only, as the fruits of Africa were well known to the ancients, and this is not noticed in the works of any of their authors who wrote on the plants of India.

That it is now found growing wild in many parts of Africa, is no proof of its being a native of that soil; it was never heard of in Europe until the discovery of America, but when once transplanted within its natural latitude, it would necessarily continue to propagate itself, or be assisted by the birds conveying the seed from place to place. The Chinese cultivated the ananas to a considerable extent, before it was attempted in Europe; and they acknowledge to have received it from South America. Parkinson writes, in 1640, that "it was first brought from Santa Cruise in Brassill, where it is naturall, into both West and East Indies, being not natural to either of them, but is only manured there, and now is growne plentifull."

Father Athanasius Kircher is the oldest author that we have met with who particularly notices this fruit; we shall therefore extract from his work, as the translation stood in 1669.

"They have in China a tree called *Kagin*, yielding fruit twice a-year, which, by inversion, thrusts forth the seed or kernels, like werts, or such excrescences, on the outside of the fruit, and is in common to the East and West Indies, who call it Ananas; but the Chinese call it *Fam-polo-Mie;* it groweth in the provinces Quantung, Kiangsi, and Fokien, and is supposed to have been brought from Peru; the tree on which it groweth is not a shrub, but an herb like unto Carduus; they call it *Cartriofoli*, on whose leaf a fruit groweth sticking unto its stalk, of so pleasant and exquisite a taste, that it may easily obtain the pre-eminency amongst the most noble fruits of India and China; the spermatick faculty is innate in all the parts thereof, for not only the seeds shed on the ground, but its sprouts and leaves being planted, produce the like fruits."

Lord Bacon mentions this fruit in his Essay on Plantations or Colonies, but does not notice that it had ever been brought to Europe in his time; nor do we meet with any mention of its having been seen in this country prior to 1657, when Cromwell the Protector received a present of pine-apples.

About two years previous to this time, the East India Company of the United Provinces sent their first embassy to the Emperor of China; and as they returned in 1657, it is probable that they were the first who brought both the fruit and plants to Europe, as John Nievhoff, who was secretary to that embassy, mentions this fruit particularly, and gives also an engraving of the plant in his History of the Embassy, and says, "Here grows a well-tasted fruit, called Ananas, which was at first brought from the West into the East Indies, where it now is to be had in great abundance. It is about the bigness of a citron, of a yellow colour, and well scented; full of juice, and pleasant in taste, if eaten when ripe; for it is much like unto strawberries with wine and sugar. Upon the top it is crowned with a cluster of flowers and leaves, and at a distance is not unlike an artichoke, but without any pricks at the corners: the middlemost stalk, being the biggest upon which the fruit grows, is about two feet high, and has fifteen or sixteen leaves. Round about this stalk grow other lesser stalks, with young fruit upon each. Whosoever will eat of this fruit, must first of all take off the outward skin, and then cut it into pieces, and so infuse them in wine or water, to draw out the biting quality that is in it, otherwise it will make blisters upon the tongue: nor is that all; for it is very dangerous to eat much of it, because it is apt to bring on dysentery. And though this fruit be hot, yet the leaves thereof are cooling, having a soure and corrosive quality, which is only found in cooling herbs; and the main hazard is produced by its pleasantness, which is such, that it will melt in the mouth like sugar."

In Evelyn's Diary, 9th August, 1661, he says, "I first saw ye famous Queen Pine brought from Barbadoes and presented to his Matie; but the first that were ever seen in England were those sent to Cromwell four years since."

In July 19, 1668, he again observes, "I was at a banquet which the King gave to the French Ambass^r^ Colbert.

"Standing by his Matie at dinner in the presence, there was of that rare fruit call'd the *King Pine,* growing in Barbados and ye West Indies, the fruit of them I had never seen. His Matie having cut it up, was pleased to give me a piece off his owne plate to taste of, but in my opinion it falls short of those ravishing varieties of deliciousness describ'd in Capt. Ligon's History, and others; but possibly it might, or certainly was, much impair'd in coming so far. It has yet a gratefull acidity, but tastes more like ye quince and melon than of any other fruit he mentions."

It was from the crowns of these pines, most probably, that Mr. Rose the king's gardener, raised the first pine-apples that fruited in England, if not in Europe. At Kensington palace is a curious picture of King Charles receiving a pine-apple from his gardener Mr. Rose, who is presenting it on his knees. The earl of Waldegrave has a similar painting in the breakfast-room of his beautiful residence at Strawberry hill, Twickenham. The painting represents king Charles the Second, in a garden before his palace at Ham, attended by two of his favourite breed of spaniels, and Rose, the royal gardener, presenting his Majesty with a pine-apple. This picture formed a part of the collection of the celebrated Horace Walpole, whose descriptive account informs us, that it was bequeathed by Mr. London to the Rev. Mr. Pennicott, of Ditton, by whom it was presented to himself. He adds, the painting is supposed to be by Daneker.

As forcing-houses had not at that period arrived at any degree of perfection, the plants were probably by the severity of the weather, or some accident, lost in this country, until they were introduced a second time, which, the Sloanean manuscripts in the British Museum inform us, was not until the year 1690, when the earl of Portland procured plants from Holland.

In the Fitzwilliam Museum, at the University of Cambridge, is a painting by Netscher, of a landscape with a pine-apple, there stated to be the first that ever fruited in England, which was in Sir Matthew Decker's garden at Richmond, in Surrey, grandfather to the late Lord Fitzwilliam. Gough says also, that it was Sir Matthew Decker, Bart. who first introduced the culture of the Ananas.

We have not been able to ascertain in what year the Ananas first fruited in Sir Matthew's garden, but surmise that it was about the year 1724 or 5, as in the year 1726 we find there was printed, "An account of the Annanus, or West Indian Pine-apple, as it now flourishes in Sir Matthew Decker's garden at Richmond, in Surrey, under the care of Henry Telende." *Ext. in ejusdem libro*: *London*, 1726.

From Lady Mary Montague's remarks, we may also conclude that it was not much before the time stated, as on her journey to Constantinople in the year 1716, this intelligent lady remarks the circumstance of pine-apples being served up in the dessert, at the electoral table at Hanover, as a thing she had never before seen or heard of; and from her ladyship's rank, we may conclude that she would naturally have met with them, or heard of the circumstance that excited so much curiosity, had they been previously ripened at Richmond.

It is stated, that the first pine-apples, raised in Europe, were by M. La Cout of Leyden; and this is probable, excepting those grown by Mr. Rose, in the time of Charles the Second.

By an engraving of the pine-apple, which was published by Robert Furber, gardener, at Kensington, in the year 1733, we may judge that the raising of pines was not then brought to any degree of perfection, as the fruit is represented short, having not more than four or five rows of pips in height; and the crown appears small and weak. From the drawings of the other fruits, which seem to be from fine specimens, it is natural to suppose that this fruit was also copied from the best pine then produced.

In Jamaica, pine-apples have become so prolific, that they are often used to flavour rum, and a wine is made from the fermented juice of the sweeter sorts, nearly equal to Malmsey. Lunan observes, in his *Hortus Jamaicensis*, that these plants grow most luxuriantly when they are associated together; and the suckers from them are stronger and finer, than when the plants are separated at a distance from each other: by this their roots are likewise kept cooler and moister.

Mr. Swinburn observes, that the ananas grows very well out of doors at Reggio near Naples. The prince of Scilla was the first that cultivated it in that part of the world. He treated it in the beginning with great chariness and precaution; but, upon trial, he found a bolder management suit it better.

In the month of February 1822, we saw exhibited at the London Horticultural Society, a moderate-sized pine-apple, which was grown in a common green-house; and Thomas Andrew Knight, Esq. tells us, in the Transactions of that Society, that, "in the month of June 1820, he gave a couple of pine-plants, which had shewn fruit at six months old, and were of small size, and no value, to a child, to be placed in a conservatory, in which no fires were kept during the summer. In July, a storm of hail destroyed nearly, or fully, half the glass of the conservatory; and its temperature through the summer and autumn had been so low, that the Chasselas grapes in it were not ripe in the second week in September. In the second week of the present month (October) one of the pine-apples became ripe, having previously swollen to a most extraordinary size, comparatively with the size of the plant; and upon measuring accurately the comparative width of the fruit, and of the stem, he found the width of the fruit to exceed that of the stem in the proportion of seven and three quarters to one. The fruit had of course, been propped during all the latter part of the summer, the stem being wholly incapable of supporting it. The taste and flavour of this fruit were excellent, and the appearance of the other, which is not yet ripe, and is of a larger size, is still more promising."

We hope these results will be profitable to those that have good vine-houses or conservatories.

We have now a considerable variety of this exquisite fruit, and new kinds are frequently procured by the curious from the seed, which is very small, of a kidney shape, and lodged like the seeds of berries in the tubercles; but the pine is chiefly propagated by planting the crowns or suckers, which latter come more quickly to maturity, and are therefore more generally preferred. The most rare kind is the green pine, which was brought from Barbadoes; the black pine is of late introduction. Of the older varieties, the sugar-loaf pine, with a yellowish flesh, is greatly preferred to the oval-shaped fruit of a paler colour. The Welbeck-seedling is a pine justly admired; as is the blood-pine, a variety grown by Mr. Wilmot of Isleworth, who makes the following just remark: "like the strawberry," says he, "pines would be better reduced to four or five varieties."

The heaviest pine-apple, we believe, that has been grown in this country, weighed eleven pounds; and the one exhibited at the London Horticultural Society and afterwards presented to his Majesty for his coronation dinner, was the largest ever seen in England, but was not quite so heavy, weighing ten pounds eight ounces. There has also been cut in the hot-house of the Right Hon. Thomas Wallace, of Carlton Hall, a pine-apple, weighing nine pounds four ounces and a half. It was brought to this high state of perfection by the skilful management of Mr. Thomas Todd, gardener.

It is stated by William Bastard, Esq. in the Philosophical Transactions for 1777, that pine-apples raised in water are larger and finer flavoured than those raised in bark beds; the plants are set in pots of earth which are kept in a pan of water that is kept full, and placed in the hottest part of the forcing-house.

Dr. Wright says, pines have a detersive quality, and are better fitted to cleanse the mouth and gums than any gargle whatever.

This fruit was long confined to the tables of the rich and the luxurious, on account of the expense of raising it in stoves; but the cultivation of the pine-apple is now so well understood in this country, that notwithstanding the bar made by the high price of glass, and the expense of fuel, this fruit is seen in our markets, at one-fourth of the price they produced a few years back: and pine-apple ices are already become as common as those of raspberry, in the shops of the London confectioners.

As the heating of pineries by steam is found to answer to the most sanguine expectation, we have only to hope that the duty on garden glass will be relinquished, when we should soon have African gardens of great extent on the banks of the Thames, and this American fruit cried through our streets, two for a crown.

The late Sir Joseph Banks says, that it does not require the foresight of a prophet to foretell, that in less than half a century we shall have forcing-houses of such an extent, that our markets will be supplied with the aki, and the avocado pear of the West Indies, the flat peaches, the Mandarine orange, and the Litchi of China; the mango, (which has already been ripened at Kew, in the autumn of 1808,) the mangostan, and the durion of the East Indies, and possibly other valuable fruits.

This fruit was for the first time imported as an article of commerce from the Bermuda islands, in the summer of 1820. The importation consisted of about 400 pine-apples of the species called the Green Providence. These were purchased by Mr. Mart, of Oxford Street, fruiterer, who informed the author that about two thirds of the quantity arrived in good condition. As this experiment has been found to answer, we may in future expect a regular supply of pine-apples, not only from the Bermudas, but also from the West India islands. We observed, that those pines which were packed with the roots, arrived in a better state than others that were cut off in the usual manner.

Monsieur Berard, of Montpelier, in a paper of the French journals, Annales de Chimie for 1821, says, "that most fruits, and especially those that do not require to remain on the tree, may be preserved for some time, and the pleasure they afford us thus prolonged. The most simple process consists in placing at the bottom of a bottle, a paste formed of lime, sulphate of iron, and water; and afterwards to introduce the fruit, it having been pulled a few days before it would have been ripe. The fruit is to be kept from the bottom of the bottle, and as much as possible from each other, and the bottle to be closed by a cork and cement. The fruit is thus placed in an atmosphere free from oxygen, and may be preserved for a longer or a shorter time according to their nature: peaches, plums, and apricots from twenty days to a month; pears and apples for three months. If they are withdrawn after this time, and exposed to the air, they ripen extremely well; but if the times mentioned are much exceeded, they undergo a particular alteration, and will not ripen at all.

Ripe fruit exposed to the air rots and decays. In this case it first changes the oxygen of the surrounding air into carbonic acid, and then liberates from itself a large quantity of the same acid gas. It appears that the presence of oxygen gas is necessary to rotting or decay of fruits; when it is absent, a different change takes place.

PLANTAIN.—MUSA PARADISIACA.

Natural order, Scitamenceæ. A genus of the Polygamia Monœcia class.

" The plantain wide his graceful foliage spreads ;
Where giant palms lift high their tufted heads."

THIS tree received its generic name in memory of Antonius Musa, the freedman and physician of Augustus, who, for curing his imperial master of a dangerous disease by the use of the cold bath, was honoured by the senate with a brazen statue, placed near that of Æsculapius. Antonius was a botanist, and is supposed to be the author of the treatise *De Herbâ Botanicâ.*

The plantain is a native of Guinea, whence it was brought to the Canary Islands; and thence it was afterwards carried to the West Indies; where it is now cultivated with much care in all the islands, the fruit being regarded as one of the greatest blessings bestowed upon the inhabitants of that climate. Dr. Wright says, the island of Jamaica would scarcely be habitable without this fruit, as no species of provision could supply its place: even flour, or wheaten bread itself, would be less agreeable, and less adapted to support the laborious negro, so as to enable him to perform his business, or to keep up his health.

Dampier calls it the king of all fruit, not excepting the cocoa itself.

The fruit of the plantain-tree is about a foot long, and

two or three inches in diameter; it forms a principal part of the food of the negroes, who either roast or boil it; and when thus cooked, it is a palatable and strengthening diet. It is often boiled in their mess of salt beef, pork, or fish, &c.; many Europeans, when accustomed to it, prefer it to bread: and those who settle in America, when they make a new plantation, generally begin with a good plantain-walk, enlarging it as their family increases; some of the trees are always to be found in fruit, and this is many times the sole food on which a family subsists. These trees thrive only in a rich flat ground; they will not prosper in a poor sandy soil. When ripe, the fruit is lusciously sweet, and makes good tarts. The Spaniards dry and preserve it as a sweetmeat, and it is thought to be the most wholesome of all confectionary. It is one of the very best foods to fatten domestic animals and fowls, giving a firmness and exquisite flavour to their flesh.

The plantain is cultivated in Egypt, and most other hot countries, where it grows to perfection in about ten months from its first planting, to the ripening of its fruit. This tree is only perennial by its roots, and dies down to the ground when it has fruited, after which it is cut down: several suckers then soon come up from the roots, which in six or eight months produce fruit, so that by cutting down the stalks at different times, there is a constant succession of fruit all the year.

When the plantain is grown to its full height, the spikes of flowers appear in the centre, which is about four feet long. The flowers come out in bunches, those in the lower part of the spike being the largest; each of these bunches is covered with a sheath of a fine purple colour, which drops off when the flowers open. The upper part of the spike is made up of male flowers, which are succeeded by the fruit. The plantain is of a pale yellow colour when ripe, and the spikes of fruit often weigh upwards of forty pounds. This plant has been reared in our stoves ever since the year 1690.

THE BANANA TREE: *Musa Sapientum.*—This tree so much resembles the plantain, that it is only known at first by the dark spots on its stem, which the other has not. It is a wholesome fruit, and is used at desserts. A pleasant drink, exceeding our cider, is made from it. When baked in tarts, or boiled in dumplings, this fruit tastes like the apple: when dried in the sun, it resembles a delicious fig. It also makes a good marmalade, which is recommended as a great relief for coughs. The fruit of the banana-tree is said to comfort the heart; is cooling, and refreshes the spirits. Labat states, that when the natives of the West Indies undertake a voyage, they make part of their provision to consist of a paste of banana, which, in case of need, serves them for nourishment and drink. For this purpose they take ripe bananas, and having squeezed them through a fine sieve, form the solid fruit into small loaves, which are dried in the sun, or in hot ashes, after being previously wrapped in the leaves of Indian flowering-reed.

The fruit of the banana-tree is about four or five inches long, of the size and shape of a middling cucumber; it generally grows in bunches, weighing upwards of twelve pounds. The Spaniards have a conceit, that if you cut this, or the fruit of the plantain athwart, or crossways, there appears a cross in the middle of the fruit, and therefore they will not cut any, but break them. Lodovicus Romanus, and Brocard, who wrote a Description of the Holy Land, call the bananas Adam's Apples, supposing them to be the fruit that Eve took and gave to Adam; which is as erroneous as the account of the Abbé Poyart and others, who state the leaves to be those of the tree from which our first parents made themselves aprons, as from their size, which is from five to seven feet in length, and from one to two feet in breadth, they could not have required sewing together for that purpose. These leaves are said to be as strong as parchment. The leaves of the plantain, as well as the banana, grow so rapidly, that by placing a thread, they will be found to grow an inch in an hour. The young leaves are so soft, that they are employed in dressings for blisters, &c. When full grown, they are so large that they are used as substitutes for napkins and table-cloths: when dried, they are made into mats and stuffings for mattresses, &c.

If a knife be thrust into a plantain-tree, there will come out a great quantity of clear water, which is very rough and astringent, stopping all sorts of fluxes.

The fruit of the banana-tree has been ripened in our hothouses; but as the tree grows very tall, the size of the leaves requires more room than most gardeners are willing to allow it in the stove.

Mr. Swinburn tells us that the Musa grows very well in the open air at Reggio.

From the rapidity of the growth of the banana, it is of too porous a nature to merit the name of wood, and the Indians have ever been accustomed to make cordage, and a kind of cloth from its fibres. The celebrated circumnavigator, Dampier, noticed the process more than a century ago as follows :—

" They take the body of the tree, clear it of its outward bark and leaves, cut it into quarters, put it into the sun, when the moisture exhales; they then take hold of the threads at the ends, and draw them out: they are as big as brown thread; and of this they make cloth in Mindanas, called *saggen*."

In Jamaica, there have been upwards of two hundred

pounds given by order of the Assembly, for the best specimens of this hemp. Dr. Stewart West gained a premium, and his process may be seen in the Hortus Jamaicensis.

From experiments tried on the hemp made from the plantain-tree fibre, which was manufactured into rope at his Majesty's dock-yard, Port Royal, in Jamaica, the following results were obtained:—

	Cwt.	*qr.*	*lb.*
King's nine-thread inch-rope broke by the weight of	6	1	14
Dr. West's specimen broke by the weight of	6	2	0
Specimen from the parish of St. Andrew .	6	1	0
Do. Do. Portland .	4	2	0
Do. Do. St. George .	3	2	0

The above specimens were all made of the same size as the king's rope.

PLUM.—PRUNUS.

Natural order, Pomaceæ. A genus of the Icosandria Monogynia class.

—— "The mealy plum
Hangs purpling, or displays an amber hue."

Plums are so numerous in their varieties, that to describe them separately would be endless; as not only every country, but almost every district, has its peculiar sorts of this fruit.

The Grecians added to their native plums those of Syria, Egypt, and Persia; and the Romans not only possessed themselves of the plums of all the known world, but employed their ingenuity in making additional varieties. Columella, in his tenth book, speaking of this fruit, says—

—— "then are the wicker baskets cramm'd
With Damask and Armenian, and wax plums."

Pliny states, in his fifteenth book, chap. 13, that there was a great variety of this fruit in Italy; and it is not long, says he, since the country about Grenada and Andalusia began to graft plums upon apple stocks, which were called apple plums; others upon almond stocks, which he calls a clever device, as it produced both fruits, the stone being like the kernel of an almond. Those grafted upon nut stocks, he states, retained the form of the mother graft; but they got the taste of the stock wherein they were set.

The wild sloe and bullace are indigenous to this country, and in all probability the only kinds that are natives; but, like the wild crab-apple, they have furnished stocks for every variety of their own species; and this fruit appears to have been attended to in early days, if we may judge from the variety that Gerard had in his garden at Holborn, in 1597. "I have," says he, "three score sorts in my garden, and all strange and rare: there be in other places many more common, and yet yeerely commeth to our handes others not before knowne. The greatest varietie of these rare plums are to be found in the grounds of Master Vincent Pointer, of Twicknam."

The damson, or damascene plum, takes its name from Damascus, where it grows in great quantities, and from whence it was brought into Italy about 114 years B. C. Pliny says, this plum required the warmer sun of Syria: we may therefore conclude, it is still inferior in our climate to what it is in Italy.

The Orleans plum takes its name from the part of France so called. This is a handsome but an indifferent fruit, and not equal to the common muscle plum in flavour, although it is more cultivated than even the greengage, which is not only the most agreeable, but also the most wholesome of all the plums. This latter plum was called the Reine Claude, from having been introduced into France by Queen Claude, wife to Francis the First of that country, but it bears various names in different parts of France. It is often called *Damas verd;* at Tours it is named *Abricot verd;* at Rouen, where it grows abundantly, they call it *la Verte bonne*. This plum received the name of Green-gage from the following accident:—The Gage family, in the last century, procured from the monastery of the Chartreuse at Paris, a collection of fruit-trees. When these trees arrived at the mansion of Hengrave Hall, the tickets were safely affixed to all of them, excepting only to the Reine Claude, which had either not been put on, or had been rubbed off in the package. The gardener, therefore, being ignorant of the name, called it, when it first bore fruit, the Green Gage. The compliment was justly due to the family for the introduction of this excellent plum, which is more acceptable to the country at large, than the trifling respect can be to the family of Gage.

Lord Cromwell brought several sorts of plums from Italy into this country, in the reign of Henry the Seventh: among them was the Perdrigon.

The Bonum Magnum is our largest plum, and greatly esteemed for preserves and culinary purposes. This appears to have been originally a Dutch fruit, or rather enlarged by their culture and soil. A plum of nearly the same size and shape, but of a yellower hue, has lately been introduced by Mr. Coe, of Brompton, and is called Coe's golden drop. In flavour it partakes both of the green-gage and the apricot. The author had several standard trees in his garden at Bayswater, which were very productive; and the fruit had the quality of keeping perfectly sound and good until near Christmas, if gathered with the stalk or a part of the branch, and suspended in a dry room.

Plums are now forced in the highest perfection, which enables the gardener to supply the spring desserts with the autumnal fruits.

John Townsend Aiton, Esq., of the Royal Gardens, Windsor, has lately communicated some useful information on the forcing of this fruit, in a letter to the Secretary of the Horticultural Society. He says, "The kinds of plums generally preferred for forcing, are the following:—Precoce de Tours, green-gage, blue-gage, white perdrigon, Orleans, New Orleans, and Morocco.

"When an early crop is desired, plums are best forced

in large pots or tubs, as this method admits of their removal at pleasure into different degrees of temperature as occasion may require; but for a general crop to ripen by the end of May, or beginning of June, it is preferable to have the trees planted in the forcing-house, and if they are intended to be forced in the first year, proper trees for the purpose, furnished with well branching wood, should be selected and planted early in the autumn, that they may establish themselves before the winter sets in. The soil to be preferred is a moderately rich loam, without mixture of manure.

"For a crop to ripen in the second week in May the house must be covered in early in January, commencing with a temperature of 42° of Fahrenheit, for the first fortnight, after which the heat may be gradually raised to 52°, at which it may continue until the flowers make their appearance; during this time frequent changes of air must be admitted, to strengthen the bloom, and the crop will be rendered more certain by keeping the trees in blossom as long as possible, by light shading when necessary; and when the petals begin to fall, gentle dews may be raised from the surface of the mould.

"As the fruit forms, the thermometer should be raised to 58°; this must be done gradually, as the consequence of a rapid rise may be a casting of the fruit. During the progress of stoning great care must be taken against sudden variations of the temperature, water being very sparingly used, and every check by fumigation, &c. given to the various insects which will be particularly active at this period. When the fruit is safely stoned, a moderate dressing of rotten manure may be spread on the surface of the mould; the heat increased to 68°, and a more liberal supply of water given. After the fruit has attained a full size, and approaches maturity, air may be freely admitted, and water should be given in less quantities, and finally discontinued a few days before gathering."

Dried plums are principally imported from Portugal, and the neighbourhood of Marseilles in France; from whence also prunes are brought: this latter variety is mostly used in medicine, and though the laxative power is diminished by drying, yet as they contain much of their acid, they have more effect than other dried fruits. They are peculiarly useful in costive habits. It is the pulp of this fruit that forms the principal part of lenitive electuary.

Plums of all kinds are considered more agreeable than wholesome, but, like the pear, they lose their bad qualities by baking. Plums in general are moistening, laxative, and emollient, except the bullaces and sloes, which are astringent. They are cooling, quench thirst, and create an appetite, and therefore agree best with hot constitutions; but they do not suit weak stomachs: in general, however, they may not only be eaten with impunity, but even with advantage, when perfectly ripe, as they tend to keep the body moderately open. In years when plums are very plentiful, and consequently much eaten, *dysenteries* generally abound: hence it appears that they ought always to be eaten very moderately, and then they should be quite ripe and sound. *(Brookes.)* The damson plum produces a tolerably pleasant wine, and an exceedingly agreeable kind of jelly called damson cheese. The wild plum was used in medicine by the ancients, and the bark of the tree is thought to be equal to the Peruvian bark in cases of intermitting fevers.

Plums should have a middling soil, neither too wet and heavy, nor over light and dry: in either extreme they seldom do well; yet we have known them occasionally flourish in a cold gravelly soil where apple-trees would not prosper. An east or south-east aspect is better for plum-trees than a full south, on which they are subject to shrivel, and to be very dry, and often extremely mealy, if exposed too much to the heat of the sun: in planting, this should be particularly attended to; as it leaves the better situations of the garden free for those fruits that require warmer suns.

The young pruner must recollect that plums do not only produce their fruit upon the last year's wood, but also upon curzons or spurs, which come out of wood that is many years old; therefore it is not necessary to shorten the branches, in order to obtain new shoots, as is requisite with the peach, &c. If plum-trees are much pruned, they grow too luxuriant to produce fruit, and often gum and spoil.

Standard plum-trees should have a situation in the pleasure-grounds, as the snowy petals are next in succession to the blushing almond, and they fill up a vacancy before the lilac flowers. We observe this peculiar character in the plum-tree, that it always blossoms in cold weather.

POMEGRANATE.—PUNICA.

Natural order, Pomaceæ. A genus of the Icosandria Monogynia class.

THIS fruit takes its name from *pomum granatum*, a kernelled apple.

The generic name is called after a part of Africa, where ancient Carthage stood, and not after the colour of the blossoms, as is generally stated; as Pliny tells us positively that the colour was named from the flower,—which seems more reasonable.

The Bible notices the pomegranate as a native of Syria. It is mentioned as one of the fruits discovered in the Land of Promise; previous to which discovery, while the Israelites sojourned in the wilderness, it was selected as the ornament to the robe of the Ephod.

The sacred history also informs us, that the two large pillars of brass, made by Hiram for the porch of Solomon's temple, were ornamented with carvings of the pomegranate; and by the writings of Solomon we may conclude, that a choice wine was made from it in Judea:

"I would cause thee to drink of spiced wine of the juice of my pomegranates."

Again it is mentioned by the Prophet Joel:

"The vine is dried up, and the fig-tree languisheth; the pomegranate-tree, the palm-tree also, and the apple-tree; even all the trees of the field are withered."

The Grecians esteemed this fruit, and described it in

their fabulous stories as growing in the Elysian Fields. When Ceres earnestly entreated Jupiter for the restitution of her daughter Proserpine, who had been carried off by Pluto, he promised to grant it on condition that she had tasted no food in the infernal regions. Unfortunately she had gathered a pomegranate from a tree, and eaten a few of the seeds, as she was walking in the Elysian Fields. This was made known by Ascalaphus, who alone had seen it; and the enraged mother turned him into an owl for his unseasonable information.

The pomegranate-tree was first brought to Rome from Carthage, in the days of the murderous Sylla. Pliny says, that the territory of Carthage claimed to itself the Punic apple, which some call pomegranate; from the flowers of which is obtained the colour to dye cloth, called Puniceus (pink or light red.). He speaks of nine varieties; describes the sweet sort, the sour, the temperate, the styptic or austere, and one kind tasting of wine. "The difference," he says, "between the pomegranate of Samos and that of Egypt, consists in their flowers; the one being white, and the other red. The rind of the sour kind is the best for tanners and curriers to dress their leather with." This author recommends pomegranates to be divided into quarters, and steeped in rain-water for three days; which, he states, makes a good drink for those who are of weak habits. The flowers, rind, and every part of the fruit, were used medicinally by the Romans; on which subject he has written at large, book vi. chap. 23.

Some authors affirm, that Grenada, in Spain, owes its name to this fruit, which was brought from Africa, and planted in that district. The capital of this province has a split pomegranate for its arms, which is seen on the gate-posts of the public walks, and is represented in carving, or by painting, on all the public buildings.

The pomegranate-tree was first cultivated in England

in the year 1548, during the reign of Henry the Eighth; and we find it mentioned among the trees that fruited in the orange-house of the unfortunate Charles the First.

It blossoms well in the warmer counties of England; but the fruit seldom comes to perfection in the open air. The kind generally planted for ornament is the double scarlet, which is very beautiful when in blossom.

Gerard writes on the medicinal qualities of this tree, and informs us, that he reared several plants from the seeds previous to 1597.

The pomegranate has been planted in the West India islands, where the fruit grows larger and finer-flavoured than in Europe. The French, in the island of St. Vincent, had a riddle on the pomegranate, on account of the resemblance which the calix bears to a crown.

"Quelle est la reine, qui porte tout son royaume dans son sein?"

Lord Bacon notices this fruit, and recommends the use of the wine of the sweet pomegranates for complaints of the liver, or, if that cannot be had, the juice of them newly expressed. He says, "let it be taken in the morning, with a little sugar; and into the glass into which the expression is made, put a small piece of green citron-peel, and three or four whole cloves: let this be taken from February till the end of March." The juice of the pomegranate is preferred even to that of oranges in cases of fever. The rind of the fruit and the flowers are the parts directed for medicinal uses: they are both powerful astringents, and have long been successfully employed as such, both internally and externally for gargles, and in diarrhœas, &c. The dose in substance is from half a dram to a dram; in infusion or decoction, to half an ounce. *(Woodville.)*

As an astringent, the rind of the fruit, boiled in water with cinnamon, port wine and guada jelly to be added, is recommended in Dancer's Medical Assistant.

The Persians make a favourite drink of the rinds of the pomegranate, with the addition of cinnamon.

The rind also produces as good ink as that made from galls.

Sloane says, that the leaves beaten with oil of roses, applied to the head, cure its aching. The rind of the fruit, together with the bark of the tree, is still used in some parts of Germany, in the preparation and dyeing of red leather in imitation of Morocco.

These beautiful trees love a strong rich soil. They are easily propagated by laying down their branches in the spring, which in one year will make good roots, when they should be planted before they begin to open their buds.

As these trees are often deprived of blossom by the ignorance of the pruner, we shall observe that the flowers always proceed from the extremity of the branches which are produced the same year. Therefore, all weak branches of the former year should be cut out, and the strongest should be shortened in proportion to their strength, in order to obtain new shoots in every part of the tree. The best time for this pruning is about Michaelmas.

The Parisians are very fond of this tree, which is to be seen in every garden in the city and its vicinity.

In Sicily it forms the hedge-rows. Russel notices, in an account of Aleppo, that "the nightingale sings from the pomegranate-groves in the day-time, and from the loftiest trees at night;" from which Moore seems to have taken the idea,

"The nightingale now bends her flight
From the high trees, where all the night
She sang so sweet, with none to listen;
And hides her from the morning star,
Where thickets of pomegranate glisten."

PUMPKIN, OR POMPION.—PEPO.

Natural order, Cucurbitaceæ. A genus of the Monœcia Syngenesia class.

THE pompion is a coarse, inferior kind of melon, which has long been known in Europe, as Pliny mentions it in his 19th book, chap. v. where he says, cucumbers of an exceeding large size are called pompions. Again, in his 20th book, chap. ii. he says, "the fruit called pompions, or melons, are eaten to cool the body, and the fleshy substance is applied to the eyes, assuaging their pain," &c.

Aiton states it to be a native of the Levant, and says it was first introduced into this country in 1570. Gerard says, "as there is a wild sort of cucumbers, of melons, citruls, and gourds, so likewise there be certaine wild pompions, which grow in Barbarie, Africa, and most parts of the East and West Indies." This author says, "the pulpe of the pompion is neuer eaten raw; but boiled in milk and buttered, is not onely a good wholesome meate for man's bodie, but, being so prepared, is also a most phisicall medicine for such as have an hot stomacke, and the inward parts inflamed:" he continues, "the flesh or pulpe of the same sliced, and fried in a pan with butter, is also a good and wholesome meate:" but he condemns the method of using it with apples in pies.

This fruit has lately been raised in the neighbourhood of London to an extraordinary size, weighing nearly two hundred weight. These are sold in the shops of the metropolis, more as a curiosity than for use. I have found them, when boiled in their own moisture, viz. without water, an excellent vegetable with meat, having a taste resembling artichokes: with the addition of the peel and juice of lemons, they make an agreeable pudding.

Pompions are used by the Jews in the Feast of Tabernacles; when they form a kind of cradles, into which they put a great number of pompions.

In Hughes's Natural History of Barbadoes, he says, "Pumpkins make a great part of the food of the poorer sort, in the summer-time, as well in Asia and Africa as in America." He adds, that they are distinguished in Barbadoes by the names of the White, the Blue, the Marbled, and the Garden Pumpkin. The latter differs from all the rest by having no seed, but is propagated by slips. He says, also, that they are boiled and eaten with flesh meat, and much used by the poorer sort in soups.

Galiffe tells us that at Venice the poorest class live almost exclusively on pumpkins, of which there are two sorts. "The first and cheapest is that round and insipid kind, which is known all over Europe; it is called *Zucca barucca*, and a slice of it costs only one centime, equal to the tenth part of a penny. It is miserable food, but five or six slices of it during the day, are sufficient to keep body and soul together. The other sort is called *Zucca Santa;* it is more substantial, less insipid, and proportionably dearer: and is the favourite and usual food of that portion of the lower classes who are just above begging. Its form is that of a very long pear, its taste is not unlike that of a carrot, and the rind, when fried, forms a sort of resinous substance, which is esteemed a great delicacy by the pumpkin eaters. These pumpkins are sold ready fried, in three or four different moveable stalls in every street; you cannot go ten paces, without meeting with some. They afford, perhaps, a less savoury, but certainly a more wholesome nourishment, than the greasy and dirty fritter, of which the Amsterdam beggars are so fond."

We are assured that the grooms in India defend their horses from the flies by rubbing them every morning with the flowers of the pumpkin.

The Jugglers, or quacks, in some parts of America, extract the pulp out of pompions, and fill them with flint stones, with which they make a great noise, and pretend to frighten away all the complaints of their superstitious patients.

QUINCE.—CYDONIA.

Natural order, Pomaceæ. A genus of the Icosandria Pentagynia class.

The Greeks called this fruit Μηλεα Κυδωνια, and the Latins *Cydonia Malus*, from Cydon in Crete, now called Candia. Cato called it *Cotonea*, from the down which covers the fruit, and which Fuchsius tells us was called *Cotton*. The Spaniards call it *Marmello*, from whence we derive the name of Marmalade. The English name of Quince seems to be a compound of the French *Coing*, and the German *Quittenbaum*.

Linnæus has joined this genus, as well as the apple, to the pear, while Miller separates it on this account: he says, "the pear will take upon the quince by grafting or budding, and so *vice versâ;* but neither of these will take upon the apple, nor that upon either of these." But we have a particular account transmitted to us by Pliny, that quinces were grafted upon apple-stocks in his time (book xv. chap. 14): he says, "as for the quince-apples that come of a quince grafted upon an apple-stock, they are called *Appiana*, after Appius, who was of the Claudian house, and who first devised and practised this mode of grafting: these apples," continues he, "have the smell of the quince, are of a red colour, and the size of the Claudian apple."

The Quince is a fruit that the ancients held in high estimation: they considered it as the emblem of happiness, of love, and of fruitfulness: it was dedicated to Venus, and the temples of Cyprus and Paphos were decorated with it. The statues of the gods also who presided at the nuptial bed, were ornamented with this fruit; and the bride, before she entered into the marriage-bed, used to eat of the quinces. Columella says, quinces not only yield pleasure, but health also: he speaks of three kinds; the Struthian, the Must Quince, and the Orange or Golden Quince.

The learned Goropius maintains that quinces were the golden apples of the Hesperides, and not oranges, as some commentators pretend. In support of his argument, he states, that it was a fruit much revered by the ancients, and he assures us that there has been discovered at Rome a statue of Hercules, that held in its hand three quinces; this, he says, agrees with the fable which states, that Hercules stole the golden apples from the gardens of the Hesperides.

Pliny speaks of quinces in his 15th book, 11th chap. and says, "There are many kinds of this fruit in Italy, some growing wild in the hedge-rows, others so large that they weigh the boughs down to the ground; some of a green hue, others inclining to gold colour: these were called *Chrysomela*, which seems to give authority to the above account of Goropius. The only kind that was eaten raw, he states to have been raised by grafting the large quince upon the stock of a small kind, called *Struthea* (the pear-quince). He adds, "All kinds of this fruit are in use now-a-days, within the waiting or presence-chambers of our great personages, where men give attendance to salute them as they come forth every morning." He also states, that they were used to garnish the images which stand about the bed's head and sides.

The same author, in his 23d book, chap. 6, writes much on the medicinal qualities of this fruit. "Quinces," says he, "when eaten raw, if quite ripe, are good for those who spit blood, or are troubled with hæmorrhage." The juice of raw quinces, he states to be a sovereign remedy for the swoln spleen, the dropsy, and difficulty of taking breath, particularly to those who cannot draw their breath but in an upright position. The flowers, either fresh or dried, he tells us, are good for the inflammation of the eyes. The root of the tree was used more as a charm than a medicine for those afflicted with the scrofula.

Quince-trees grow wild on the banks of the Danube, and they are stated to have been brought into this country from the island of Crete, now called Candia. They have long been cultivated in this kingdom, as our earliest authors on this subject mention them. Gerard says, they were often planted in hedges and fences to gardens and vineyards in his time. By the Hortus Kewensis it appears, that the quince was first introduced in the reign of Henry the Eighth, 1537, which is evidently an error, from the circumstance above related by Gerard, who was then an old man.

Rea's Pomona notices (in 1665), that we then cultivated in this country, "in addition to the English Quince, the Portugal Apple-Quince, a large yellow quince, which was apt to split, but so tender as to be eaten raw. The Portugal Pear-Quince for baking or preserving.

"The Barberry Quince, which was smaller both in fruit and tree.

"The Lion's Quince, a large fruit of a deep yellow colour, the sides ribbed with a deep hollow crown.

"The Brunswick Quince, large and round, but a whiter fruit than any of the others."

Coles also mentions these varieties in 1657.

Quinces are used in medicine, being of an astringent and stomachic quality. The expressed juice of this fruit, in small quantities, as a spoonful or two, is of service in nausea, vomiting, &c. Lord Bacon says, "It is certain that the use of quinces is good to strengthen the stomach; but we take them to be better, if they be used in that which they call *quiddeny* of quinces, than in the bodies of quinces themselves, because they lie heavy in the stomach; but those quiddenies are best taken after meals alone; before meals, dipped in vinegar."

Quinces grow in such abundance in some parts of the wealds of Sussex, as to enable private families to make quince-wine in quantities of from one to two hundred gallons in a season. It is an agreeable wine, that improves much by keeping, and is greatly esteemed by asthmatic persons. A gentleman residing at Horsham, in Sussex, assured the author that he was not only relieved in an asthmatic complaint of long standing, but completely restored to his health by the use of this wine, which was made after the following receipt:—

"Cut large quinces in quarters, and core them, as the seeds give the wine an unpleasant flavour; grind them in the same manner as apples for cider, and put to every gallon of pummis a gallon of water; let it stand a day or two, then strain it off. Should the pummis smell very strong of the fruit, it will bear a little more water, and to every gallon put three pounds and a quarter of moist sugar; tun it, and stop it quite close in the following March; rack it off; cleanse the cask from the sediment, and put it back again; and in the second year bottle it off."

Quince-marmalade is greatly admired by those who are fond of the fruit. It is the most esteemed among the various comfits which the Greeks and other Christians in the Levant offer their guests.

The Portugal quince is reckoned the best. In the pruning of the quince-tree little is required, except to keep the stem free from suckers, and to cut all branches that rub each other.

It was formerly much more in use in this country than at present. Coles says, " Marmalade of quinces is toothsome, as well as wholsome, and therefore I cannot blame such gentlemen which are seldom without it in their closets."

RASPBERRY-BUSH.—RUBUS IDÆUS.

Natural order, Senticosæ. A genus of the Icosandria Polygynia class.

The raspberry was but little noticed by the ancients, and that principally on account of its medical virtues. Pliny does not consider it of so much importance as the bramble, in mentioning which he says, "there is a third sort of bramble, which the Greeks call *Idæa*, after Mount Ida. This fruit is smaller than the other bramble-berries, with less thorns on the stem, and these not so sharp or hooked. The flowers of this raspis," he continues, "being tempered with honey, are good to be laid to watery and blood-shotten eyes, as also in the Erysipelas. Being taken inwardly, and drunk with water, it is a comfortable medicine to a weak stomach."

The red raspberry is indigenous to this country, and is often found wild in the northern counties. We have also seen it in the wild state growing freely in some woods on the South Downs of Sussex. It is a fruit that appears to have been much improved by cultivation, as Gerard writes on it, previous to 1597, as not being equal to the blackberry, although he says it is planted in gardens. He calls it Raspis, or Hindberry: "the fruit," he adds, "is in shape and proportion like that of the bramble; red, when it is ripe, and covered over with a little downiness, of taste not very pleasant." He does not mention the white raspberry; nor has Tusser, who wrote in the previous reign.

Dr. Turner says, in his Herbal of the year 1568, "the raspis is found in many gardines of England; the berries are rede."

The large kinds of raspberries, both red and yellow, were brought from Antwerp to this country.

The yellow, or white raspberry, is most admired at the dessert: indeed all the white fruits of the berry kind are sweeter than the coloured, but other fruits that are coloured are generally sweeter than the white.

The red raspberry is considered the finest for flavouring ices, jams, &c. A third kind is cultivated, which produces two crops a-year, but we have seldom met with the October raspberry possessing much flavour.

Raspberries are much cultivated in the neighbourhood of Isleworth and Brentford; from whence those are sent to London in swing carts, which are used by the distillers for making raspberry brandy, raspberry vinegar, &c. as also those used by confectioners and pastry-cooks; but the raspberries which are intended for the table, are brought by women on their heads: their load consists of a round, or basket, containing twelve gallons, of three pints to a gallon; and although the distance is ten miles from Isleworth to Covent-Garden market, they regularly perform the journey in two hours, for which they are paid three shillings and sixpence. From Hammersmith these industrious women will take a load three times a-day, for which they receive eighteen-pence per load. These female fruit-porters come to the vicinity of London for the season, from Wiltshire, Shropshire, and Wales: in their long journeys they seldom walk at a less pace than five miles per hour.

The dietetic and medicinal virtues of raspberries being the same as those of the strawberry, will be noticed in the history of that fruit.

"Raspberry and strawberry wines," says Dr. Short,

"are of all made-wines the most delicious to the taste: they lightly and pleasantly stimulate the nerves of the mouth and nose with a most agreeable smell and taste, which proceeds from a mixture of their essential salt and fine oil." This author recommends these wines in scorbutic disorders as a purifier and sweetener of the blood. "Mixed with water," he says, "they make a good reviving draught in ardent fevers."

The wood of the raspberry-bush produces fruit but one year, therefore that should be carefully cut down below the surface of the earth, and the young shoots should be shortened to about two feet in height; and we would recommend not more than three or four of the shoots to be left to each root, as these will produce a greater number of berries, and larger fruit, than would be obtained if twice that number of suckers were left. The middle or end of October is the proper time for this pruning. The fruit is produced from young branches out of the last year's shoots or suckers.

The plants raised by layers are much preferred to those taken from suckers; they should also have plenty of room, for when there is not space for the air and light to pass between the rows, the fruit will be small, and not ripen well. They require a fresh strong loam, for in warm light ground they produce but little fruit.

We have seen raspberries make extraordinary strong wood, and produce abundant crops of fine berries, from being manured with swine's dung only.

STRAWBERRY-PLANT.—FRAGARIA.

Natural order, Senticosæ. A genus of the Icosandria Polygynia class.

"The blushing strawberry
Which lurks, close shrouded from high-looking eyes,
Shewing that sweetness low and hidden lies."

THE Latins named this fruit *Fragaria*, from its fragrance. It was also called *Morum terrestre*, ground mulberry, from the similarity in the form of the fruit.

The late Sir J. Banks concludes, that their English name was derived from the practice of putting straw under them when the fruit began to swell, as the plant has no relation to straw in any other way, and no other European language applies the idea of straw in any other shape to the name of the berry, or to the plant.

But as we find not only the oldest, but all the English writers call it by the same name, we are of opinion that it had this appellation prior to its being cultivated in our gardens, and that the name of strawberry originated from the old practice of threading these berries on straws of grass, in which shape they were brought from the woods. It is still practised by children in many country places where the wild strawberry abounds, who offer you the fruit, so many straws of berries for a penny.

This most agreeable fruit does not appear to have been cultivated by the ancients; and it seems only to have grown in the mountainous parts of Greece and Italy, the climate being too warm in the other parts of these countries. It is slightly mentioned by Virgil, Ovid, and Pliny, and even the latter author does not speak of the fruit as a diet or medicine. In speaking of the arbutus tree, book 15, chap. 24, he says, "the tree is termed the strawberry-tree; and there is not any other tree that gives fruit which resembles the fruit of an herb growing on the ground." Again he says, speaking of the bramble-berry, —"as the ground-strawberry differs in carnosity from the fruit of the arbutus-tree."

The red-wood strawberry is a native of this country; and several modern writers state, that the white strawberry, as well as the green strawberry, are indigenous to these kingdoms. The latter is often called the pine-apple strawberry, from its excellent flavour.

That our native strawberries have long been cultivated in the gardens of this country, we find from Tusser's advice to the Farmer, who, in the work he points out to be done in the month of September, says,

> "Wife, into the garden, and set me a plot
> With strawberry-roots, of the best to be got:
> Such growing abroad, among thorns in the wood,
> Well chosen and pricked, prove excellent good."

Gerard seems to consider only the red strawberry as a native of this climate. He says, "strawberries do grow upon hills and valleys, likewise in woods, and other such places that bee something shadowie. They prosper well in gardens: the red strawberry euery where; and the other two, white and green, more rare, and are not to be founde saue onely in gardens."

Shakspeare says, in Henry V.—

"The strawberry grows underneath the nettle;
And wholesome berries thrive, and ripen best,
Neighbour'd by fruit of baser quality."

From another of his dramatic pieces we are told how early they were cultivated in Holborn:—

"My Lord of Ely, when I was last in Holborn,
I saw good strawberries in your garden there,
I do beseech you send for some of them."

The scarlet strawberry is a native of Virginia, where it grows wild; and was brought to this country about the year 1625. Parkinson observes, in 1629, "it hath been with us but of late days. Master Quester, the post-master, first brought them over into our country; but I know no man so industrious in the careful planting and bringing them to perfection in that plentiful manner, as Master Vincent Sion, on the Bankside, near Paris-garden stairs, who from seven roots, in one year and a half, planted half an acre of ground with the increase from them, besides those he gave away to his friends." This is the earliest sort, and is the best strawberry for forcing.

The hautboy-strawberry was, according to Miller, procured also from America; from which we have raised the improved kind, called the globe-hautboy.

The Chili strawberry takes its name from the part of America so called, from whence it was brought by M. Frazier, engineer to the French king. It was cultivated in the royal gardens at Paris, from whence some of the plants were conveyed to Holland, and from the latter place they were brought to England, by Mr. Miller, in the first year of the reign of King George the Second, 1727.

The Alpine strawberry is a native of Germany, and was planted in England in the year 1768.

The varieties of the strawberry have, like those of other fruits, been so increased, that, to describe them distinctly, would be almost impossible, even with the assistance of coloured drawings. The president of the Horticultural Society, Thomas Andrew Knight, Esq., states, that he has at this time not less than 400 varieties of this fruit in his garden. Among those which he has raised, is one from the white Chili strawberry and the pollen of the black strawberry.

Mr. Keen of Isleworth, in the county of Middlesex, who is one of the greatest growers of strawberries for the London market, has obligingly furnished us with his observations on the culture of this fruit, which afford a strong instance of the advantage of botanical knowledge. Mr. Keen states, that the want of education deprived him of the benefit of written information; but it will be found that he has studied the book of nature to advantage. "I observed," says Mr. Keen, "that some of my strawberry plants gave out abundance of male blossoms, but produced no fruit. I therefore, in the year 1809, had all these plants taken from my beds, and had other beds made with the fruit-bearing, or female plants only; but finding my crop entirely fail, and suspecting the error I had made, I procured some blossoms of the male plants, which having put into a bottle of water, I placed on one of my beds, and in a few days perceived the fruit began to swell and thrive on all the plants contiguous to the bottle.

"Having tried the same experiment in several parts of my garden with the like effect, I was convinced of the necessity of the male plants in producing fruit; since which time, I have planted about one male plant to ten female plants, which I find to be the most profitable proportion, as my beds have since been so productive, that it has been scarce possible to gather the fruit without bruising others. Some strawberry plants have both male and female flowers on the same plant. These are not so profitable; and I find it more advantageous to raise my plants from seed than by suckers. When the fruit is quite ripe, I sow them in a rich moist soil, and in one year the Alpines produce fruit, but the other kinds require two years." From the seed, Mr. Keen has procured a new variety of this fruit, to which he has given the name of Imperial Strawberry; it is of a dark ruby colour, and, in appearance, the most beautiful of all the strawberries; but I find the flavour of it is not superior to that of other kinds. Mr. Keen recommends the month of March, as the best season for making new beds.

The strawberry is our earliest fruit, and, as the harbinger of the *fructus horæi*, its appearance is as welcome, as its flavour is agreeable.

It has also of late years formed a part of the autumnal and winter desserts. The alpine variety having been obtained from cold mountains, and the seed sown, is found to produce abundance of fruit in the open air, even as late in the season as December; and it is not an uncommon thing now, to hear them cried through the streets of London in November. Thus by the improvement in horticulture, we are now enabled to enjoy these fragrant berries in every month of the year, the hot-house affording them from January until the arrival of the earliest varieties in the open garden. The August and September strawberries are procured, by planting well-rooted runners of the Roseberry, Wilmot's late Scarlet, or the Common Scarlet, in beds and in open situations, about the middle of May.

The treatment of these plants having varied so much of late years, and the size and quantity, as well as the quality, having been so much improved, we shall notice the principal cause, for the information of those who have not regular gardeners.

It is no uncommon thing, in many parts of the country, to see strawberry-beds that have not been renewed for ten or twenty years; these, of course, will not produce so much fruit in ten years, as may be obtained in one year by attention. Strawberries in general prosper in hazelly loam; if the soil is too rich, the plants run more to leaves and suckers than to fruit; it should also not be too dry, for watering will not answer so well as a moist mould; but the different kinds of strawberries require different soils. For instance, the Chili strawberry is found to succeed best in a strong brick earth approaching to clay. The situation of the beds should be well exposed to the sun and air, without which, fine-flavoured fruit cannot be expected; the crops are too frequently destroyed by an improper mode and time of watering, as many persons, without considering how necessary it is that the blossoms should receive impregnation, wash all the prolific powder from the flowers, and thus, disabling nature to fulfil its office, deprive themselves of a crop of fruit. When the fruit is set, watering may greatly assist the size of the berry. Should excessive droughts prevail when these plants are in flower, the ground should be watered without sprinkling the plants, and which will well repay the extra time and care required.

The Rev. Thomas Gardiner having succeeded in growing abundant crops of fine strawberries, we shall notice the information he gives on the subject, as laid before us in the Transactions of the Horticultural Society. "The soil consists of a dark sandy loam, of about two feet in depth, having a very fine white sand for the sub-soil, which I take care never to disturb. In preparing the ground for my crops, I trench it all over two spades deep, and then lay upon the surface a dressing, about two inches thick, of rich yellow loam, rotten dung, and bog-earth, mixed together in equal proportions, and which is afterwards well dug in with a fork; I then form the beds four feet four inches wide, with alleys at least two feet wide between them. The runners of most varieties are set out eighteen inches from plant to plant, and the same distance from row to row: the roseberry and common scarlet do not require so much room; I consequently set them sixteen inches from plant to plant, and only allow a foot between the rows, which I find quite sufficient for their growth. The sorts I prefer and cultivate chiefly, are the Pine, Downton Castle, Hautboy, Hudson's Bay, Wilmot's late Scarlet, Common Scarlet, Keen's Imperial, and two sorts of Chili; but I never suffer any of the varieties to remain in the ground more than one year. Early in August, as soon as the gathering is over, I destroy all my beds, and proceed immediately to trench, form, and manure them in the manner before directed, to receive the plants for the crop of the ensuing year, taking care to select for that purpose the strongest and best-rooted runners from the old rejected plants. If at this season the weather should be particularly hot, and the surface of the ground much parched, I defer the operation of preparing my beds and planting them, till the ground is moistened by rain."

The covering of strawberry-plants with sea-weed in the winter, has been found to increase the size of the fruit to a prodigious degree. This is much practised in the Island of Jersey.

The old practice of putting clean straw round strawberry plants, is still continued in some parts of Suffolk; and its utility is very evident, as in dry, parching weather, it is the means of keeping the plants moist; and in wet, showery weather, it both keeps the fruit clean, and prevents its rotting so rapidly.

We have found the short grass mowed from lawns answer this purpose, and which has a neater appearance.

As a dietetic fruit, the strawberry affords but little nourishment; the moderate or even plentiful use of it is salubrious, and recommended to those of inflammatory or bilious habits. Boerhaave considers the continued use of this fruit, as one of the principal remedies in cases of obstruction and viscidity, and in putrid disorders. Hoffman furnishes instances of some obstinate diseases being cured by strawberries, and other mild sweet subacid fruits, and affirms that he has known consumptive people cured by them. Linnæus informs us, that by eating plentifully of strawberries every day, he kept himself free from the gout. They promote perspiration, and dissolve the tartarous incrustations upon the teeth. Strawberries should be taken sparingly by those of a cold inactive disposition, where the vessels are lax, the circulation languid, or digestion weak. Many persons are fearful of being poisoned by the saliva of toads and other reptiles which is found on this fruit; M. Haller says, there is no animal in Europe whose saliva can injure, unless instantaneously introduced into the blood.

This fruit is generally sent to dessert in its natural state, although often with cream and sugar; but it is more esteemed when Burgundy or claret wine is substituted for the cream. Strawberry jam is much admired; and for ice-creams the flavour is generally preferred to that of raspberries.

The pine strawberries make an agreeable dessert wine, as rich as mountain; but possessing greater fragrance and acidity: the latter quality is generally too predominant in our English made-wines, which proceeds more from the want of attention in the making of wines than from the quality of the fruits.

In the coffee-houses of Paris they make a very agreeable drink of the juice of strawberries, lemons, sugar, and water, which is called *bavaroise à la grecque.*

In the monastery of Bathalla, in Portugal, is the tomb of Don John, son of King John the First, of Portugal, which is ornamented by the representation of strawberries; this prince having chosen them for his crest, to shew his devotion to St. John the Baptist, who lived on fruits.

The yellow-flowered strawberry, *fragaria indica*, is a native of the mountains of the Indian continent; it was first discovered by Dr. Buchanan on the sand by the sides of rivers in Nepaul; and was introduced into this country by Mr. Charles Grevill, who cultivated it at Paddington in 1804. We have tasted this fruit in the nursery-grounds of Mr. Hugh Ronalds at Brentford, but found the strawberry pithy and still more disagreeable than insipid; its only merit as a fruit is novelty: as a plant it is curious, possessing the bloom of the cinquefoil and the fruit of the strawberry, which is of a bright poppy colour, and in shape more like the fruit of the arbutus than that of the strawberry, being quite globular. In the greenhouse it is ornamental, as its red tendrils trail over the shelves, and embellish them with its bright yellow flowers and glowing red fruit at the same time.

SERVICE-TREE.—SORBUS.

Natural order, Pomaceæ. A genus of the Icosandria Trigynia class.

THIS fruit, which is a native of England, is now as little known, and as rare in the London market, as the fruits of the most distant parts of the world; and the serviceberry-tree is now so thinly scattered over the country, that many farmers are ignorant of its existence.

It is difficult to ascertain whether the English name is a corruption of the Italian *Sorbe*, the French *Sorbes*, or the Spanish *Servas*, or like them is derived from the Latin *Sorbus, à sorbendo, quia caro matura sorbetur;* the pulp being supped or sucked in.

Pliny writes of it as a fruit held in esteem by the Romans. He mentions four sorts, some round, resembling apples, others shaped like pears, others like an egg, and one variety which was only used medicinally. He states, that Cato would have service-berries preserved, (book xv. c. 21), and in the 17th chapter of the same book he gives directions for preserving them in two different ways: again he mentions them in his 23d book, 17th chap. and says, their medicinal virtues are the same as those of the medlar.

Gerard describes two kinds, and says, "they are found in woods and groves in most places of England. There be many small trees thereof, in a little wood a mile beyond Islington: in Kent it groweth in great abundance, especially about Southfleete and Gravesend."

The service-tree is still occasionally to be met with in the hedge-rows in Kent, and in the wealds of Sussex, of the size of a moderate oak-tree; as also in the north of England and Wales.

The service-berry, which is an umbilicated fruit, partakes of the quality of the medlar, both in the green and in the ripe state. It is gathered in bunches, and put into, or hung on, a cleft stick of about a yard long, which becomes a mass of berries: in this state the fruit is sold by the country people, and then hung up in a garden to receive the damp air of the night, which causes it to undergo a kind of putrefactive fermentation, and in this soft state it is eaten, and has a more agreeable acid than the medlar. Chancellor Bacon speaks of service-berries in his time as a garden fruit. In Italy and the south of France, they are still served up in the dessert.

Perhaps the great size of the service-tree has been the cause of excluding this fruit from our gardens: but it is, from its beauty, particularly when in blossom, a desirable tree for planting in parks or paddocks; and as the timber is so valuable, and now become so rare, we hope to see it more cultivated. There is a remarkable fine tree of this kind now growing at Kingsfold farm, in the parish of Rusper, near Horsham in Sussex.

It is known that many noblemen and gentlemen object to fruit-bearing trees being planted on their estates, on the principle that it encourages depredators to injure their plantations: but this seems but a poor excuse for depriving themselves and the public of the beauty and variety which the blossoms give at one season of the year, and the fruit at another, particularly to those who have park-keepers or bailiffs on the premises.

A great number of large service-trees grow wild about Aubigny in France, whence the late Duke of Richmond brought a large quantity of the fruit, and from the seeds raised a considerable number of young plants at Goodwood in Sussex.

St. Pierre says, he found the service-tree growing between Sweden and Russia. It is also found in the island of Jura, where the juice of the fruit is employed as an acid for punch.

Furber of Kensington, who in 1733 published his twelve engravings of fruits for the desserts of each month, gives a representation of the Italian services for October, and the English maple-leaved service-berries for the month of November.

This fruit is considered to be very restringent, and useful for all kinds of fluxes; but when ripe it is not altogether so binding.

The timber of the service-tree is of a fine hard grain, and the variations pleasing when wrought into cabinet goods; it is esteemed by the turner and carver, as well as for the making of gun-stocks. It is used by mill-wrights for cogs to wheels, &c. in preference to any other wood: it is also a very durable wood for buildings that are exposed to a northern aspect. Evelyn says, he saw a room curiously wainscotted with this wood.

TAMARIND.—TAMARINDUS

Natural order, Lomentaceæ. A genus of the Monadelphia Triandria class, and not of the Triandria Monogynia, as classed by Linnæus.

———— " Lay me reclined
Beneath the spreading tamarind that shakes,
Fanned by the breeze, its fever-cooling fruit."

This name is derived from *Tamar*, the Arabic name for the date; and it is to the Arabians that we owe a knowledge of the use of this fruit in medicine. The ancient Greeks knew nothing of it, and the first authors who prescribe the tamarind are Serapion, Mesue, and Avicenna.

The tamarind-tree is a native of both Indies, and thrives also in Egypt, Palestine, Arabia, and other parts of Asia; and it appears, by Johnson's edition of Gerard, to have been cultivated in England previously to 1633. Miller states, that he has had it grow upwards of three feet high in one summer, and produce flowers the same year it was sown; but this must have been accidental, for none of his older plants blossomed, although he had them twelve feet high, and eighteen years old. There is a fine healthy tree of this species now in the Royal Botanic Gardens at Kew, which flowered a few years back for the first time.

The tree grows to a great size, with large spreading branches, and a thick and beautiful foliage. The leaves are pinnate, composed of sixteen or eighteen pairs of leaflets, without a single one at the end: they are ovate-oblong, quite entire, smooth, sessile, of a bright green, spreading during the day, but closing, so as to lie over each other in the night: they have an acid taste. The flowers come out from the sides of the branches, on a long, upright, common peduncle, six or eight together, in loose bunches, of a yellow colour, veined with a reddish purple.

What we style the fruit of the tamarind is only the pistil of the flowers, which become pods, that are thick and compressed, from two to five inches in length, with from two to four or six seeds: these pods become of a reddish brown as they ripen. The fruit is, properly speaking, composed of two pods: the outer pod is fleshy, and the inner one thin as the finest parchment; between these two there is a space of about a quarter of an inch all the way, which is filled up with a soft pulpy substance, of a tart but agreeable taste, which is what we use as the fruit: this, and the stones which are enclosed in the inner pod, are fastened together by a great many slender fibres from the woody stalk which runs through the pod, and conveys the vinous juice, that afterwards hardens, into the viscous matter of the pulp. Lunan says, the tree is exceedingly common in Jamaica, where it grows to vast bulk; and he gives the following account of preparing the fruit. "The pods are gathered when full ripe, which is known by their fragility, or easy breaking on a small pressure between the finger and the thumb. The fruit is taken out of the pod, cleared from the shelly fragments, and placed in layers in a cask; and the boiling syrup from the teache, or first copper in the boiling-house, just before it begins to granulate, is poured in till the cask is filled: the syrup pervades every part quite to the bottom, and, when cool, the cask is headed for sale. The more elegant method is with sugar, well clarified with eggs, till a clear transparent syrup is formed, which gives the fruit a much pleasanter flavour.

The East-India tamarinds are preserved generally without sugar, and are better adapted for an ingredient in medical compositions. The best method of preserving them is said to be by putting alternate layers of tamarinds and powdered sugar in a stone jar: by this means the tamarinds preserve their colour and taste more agreeably.

In the Indies, and in some parts of Africa, tamarinds are used as food, and are made into a sort of confection with sugar, and eaten as a delicacy, which in the violent heats of these climates is cooling, and at the same time keeps the bowels in a proper state of laxity. The fruit is also frequently made an ingredient in punch, and seldom fails to open the body. A very agreeable cooling drink is made by simply mixing water with a few spoonfuls of it when preserved. Dr. Cullen was of opinion, that it was best to preserve tamarinds in the pods. They contain a larger proportion of acid, with saccharine matter, than is usually found in the acid dulcet fruits, and are therefore not only employed as a laxative, but also for abating thirst and heat in various inflammatory complaints, and for correcting putrid disorders, especially those of a bilious kind, in which the cathartic, antiseptic, and refrigerant qualities of the fruit have been found equally useful. When intended merely as a laxative, it may be of advantage to join them with manna, or purgatives of a sweet kind, by which their use is rendered safer and more effectual. Three drams of the pulp are usually sufficient to open the body; but to prove moderately cathartic, one or two ounces are required. The leaves are sometimes used in sub-acid infusions; and Alpinus says, a decoction of them kills worms in children. *(Wright.)* Dr. Zimmerman prescribes tamarinds in putrid dysentery.

The sour taste of tamarinds proves that acid particles

abound greatly in them, and a chemical analysis gives farther proof of this. There is indeed no alkali to be obtained from this fruit, otherwise than by distilling it in a retort with quicklime. A simple analysis of it yields no other principle but acid and sulphur.

It is not uncommon to find an essential salt crystallized on the branches of the tamarind tree, which greatly resembles cream of tartar in all respects, and is no other than the genuine salt of the plant, formed by the sun's drying up the accidental extravasated juices.

The leaves of the sycamore, in hot seasons, are often found thus covered with crystals of their essential salt, which is sweet, and very much of the nature of sugar. The lime-tree produces a like saccharine matter, which, being given to a person to drink, will be found of the same purgative virtue as manna.

Tamarinds are an ingredient in the well-known medicine called lenitive electuary.

WALNUT.—JUGLANS.

Natural order, Amentaceæ. A genus of the Monœcia Polyandria class.

THE walnut-tree is evidently a native of the northern parts of Persia and China, where it grows wild; and the Grecian names for this fruit, Persicon and Basilicon, Persian or Royal Nut, bespeak it to have been brought from Persia, either by the monarchs of Greece themselves, or sent thither from the kings of Persia. According to Pliny's account, book 15, chap. 22, "the Greeks afterwards called them *Caryon*, on account of the heaviness of the head which their strong smell caused."

"Walnuts were first brought into Italy by Vitellius, a little before the death of Tiberius the emperor; and the Romans," continues Pliny, "honoured them with the name of *Jovis-glans*, acorn or mast of Jove." Some of the later Greeks also called them Διος βαλάνος, and the Latins *Diu-glans*, whence was formed the word *Juglans*.

These nuts appear to have been first brought to this country from France, and were therefore called Gaul nuts; from which by a common transition, the English formed the word Walnut.

Pliny has written much on the medical virtues of these nuts, book 23, chap. 18, wherein he says, that "the more walnuts one eats, with more ease will he drive worms out of his stomach; and that, eaten before meals, they lessen the effects of any poisonous food; eaten after onions," he states, "they keep them from rising, and prevent the disagreeable smell."

The bark of the walnut-tree was considered a sovereign remedy for the ringworm. The leaves bruised and stamped with vinegar, and so applied, removed the pain of the ears.

After Mithridates was vanquished, Cneius Pompeius found in his secret closet or cabinet, among many precious jewels, the receipt of a certain antidote against poison, written in the hand-writing of Mithridates, in his private note-book, as follows :—

"Take two dry walnut kernels, as many figs, of rue twenty leaves; stamp all these together into one mass, with a grain or corn of salt. Whoever eats of this confection in a morning, fasting, no poison shall hurt him that day."

Walnuts are considered stomachic: their oil is a good medicine for the stone and gravel, and is of extraordinary use to the painter, in mixing white and other delicate colours, also for gold, size, and varnish. They eat it instead of butter, at Berry in France, and burn it in lamps, therefore these trees are cultivated with great care in that neighbourhood.

The oil of walnuts does not congeal by cold, and answers the medicinal purpose of the oil of almonds. One bushel of nuts will yield about fifteen pounds of peeled and clear kernels, and that half as much oil, which the sooner it is drawn the more in quantity, though the drier the nut the better the quality.

The bark of the tree is a strong emetic, either green, or dried and powdered. The unripe fruit is used in medicine for the destruction of worms, and is administered in the form of an extract. If the water in which the outside covering of walnuts has been steeped, be thrown on the ground, the worms will immediately come out of the earth: anglers often use this means to obtain bait for fishing.

The ancients considered that walnuts chewed by a person fasting, would cure the bite of a mad dog.

The green nuts are cordial, alexipharmic, and said to be of great use in all contagious, malignant distempers, and the plague itself.

The unripe fruit has long been used as a pickle, and the vinegar in which they are preserved, makes a very useful gargle.

The kernel of ripe walnuts is similar in qualities to the Almond; therefore may be eaten in moderation to advantage.

The nuts, preserved young, are an excellent sweetmeat, and are good to be eaten in a morning, in time of pestilential distempers, to prevent infection. We have been favoured by the following receipt for preserving young walnuts, by a family who assure me that they have known them succeed in obstinate costiveness when all other remedies have failed: even a small part of one of these sweetmeats will give relief.

Take green walnuts, in the proper state for pickling, and boil them till tender; take them out, and stick a piece of lemon-peel to every nut; and to every fifth one, a clove and a small piece of mace. To every pound of nuts, add one pound of moist sugar with water enough to make a good syrup; put in the nuts, and simmer them till the syrup is thick, and let them stand ten days; then clarify half the above quantity of sugar, and boil as before; and, when cold, cover them close for use. By keeping, the syrup will shrink, so that after a year or two it will be necessary to add a little more syrup.

Gerard says, "the green and tender nuts, boyled in sugar, and eaten as suckarde, are a most pleasant and delectable meate, comfort the stomache, and expell poyson."

The effluvia of walnut-trees is hurtful to the head, on

which account it is not safe to sit uncovered beneath them, nor is it desirable to plant them too near dwelling-houses. Pliny says, "the oak will not thrive near the walnut-tree;" and Mr. Keen, who is so justly celebrated for growing strawberries, informs me, that the walnut-tree is so injurious to strawberry beds, that they seldom bear fruit in the neighbourhood of that tree.

The largest plantation of walnut-trees in England, at the present time, is in the county of Surrey.

Gerard says, "the walnut-tree groweth in fields neere common highwaies, in a fat and fruitful ground, and in orchards." It therefore appears to us, that it must have been introduced earlier than the date mentioned in the Hortus Kewensis (1562), as this was only about thirty years before Gerard wrote his account, when these trees seem to have been very common in the fields; and Turner says in his Herbal of 1564, that it is so common that it needs no description.

Evelyn says, Burgundy abounds with walnut-trees, where they stand in the midst of goodly wheat lands, at sixty and a hundred feet distance; and so far are they from hurting the crop, that they are looked upon as great preservers by keeping the ground warm; nor do the roots hinder the plough. Whenever they fell a tree, which is only the old and decayed, they always plant a young one near him. In several places betwixt Hanau and Frankfort in Germany, no young farmer is permitted to marry a wife, till he brings proof that he has planted a stated number of walnut-trees.

The walnut-tree was formerly cultivated in England for the sake of the wood, which was in great esteem for cabinet goods, before mahogany and other curious woods were imported from America into this kingdom, which was about the beginning of the eighteenth century, when the use of mahogany was discovered by the following chance:—Dr. Gibbons, an eminent physician, was building a house in King-street, Covent Garden. His brother, who was a West India captain, brought over some planks of this wood as ballast, which he thought might be of service in the Doctor's building; but the carpenters finding the wood too hard for their tools, it was laid aside as useless. Soon after, Mrs. Gibbons wanting a candle-box, the Doctor called on his cabinet-maker (Wollaston, in Long Acre) to make him one of some wood that lay in his garden. Wollaston also complained that it was too hard; but the Doctor insisted on having it done; and, when finished, it was so much liked, that the Doctor ordered a bureau to be made of the same wood, which was accordingly done; and the fine colour, polish, &c. were so pleasing, that he invited all his friends to see it. Among them was the Duchess of Buckingham. Her Grace begged some of the same wood of Dr. Gibbons, and employed Wollaston to make her a bureau also. On this the fame of mahogony and Mr. Wollaston was much raised; and furniture made of this wood became general.

The timber of the walnut-tree is much esteemed by coach-builders, and also for making gun-stocks.

The late long war, which has caused such revolutions in the customs and manners of the English people, has also nearly thinned the country of walnut-trees, the great sums given by the gun and pistol-stock makers for this timber being an inducement to fell them, and the high price of all agricultural productions acting at the same time against replanting; but surely, while we were reaping so amply the fruits of our fathers' cultivation, we ought in justice to have planted for our children.

In the plains of Naples it is customary for a peasant, on the birth of a daughter, to plant a row of poplar-trees, which are cut down and sold at the end of seventeen years, to make up a fortune for her. Were the English farmer to plant a single walnut-tree on the same occasion, we should neither want gunstocks for our wars, nor walnuts for our weddings. Where young trees are not to be procured easily, let a walnut be planted; and with what delight will the mother watch the progress of her infant's tree, until the child can take the charge from her.

A walnut-tree, which was planted in the garden of Mrs. Maxwell, of Terraughtie, by her present gardener about twelve years ago, produced this last season a pretty full crop of walnuts, which, for flavour and size, are believed to be little, if any thing, inferior to the same kind of fruit grown in the south of England.

There are at this time seven walnut-trees growing in a little meadow at Greenwich, not exceeding three quarters of an acre of land, the fruit of which has been sold, for some years past, to one person at thirty pounds per annum. The owner of these trees refused a thousand guineas for the timber during the late war; and we observed, that the grass did not seem in the least injured by the shade of the trees, which are of a great bulk, but carry their branches high from the ground. We were somewhat surprised, and greatly pleased to learn, that these trees, which have no other fence than an indifferent hedge, have never been robbed of their fruit by the idle boys of that populous neighbourhood.

Evelyn says in his Sylva, "How would such plantations improve the glory and wealth of a nation! But where shall we find the spirits among our country? Yes, I will adventure to instance in those plantations of Sir Richard Stidolph, upon the Down, near Leatherhead in Surrey; Sir Robert Clayton, at Marden, near Godstone, and as about Cassaulton, where many thousands of these trees do celebrate the industry of the owners, and will certainly reward it with infinite improvement, as I am assured they do already, and that very considerably; besides the ornament which they afford to those pleasant tracts, for some miles in circumference."

The same excellent author, whose desire to benefit his country and countrymen was only exceeded by his steady perseverance in his religious duties, to make himself as acceptable to his Maker as he was to his fellow-creatures, writes in his Diary, "27 July, 1655. From Boxhill I walked to Mickleham (in Surrey) and saw Sir F. Stidolph's seat environed with elme-trees and walnuts innumerable, and of which last he told me they received a considerable revenue." On the 27th September, 1658, he notes, "Went to Casshalton (Surrey), full planted with walnut and cherry-trees, which afford a considerable rent." And on the 16th March, 1683, "I went to see S[r] Josiah Child's prodigious cost in planting walnut-trees about his seat," (where Wanstead House now stands.)

Evelyn notices the grafting of walnut-trees in his time; and the advantage of this practice is now completely established by the uniform practice in Dauphiny, Anjou, the Lower Limousin, Perigord, and Swisserland, the produce being thus increased about ten-fold.

Worlidge tells us in his Vinetum Britannicum, which was published in 1675, that Petersfield in Hampshire was celebrated for its walnuts; he says, "There is also the early walnut that ripens above a fortnight before any of the other, and is of as thin a shell and pleasant a taste as any of the other. This fruit I have not observed any where, but at Petersfield in Hampshire. Also there is a very small sort of this fruit, round, and but little bigger than a filberd, growing at the same place."

Some specimens of walnuts were exhibited at the Horticultural Society in 1820, of a long oval shape, with a shell so very thin, that the slightest pressure of the fingers crushes it. The kernel is full, white, very tender, and high-flavoured; and as it is thought to be by far the best walnut grown, we hope to see it engrafted on those trees that at present produce but ill-flavoured nuts. These walnuts are called the *Highflyer walnuts,* and were grown in a small garden at the back of the house of Mr. Jackson, a grocer at Thetford; they seem to have been originally confined to the neighbourhood of that place, and of Bury St. Edmund's.

All the sorts of walnuts which are propagated for timber, should be sown in the place where they are to remain; for the roots of these trees always incline downwards, which being stopped or broken, prevent their aspiring upward, so that they afterwards divaricate into branches, and become low spreading trees; but such as are propagated for fruit, are greatly mended by transplanting; for hereby they are rendered more fruitful; and their fruit is generally larger and fairer; it being a common observation, that downright roots greatly encourage the luxuriant growth of timber in all sorts of trees; but such trees as have their roots spreading near the surface of the ground, are always the most fruitful and best flavoured. *(Miller.)*

Evelyn says, that those who plant nuts for the sake of the fruit, should place a tile below the nut, that the roots may be obliged to spread.

The walnuts that are intended to be planted, should be preserved in their outer covers in dry sand until February, when they may be planted with less danger of being injured by vermin, than if planted in the autumn; but they will be greatly secured from mice, &c. if chopped furze is buried with the nut.

In transplanting these trees, care should be taken not to prune either their roots or large branches, both which are very injurious to them. These trees require but little pruning; and they are often injured by cutting and lopping the branches while growing; but when there is a necessity for cutting any of their branches off, it should be done early in September (for at that season the trees are not so subject to bleed), that the wound may heal over before the cold increases.

The best time for transplanting these trees is just as they have lost their leaves. The walnut-tree thrives well in a firm rich loamy soil, or such as is inclinable to chalk or marl; and will also do very well in stony ground.

Walnuts may be preserved in sand, as we have directed for oranges; or they may be put into jars, and buried in the earth. When this has been omitted, and they are become very dry and acrid, the best way is, to soak them for a day or two, when the kernels will swell, and the brown skin, which causes the acrid taste, may be taken off; they are then tolerably good.

WHORTLE-BERRY.—VACCINIUM;

Often called HURTS, or HURTLE-BERRY, and BILBERRY.

Natural order, Bicornes. A genus of the Octandria Monogynia class.

THIS berry was called *Vaccinium* by Virgil as well as Pliny, to which modern authors add *Myrtillus*, because the old German physicians and apothecaries mistook it for a true species of myrtle.

There are several varieties of this fruit, some of which are black, others red, and some white. The whortle shrub is a native of this country, and grows on most of our wild heathy commons and uncultivated hills: it is found on Portland heath, the highest spot in Norfolk, and in great abundance on Leith Hill, which is the most elevated part of Surrey. The fruit seldom reaches the London market, although it is much admired by many people either in tarts or with cream. The berries are gathered by the children of the cottagers, and by them carried to the nearest market-towns, and often in quantities that load several asses.

The Highlanders eat them with milk, and make them into tarts and jellies, which last they mix with whiskey to give it a relish to strangers.

The variety with white berries was discovered by the Duke of Athol in the woods about midway between his two seats of Dunkeld and Blair.

Gerard says, they formerly grew in Finchley Wood, near Highgate, and on Hampstead Heath. The red kind, which makes the fine purple dye, is found abundantly in several parts of Westmoreland, and the white whortle-berries principally in Lancashire; but most of our northern hills abound with some of the varieties. From their growing in high bleak situations, they are often called wind-berries.

We have never seen this shrub cultivated, although it is more ornamental than many foreign shrubs that are raised with difficulty.* The berry, which is a size larger than that of the juniper, is covered with a fine blue powder, similar to the bloom of our finest purple plums.

There is also another species of heath-berry, growing on the mountainous parts of the northern counties, as well as in Scotland, on which the heathcocks and grouse feed.

There have been no less than fifteen species of the whortle-berry brought into this country from North America, between the years 1761 and 1796. (*Hortus Kewensis.*)

* Since the first edition of this work has been published, these shrubs have been cultivated in Devonshire with success by Robert Hallet, esq.

THE FRUIT OF THE LOTUS-TREE

OF THE ANCIENTS

Has been made so interesting to us, by the inimitable verses of Homer and Ovid, as well as by the mention made of it by Herodotus, Strabo, Pliny, and other authors of antiquity, that we are induced to give their accounts of this celebrated fruit; although it is now either entirely lost, or so much degenerated, as not to be known by their descriptions.

Some authors suppose it to have been a fabulous fruit, and only to be found in the poet's imagination. This idea is absurd. Ovid has described it as particularly as any other fruit mentioned in his Metamorphoses.

The Lotus-tree was evidently a native of Africa; and, in all probability, was improved by being cultivated on the sands of the coast, where, not being indigenous, it has been lost from the neglect of the inhabitants, during the revolutions which that part of the world has undergone. If this fruit has not already been discovered under some other appellation, we may still expect that our researches in the interior of Africa will restore the lost treasure. It is now about two thousand seven hundred years since Homer related the enchanting effects this fruit had on the followers of Ulysses:

Nine days our fleet th' uncertain tempest bore,
Far in wide ocean, and from sight of shore;
The tenth we touch'd, by various errors tost,
The land of Lotus and the flowery coast.

We climb'd the beach, and springs of water found,
Then spread our hasty banquet on the ground.
Three men were sent, deputed from the crew,
(An herald one) the dubious coast to view,
And learn what habitants possess the place.
They went, and found a hospitable race;
Not prone to ill, nor strange to foreign guest.
They eat, they drink, and nature gives the feast;
The trees around them all their fruit produce,
Lotos the name, divine, nectareous juice!
(Thence called Lotophagi), which whoso tastes,
Insatiate riots in the sweet repasts,
Nor other home, nor other care intends,
But quits his house, his country, and his friends:
The three we sent from off th' enchanting ground,
We dragg'd reluctant, and by force we bound;
The rest in haste forsook the pleasing shore,
Or, the charm tasted, had return'd no more.

Hom. Odyss.

From Ovid's elegant fable of Dryope, we learn the traditional origin of the name of this tree:

Not distant far, a wat'ry lotus grows;
The spring was new, and all the verdant boughs,
Adorn'd with blossoms, promis'd fruits that vie
In glowing colours with the Tyrian die.

* * * * * * * *

Upon the tree I cast a frightful look,
The trembling tree with sudden horror shook.
Lotis the nymph (if rural tales be true),
As from Priapus' lawless lust she flew,
Forsook her form; and fixing, there became
A flow'ry plant, which still preserves her name.

Theophrastus mentions the lotus fruit in his 4th book, where he says, that it is of the size of a bean, and changes its colour as it ripens. This author affirms, that the tree is by its nature everlasting.

Strabo, in his 17th book, informs us, that Syrtis as well as Menynx was said to be Lotophagitis. The compass of the gulf, says this geographer, where the lotus grows, is almost one thousand six hundred furlongs; the breadth of the mouth six hundred: by the capes there are islands near to the main land. It is thought, continues he, that Menynx was the country of the Lotophagi, or those that feed on the lotus-trees, of which country Homer makes mention; and there are certain monuments seen, and Ulysses's altar, as well as abundance of lote-trees, the fruit of which is exceedingly sweet.

Pliny has furnished us with an account of the lotus-tree, in his 13th book, c. 17. According to this author, the finest trees of this kind grew on two large sand-banks on the Mediterranean coast of Africa, not far from Leptis and Carthage. He mentions them as being the size of pear-trees, but states that Cornelius Nepos described them as shrubs. The leaves, says Pliny, are thick, cut, and indented: otherwise they are like those of the ilex or holm-tree. There are many varieties of this fruit, but he describes the generality of them as being of the size of a bean, and of the colour of saffron; yet, says he, before it is quite ripe, the fruit changes into a variety of colours like grapes. It grows thick among the branches of the tree, in the manner of myrtle-berries, and not, says he, like cherries. This fruit in Africa, continues Pliny, is so sweet and pleasant, that it has given the name both to a nation and country, as the people are called Lotophagi; and so welcome are all strangers there, and so well contented with their entertainment, that they forget their own native soil, for the love they have for this fruit, when once they have taken to it. By report, (adds this author) those who eat of it, are free from all diseases of the stomach.

Those lotuses were accounted the best that had no

kernels within; for there is a kind, says Pliny, that has a kernel as hard as a bone. From this fruit was pressed a wine similar to mead, which he states, on the authority of Nepos, would not keep above ten days. The Lotophagi pressed the berries of this fruit, with wheat or frumenty, into a paste; and so put it up in great barrels or vessels for food. We have heard, says Pliny, that whole armies passing to and fro through Africa have fed upon it, having no other food.

The wood of the lotus-tree, according to the account of Pliny, was of a black colour, and was, says he, much sought after for making musical pipes. Shafts of daggers and knives, &c. were made of the roots. This author says, "it is growing in Italy, but with the change of soil it has changed its nature;" but in his 16th book, chap. 30, he says, "the lotus-tree is planted about the finest houses in the court-yards, because the boughs spread so large. Although the body is short and small, it affords much shade; yet there is not a tree that gives shade for so short a time, as the leaves fall at the approach of winter, when it admits the sun." The bark is described as of a pleasing hue, and was used to colour skins and leather; the root to dye wool.

"The fruit," says he, "resembles the snouts or muzzles of wild beasts, and many of the smaller berries seem to hang to those that are larger."

The same author, in writing on the age of trees, (book 16, chap. 24) says, "At Rome, in the court-yard belonging to the chapel of the goddess Diana Lucina, there is yet to be seen a lote-tree standing before the chapel which was built in the year of the Anarchy, when Rome was desolate of all magistrates, which was three hundred and sixty-nine years after the foundation of the city; but how much more ancient this tree is than the chapel, God knows! for older it is without all question, as from the trees there growing, which the Latins call *Lucus*, the goddess Diana took her name Lucina, which was about four hundred and fifty years back, and doubtless this tree is so old."

"Another lote-tree there is," says he, "still older, but the age of it is likewise uncertain: it is known by the name of *Capillata* (hairy), and so called, because the hair of the vestal virgins' heads is usually brought thither to be consecrated. There is a third lotus at Rome, in the court-yard and cloister about the temple of Vulcan, which Romulus built for a perpetual monument and memorial of a victory, and defrayed the charge out of the tenth of the pillage and spoil that he obtained from his enemies; and this tree is at least as old as the city of Rome."

Pliny writes on the medicinal qualities of the lotus, in his 24th book, chap. 2, and says his countrymen called it the Greek bean. He says the fruit is sweet, but that nothing is more bitter than the shavings of the wood.

Mr. Mungo Park discovered what is supposed to be the lotus of the ancients, and says it abounds in all parts of the interior of Africa. Agreeably to his account, it is rather a thorny shrub than a tree. The fruit is a small farinaceous berry, which being pounded and dried in the sun, is made into excellent cakes, resembling in flavour and colour the sweetest gingerbread. This traveller observes, that a sweet liquor is obtained from the lotus, which, we may conclude, was reputed to possess the bewitching qualities described by the ancients.

Desfontaines states, in the Journal de Physique, October 1788, that the lotus of the ancients is a shrub, a species of the wild jujube-tree, which grows in several parts of Barbary.

A species of the lotus, or nettle-tree, *celtis*, has long been cultivated in this country: as Gerard says, "this is a rare and strange tree in both the Germanies: it was brought out of Italy, where there is found store thereof; as Mathiolus testifieth : I have," says he, "a small tree in my garden : there is likewise a tree thereof in the garden vnder Londonwall, sometime belonging to M. Gray, an apothecary of London; and another great tree in the garden neere Colman streete, being the garden of the queen's apothecary, called Mr. Hugh Morgan, a curious conseruer of rare simples. The lote-tree doth also grow in Affricke, but it somewhat differeth from the Italian lote in fruit." Gerard adds, that the fruit ripens in September: the berries, he says, are round, and hang on stalks like cherries, and not like the African lotus. "They are," says he, "of a yellowish white colour at the first, and afterwards red, but when they be ripe they be somewhat blacke."

The lotus-flower, that is now become so fashionable in ornamenting furniture, from the circumstance of its having been selected as the decoration of the superb Chinese chandeliers made for his majesty's Pavilion at Brighton, is not the blossom of the lotus-tree, but of the *Nymphæa Nelumbo*, or Chinese water-lotus. This water-lily is called *Nymphæa*, from its growing in the water, which the poets feign to be the residence of the Nymphs. In China, where it was always held in such high value, that at length it has become regarded as sacred, it is called *Lien-wha*. Puzza, a Chinese divinity, is represented as seated on the flowers of the lotus. The gods of Japan, which are exhibited of a gigantic figure, are also seated on the blossoms of this plant. The ponds in China are generally covered with this beautiful aquatic blossom, which is also grown in large vases in the houses of the Mandarins. The roots and seeds are served up on ice at their breakfasts as a delicacy, mixed with the kernels of fruits.

Nievhoff says, "in the province of Huquang, near the

city Tan, in China, is a great cataract which occasions a mire, wherein grow flowers of a saffron colour, whose like is no where else to be seen in all those countries. Several of these flowers grow upon one root; they are something bigger than a lily of Europe, and much handsomer; for fashion, resembling tulips; the leaves of the stalks are large and round, and drive upon the water, as the leaves of some weeds do in Europe, which at their occasion they gather and dry, and by this means are fit to be used by shopkeepers instead of paper, to put up their wares in. There are in some places whole pools abounding with these flowers, which, to say truth, grow not there naturally, but have been sowed by one or other, for they are in great request amongst them."

Sonnini in speaking of the lotus *Nymphea* in his Travels in Egypt says, " this plant is the *Noufar* of the Arabians; it is a water lily of white and odoriferous flowers. Its roots form one of the most common aliments of the Egyptians, particularly in the neighbourhood of Rosetta, where the numerous ditches of the fields are covered with them; they yield a kind of tubercle, which is gathered when the waters are withdrawn; those which are accidentally left are sufficient to reproduce the plant. They are dried and preserved to be eaten; boiled like our potatoes, which they nearly resemble in taste; but they have less consistency, and are not so spungy, so that they are swallowed with difficulty, and it would not be easy to eat more than one of them without being obliged to drink.

" They are sold ready dressed, and at a very low price, in the streets of Rosetta, where the lower classes eat them in great quantities."

The Romans made repeated efforts to raise this plant, without success, which the ancients have celebrated in their writings. Homer mentions it with other flowers, as composing the genial bed of Jupiter and Juno; and the lotus-herb is said to have formed the green food of Achilles's horses.

Antiquaries assure us, that they recognise this flower on the head of Harpocrates.

Belzoni says in his work on Egypt, "At Eduf are the ruins of a superb temple, which is covered with hieroglyphics and figures. On the side wall of the pronaos I observed the figure of Harpocrates, which is described by Mr. Hamilton, seated on a full-blown lotus, with his finger on his lips, as in the minor temple at Tentyra.

Isis has been represented holding a lotus flower in her left hand.

The Indians, says Pennant, feign that Cupid was first seen floating down the Ganges on the *Nymphæa Nelumbo*.

> "Down the blue Ganges laughing glide
> Upon a rosy lotus wreath,
> Catching new lustre from the tide,
> That with his image shone beneath."
>
> *T. Moore.*

Mrs. Graham notices in her Journal of a Residence in India, "On the waters float multitudes of the beautiful red lotus; the flower is larger than that of the white water-lily, and is the most lovely of the nymphæas I have seen."

"This," says Mr. Maurice, "is the majestic lotus, in whose consecrated bosom Brahma was born, and Osiris delights to float."

Sir W. Jones has noticed the veneration paid to this plant, which was anciently revered in Egypt, as it is at present in Hindoostan, Tibet, and Nepal.

Pliny describes the Egyptian lotus as a plant which grows in the marshes of that country, and which came up in the flats when the waters of the Nile returned to their natural channel. "They have heads," says he, "like those of the poppy, within which are seeds resembling millet, of which the inhabitants make bread." He relates, that "it is reported that when the sun goes down, those heads close up with leaves, and sink under the water, where they remain shut until the morning, when they appear above the surface and open, continuing this course until they are ripe, when the flowers (that are white) fall off of themselves. This lotus," says he, "has a root as big as a quince, covered with a black rind or bark, much like the husk of a chesnut. The substance within is white, and delicious to eat, particularly boiled in water or roasted in embers. The bread made from the seeds of this lotus," says Pliny, "is worked with water or milk. There is not any bread in the world (says report) more wholesome and lighter than this, so long as it is hot; but once cold, it is hard of digestion, and becomes weighty."

This plant was introduced into this country by the late Sir Joseph Banks, in 1787, and is of the Polyandria Monogynia class, and natural order of Succulentæ.

AN EXPLANATION

OF THE

TECHNICAL TERMS IN BOTANY,

USED IN THIS WORK.*

"THE Sexual System, as invented and given to the world by Linnæus," says Miller, "is built or founded on the male and female parts of *fructification*. By fructification is meant flower and fruit; and it is disposed according to the number, proportion, and situation of the stamens or pistils, or the male and female organs.

"For the sake of brevity of expression, he has had recourse to the Greek language. *Aner*, a husband, he has applied to the stamen; and *Gyne*, a wife, to the pistil. The stamen consists of two parts. The 1st. Filament, is that part which elevates the anthera. 2d. The anthera is the part that bears the pollen, or farina fecundans, that impregnates the pistillum or germen.

"The pistillum consists of three parts—1st. The germen, or embryo, of a future fruit. 2d. The style, which elevates the stigma. 3d. The stigma or summit, which is covered with a moisture, that dissolves the farina fecundans of the anthera; fitting it for vivification.

"The orders are taken from the females or pistils, as the classes are from the males or stamens."

---

* See Plates 2 and 3.

Androgynous plant.—Bearing male and female flowers on the same root, without any mixture of hermaphrodites.

Anther.—A part of the flower, big with pollen or farina, which it emits or explodes when ripe; or big with granulated pollen, and that with favilla. It forms a part of the stamen, and is placed on the top of the filament.

Calyx.—The outward covering of the flower, or the first of the seven parts of fructification.

Chive.—Properly the stamen.

Decandria.—Ten-stamened.

Diœcia.—The twenty-second class in Linnæus's system, comprehending those plants which have no hermaphrodite flowers; but male and female flowers on distinct plants of the same species.

Favilla.—A fine substance, imperceptible to the naked eye, exploded by the pollen in the anthers of flowers.

Hermaphrodite flowers.—Having both anther and stigma. An hermaphrodite plant is that which has only hermaphrodite flowers.

Hexandria.—The name of the sixth class in Linnæus's system; comprehending those plants which have hermaphrodite flowers with six equal stamens. This is a natural class.

Icosandria.—The name of the twelfth class in the Linnæan system; comprehending those plants which have hermaphrodite flowers, with twenty or more stamens, growing on the inside of the calyx, not on the receptacle; the situation, and not the number of the stamens, is here to be attended to. The calyx also is monophyllous and concave in this class; and the claws of the petals are fixed into the inside of the calyx.

Monœcia.—The name of the twenty-first class in the Linnæan system; comprehending the androgynous plants, or such as produce male and female flowers on the same individual, without any mixture of hermaphrodites.

Monogynia.—The name of the first order in each of the thirteen first classes of the Linnæan system; comprehending such plants as have no pistil, or stigma only, in a flower.

Monophyllum.—A monophyllus, or one-leafed perianth. All in one; if cut, not separated to the base.

Octandria.—The name of the eighth class in the Linnæan system; comprehending those plants which have hermaphrodite flowers with eight stamens.

Pentagynia.—Comprehends those plants which have five pistils in an hermaphrodite flower.

Pentandria.—The name of the fifth class in Linnæus's system; comprehending those plants which have hermaphrodite flowers with five stamens.

Pistillum.—Pistil or pointal; a viscus or organ adhering to the fruit, for the reception of the pollen. It is the fourth part of the fructification. Its appearance is that of a column, or set of columns, in the centre of the flower; and when perfect, it consists of three parts,—1st. Germen, germ, or ovary; 2d. Stylus, the style; 3d. Stigma.

Petalum.—A petal: the corollaceous integument of the flower.

Polyandria.—The name of the thirteenth class in the Linnæan system; comprehending those plants which bear hermaphrodite flowers with many stamens (from twenty to a thousand) growing single on the receptacle.

Polyadelphia.—The name of the eighteenth class in the Linnæan system; comprehending those plants which bear hermaphrodite flowers with three or more sets of united stamens.

Polygamia.—The name of the twenty-third class in the Linnæan system; comprehending those plants which

Plate 2

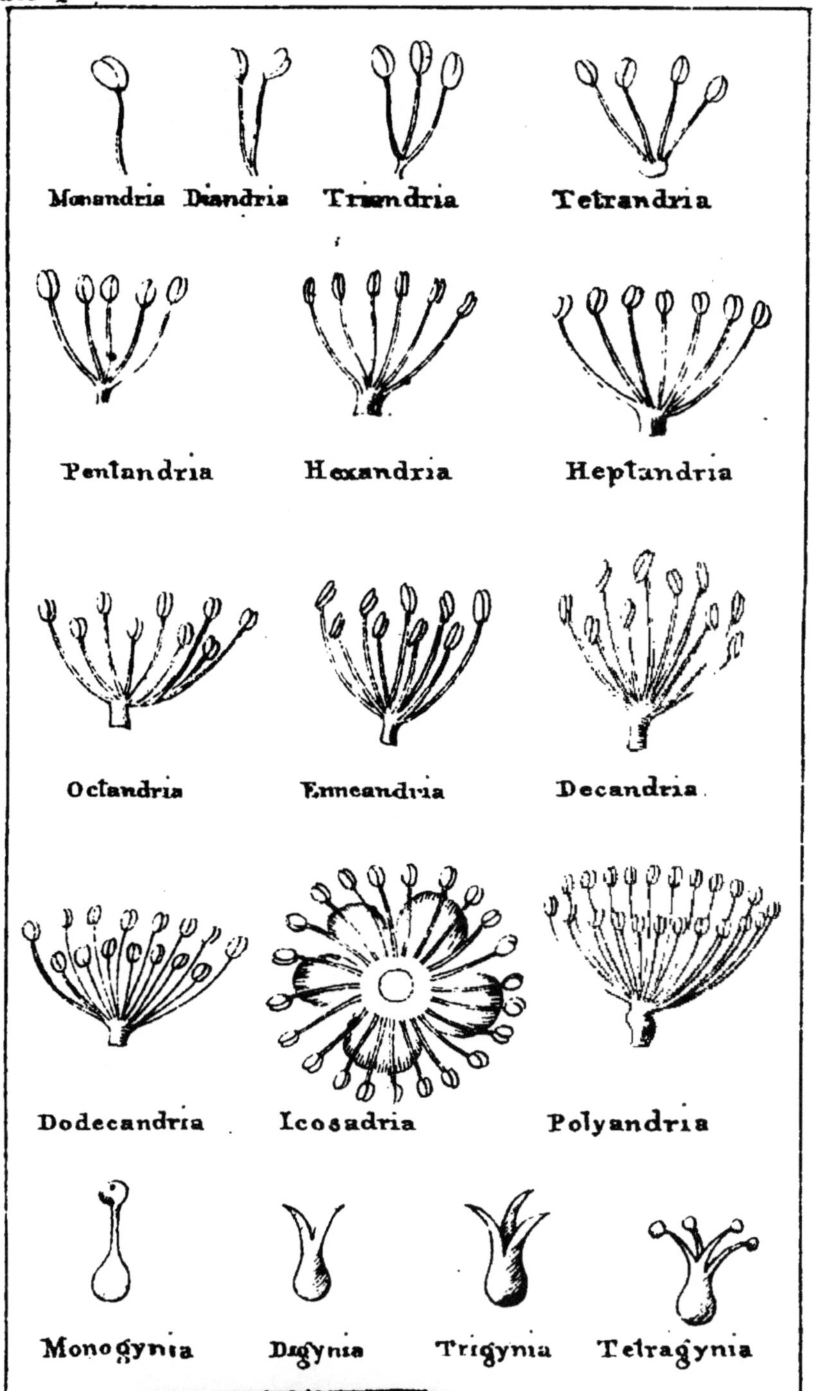
Monandria
Diandria
Triandria
Tetrandria
Pentandria
Hexandria
Heptandria
Octandria
Enneandria
Decandria
Dodecandria
Icosadria
Polyandria
Monogynia
Digynia
Trigynia
Tetragynia

Plate 3

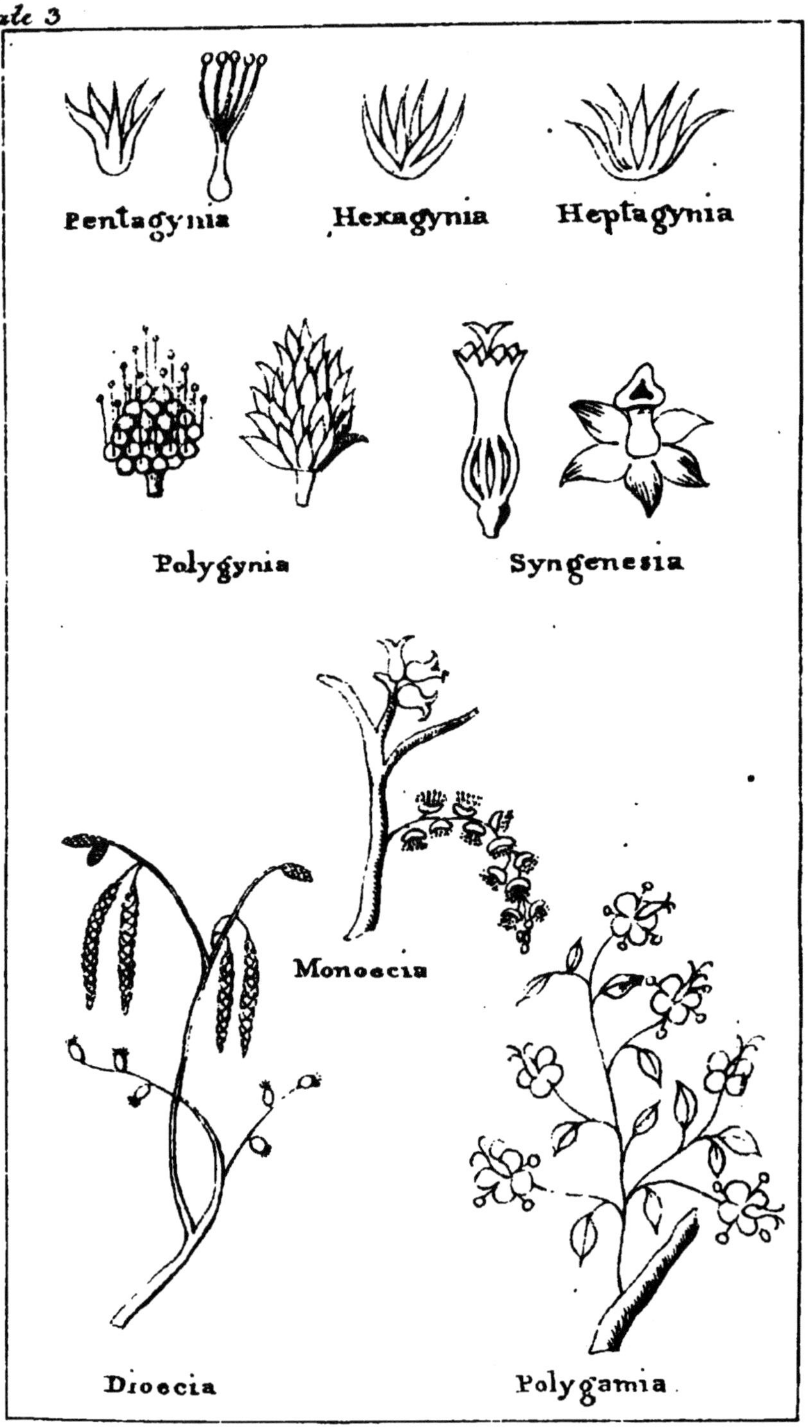
Pentagynia
Hexagynia
Heptagynia
Polygynia
Syngenesia
Monoecia
Dioecia
Polygamia

bear hermaphrodite flowers, accompanied with male or female flowers, or both; not inclosed within the same common calyx, but scattered either on the same plant, or on two, or on three distinct individuals: whence the three orders of this class,—1. *Monœcia*, 2. *Diœcia*, 3. *Triœcia*.

Polygynia.—The name of one of the orders in the fifth, sixth, twelfth, and thirteenth classes in the Linnæan system; comprehending those plants which have flowers with many pistils.

Receptaculum.—A receptacle; the base by which the other parts of the fructification are connected.

Stamen.—An organ, or viscus, for the preparation of the pollen; and formed from the wood. It is the third in the fructification, and consists of the filament and anther.

Syngenesia.—The name of the nineteenth class in Linnæus's artificial system; comprehending those plants which have the anthers united into a cylinder.

The following anecdote, as related by Ray, will prove how necessary it is for all classes of men to be in some measure acquainted with botany: the counsellor who would be a judge, the student who would be a pleader, the juryman who would give an honest verdict, and the party who would gain his cause, will, in this instance, see the importance of botanical information.

"Baal, who was a gardener at Brentford, in Middlesex, having cultivated a remarkably fine cabbage, sold a large quantity of the seeds to several gardeners about the suburbs of London. They committed them to the ground after the usual manner; but, instead of the sort Baal had made them believe would spring up, they proved to be chiefly the brassica longifolia, instead of the florida. His incensed customers, in a body, instantly commenced, in Westminster Hall, a prosecution against him. The unfortunate man being unable to prove his innocence before the judges, the Court found him guilty of fraud; and he was condemned, not only to restore the price given for the seeds, but was likewise obliged to pay each gardener for the loss of time, and for the ground that had been uselessly occupied. His character and circumstances were consequently ruined; which impaired his health, and caused him to pay an untimely debt to nature. Had the judges been at all apprized of the sexual hypothesis, or had this honest man known, from careful observation, the use of the farina in rendering the pistillum productive, Baal would not have been found guilty of a crime, but the accident would have been attributed to the true cause,—the fortuitous impregnation of the brassica florida by the farina of the brassica longifolia growing in the neighbourhood."

INDEX.

THE END.

LONDON:
PRINTED BY S. AND R. BENTLEY, DORSET STREET.

9. THE MANUSCRIPT of 1814, written at the command of Napoleon. By BARON FAIN, Secretary of the Cabinet at that epoch, Master of Requests, &c.; and Illustrated by Private and Official Correspondence. 1 vol. 8vo.

10. LETTERS FROM SPAIN. By DON LEUCADIO DOBLADO. 8vo. 15s.

"This is an invaluable Work.—The Scots are not pourtrayed with more fidelity by their great novelist, than are the interesting people of the Peninsula, by the gentleman to whom we are indebted for these Letters."—*Morning Chronicle.*

11. ITALY. By LADY MORGAN, Author of "France," "Florence Macarthy," "O'Donnel," &c. The Third Edition revised, in 3 vols. 8vo. Price 2*l.* 2s.

"This is not merely a work of opinions expressed in the ornamental style of the writer. It is a substantial account of Italy, and may be consulted for its facts by the historian, the traveller, and the topographer." *Monthly Magazine.*

12. MEMOIRS of BENVENUTO CELLINI. Written by himself. Containing an unreserved account of his intimacy with Michael Angelo, Titian, and all the great Italian sculptors and painters of the age; his connexions with Francis I. of France, the Emperor Charles V., Popes Clement VII. and Paul III., and many of the princes, statesmen, and ecclesiastics of that important era. Revised from the Italian, with Notes. By THOMAS ROSCOE, Esq. Third Edition, in 2 vols. 8vo. with Portrait, 24s.

13. THE LIFE, CORRESPONDENCE, and POSTHUMOUS WRITINGS of BENJAMIN FRANKLIN, LL.D. F.R.S. &c. published from the original MSS. by his Grandson, WILLIAM TEMPLE FRANKLIN, Esq Complete in 6 vols. 8vo. with a Portrait and other Plates. Price 3*l.* 12s. boards.

Vols. 1 and 2 contain the Life.
—— 3 and 4 ——— the Private Correspondence.
—— 5 and 6 ——— Select and Posthumous works.

Any of the volumes may be had separately; and the Public are advised to complete their sets without delay.

14. MEMOIRS OF JOHN EVELYN, Esq. the celebrated Author of "Sylva," &c. illustrative of his Life, Times, and Writings, and comprising his Diary from the year 1641 to 1705-6: a Selection of his Familiar Letters, &c. &c. To which is subjoined The Private Correspondence between King Charles I. and his Secretary of State, Sir Edward Nicholas, whilst his Majesty was in Scotland, 1641, and at other times during the Civil War; also between Sir Edward Hyde, afterwards Earl of Clarendon and Sir Richard Browne, Ambassador to the Court of France, in the time of King Charles I. and the Usurpation. The whole now first published from Original MSS. By WILLIAM BRAY, Esq. Fellow and Treasurer of the Society of Antiquaries of London. Handsomely printed, in 2 vols. royal quarto, embellished with Portraits and other Engravings, by the first artists, price 5*l.* 15s. 6d. boards.

15. AN HISTORICAL ACCOUNT of the CAMPAIGN in the NETHERLANDS, in 1815, under his Grace the Duke of Wellington and Prince Blucher, comprising the Battles of Ligny, Quatre Bras, and Waterloo. With a detailed Narrative of the Political Events connected with those memorable Conflicts, drawn up from the first Authorities, and dedicated to the Duke. By WILLIAM MUDFORD, Esq. Illustrated by numerous public and private Official Documents, and other Papers hitherto unpublished, communicated by Officers of the highest distinction. Elegantly printed in 1 vol. imperial 4to., embellished with 30 coloured Plates, Portraits, Maps, Plans, &c. price 6*l.* 6s. boards, or in Four Parts, at 1*l.* 11s. 6d. each, the last three of which are sold separately, to complete sets.

16. LETTERS from the COURT of TRIPOLY, written during a Ten Years Residence in that Country. Published from the Originals, in the possession of the Family of the late RICHARD TULLY, Esq. the British Consul. In 2 vols. 8vo. with coloured plates, price 28s. Third Edition.

"This work boasts an interest peculiarly its own, and not depending upon any locality of circumstance whatever. It is beyond doubt the most delightfully entertaining work that has for a long time appeared; the finished picture that is given of the Moors, Turks, and Arabs, reminds us of the most splendid fictions of the *Arabian Nights*, and gives to us, arrayed in all the reality of truth, those delightful scenes, and that glowing imagery, which we have never been accustomed to consider, otherwise than as the workings of a brilliant imagination."

17. THE PHILOSOPHY of LIFE. By SIR CHARLES MORGAN, M.D. and Fellow of the Royal College of Physicians of London. 8vo. 14s.

"Sir C. Morgan has here presented us with a book containing a great deal of useful and entertaining information. The work contains many plain and sensible lessons, on the best methods of keeping both mind and body in a healthy state."

Also, by the same Author,

18. THE PHILOSOPHY of MORALS. In 1 vol. 8vo. 14s.

"In our present state, the operations of the mind so far depend on the right tone and good condition of its instrument, that any thing which greatly contributes to preserve or renew the health of the body, is well worth the attention of the mind."—*Bishop Berkeley.*

19. TABLE TALK; or, ORIGINAL ESSAYS. By WILLIAM HAZLITT, Volume the SECOND, 8vo. price 14s.

Contents.—1. On a Landscape of Nicholas Poussin—2. On Milton's Sonnets—3. On going a Journey—4. On Coffee-house Politicians—5. On the Aristocracy of Letters—6. On Criticism—7. On Great and Little Things—8. On Familiar Style—9. On Effeminacy of Character—10. Why distant Objects Please—11. On Corporate Bodies—12. Whether Actors ought to sit in the Boxes—13. On the Disadvantages of Intellectual Superiority—14. On Patronage and Puffing—15. On the Knowledge of Character—16. On the Picturesque and Ideal—17. On the Fear of Death.

N.B. Either Volume may be had separately.

"This work contains some of the most valuable of those treasures which its author has produced from his vast stores of feeling and of thought."—*Edinburgh Review.*

20. THE ETONIAN. A Series of Essays, Criticisms, and Delineations, of Life and Manners. Third Edition, in 3 vols. post 8vo. 31s. 6d.

"So much ingenuity, good taste, good sense, and good feeling, are displayed, that Eton has reason to be proud of her sons, and their labours deserve extended patronage." —*New Times.*——High eulogiums on this interesting work will also be found in the Quarterly and Monthly Reviews, &c.

21. POETICAL WORKS of BARRY CORNWALL, now first collected. In 3 vols. foolscap 8vo. 21s.

"It is delightful to turn awhile from moral and political animosities to the unalloyed sweets of such poetry as Mr. Cornwall's; and to refresh our fancies, and strengthen and compose our good affections, among the images of love and beauty, and gentle sympathy and sorrow, with which it every where presents us."—*Edinburgh Review.*

22. THE HERMIT in LONDON; or, SKETCHES of ENGLISH MANNERS. The Fourth Edition revised, in 3 vols. 21s.

23. THE HERMIT in the COUNTRY; or, SKETCHES of ENGLISH MANNERS. By the celebrated Author of "The Hermit in London." The third edition, in 3 vols. price 21s.

"Quite weary grown
Of all the follies of the town,
And seeing in all public places
The same vain fops, and painted faces."

24. HISTORY of CULTIVATED VEGETABLES. By HENRY PHILLIPS, F.H.S. Author of The Pomarium Britannicum, or History of Fruits known in Great Britain. Second Edition, in 2 vols. 8vo. 21s.

In this Work, the object of the Author has been to render the knowledge of Plants entertaining and useful, not only to Botanists, but to those who have hitherto deemed it a difficult and uninteresting science. He has endeavoured to ascertain of what Countries the Vegetables now cultivated are natives, the earliest account of their cultivation, and how far they have improved by attention, or degenerated by neglect; also the various uses made of them by the Ancients, as well as the Moderns, of different Countries.

25. THE FLORISTS MANUAL; or, Hints for the construction of a Gay FLOWER-GARDEN, with Directions for preventing the depredations of Insects. By the Authoress of Botanical Dialogues, and Sketches of the Physiology of Vegetable Life. Second Edition, corrected and enlarged. In small 8vo. with six coloured Plates, 5s. 6d. boards.

26. A NEW SYSTEM OF PRACTICAL ECONOMY; founded on Modern Discoveries, and adapted to the Purposes of Domestic Life. To which are now first added, ESTIMATES OF FAMILY EXPENSES, founded on Economical Principles, and adapted to Families of all Descriptions. The Third Edition, much improved and enlarged, in one thick vol. 12mo. price 8s. 6d.

"This work contains a variety of new and useful information, calculated at once to increase our comforts and diminish our expenses."—*New Monthly Magazine.*

27. THE ART of EMPLOYING TIME to the greatest Advantage—the true Source of Happiness. The Second Edition, 8vo. price 9s. 6d. boards.

"Dost thou love life?—then do not squander time, for that is the stuff life is made of."—FRANKLIN.

We have the author's authority for stating, that several persons have already practised this method of regulating the employment of time, for some years, with perseverance and success. It is particularly adapted to young people of the age of fifteen or sixteen years to twenty-five, but it is also calculated to confer advantages on persons of all ages and professions—in all classes of society, and in all circumstances of life. It tends to form the heart, the judgment, the understanding, the style and the memory, to preserve health, to neutralize or to give a beneficial direction to the passions, in short to make man more virtuous, more enlightened, and more happy.

28. THE NEW MONTHLY MAGAZINE.

The Public are respectfully informed that the Numbers of this Work, which were out of print, having been reprinted, COMPLETE SETS, from the commencement in 1821, may now be had, price 3s. 6d. each Number, or in Volumes, handsomely half-bound, price 14s. each, and those who desire to commence taking it, are requested to send their orders forthwith to any Bookseller, Stationer, or News-vender, in their neighbourhood, by whom it will be regularly supplied. It may also be exported to Friends abroad, by application to the General Post Office, or to any local Post Master.

This Magazine, which was commenced on the 1st January, 1821, on a new and very improved plan, has the advantage of being conducted by a gentleman of distinguished eminence in the Literary World, aided by an extensive circle of contributing friends, among whom are also many of the first celebrity in the Republic of Letters.

Each Number contains about 150 pages of letter-press, handsomely printed, (comprising more matter than is usually contained in an ordinary octavo volume,) 100 pages of which are devoted to ORIGINAL PAPERS on Subjects of Literature, Philosophy, Morals, Manners, &c. and the remaining 50 to a REVIEW of all interesting NEW PUBLICATIONS, Foreign as well as English—BIOGRAPHICAL NOTICES of Distinguished Characters—Essays on the FINE ARTS, MUSIC, and the DRAMA—LITERARY and SCIENTIFIC VARIETIES, NEW INVENTIONS, DISCOVERIES, and IMPROVEMENTS—RURAL ECONOMY—Meteorological, Agricultural, and Commercial REPORTS, POLITICAL EVENTS, and IMPORTANT OCCURRENCES, throughout Great Britain, arranged under the several Counties.

London: Printed for HENRY COLBURN and Co. Conduit-street; and sold by Bell and Bradfute, Edinburgh; and John Cumming, Dublin.

Lightning Source UK Ltd.
Milton Keynes UK
15 March 2010

151426UK00001B/76/P